THE KEY

STUDENT STUDY GUIDE

lish 20-1

THE KEY student study guide is designed to help students achieve success in school. The content in each study guide is 100% curriculum aligned and serves as an excellent source of material for review and practice. To create this book, teachers, curriculum specialists, and assessment experts have worked closely to develop the instructional pieces that explain each of the key concepts for the course. The practice questions and sample tests have detailed solutions that show problem-solving methods, highlight concepts that are likely to be tested, and point out potential sources of errors. ***THE KEY*** is a complete guide to be used by students throughout the school year for reviewing and understanding course content, and to prepare for assessments.

Publisher
Gautam Rao

Contributors
Ute-Brigitte Blunck
Brigitta Braden

Rao, Gautam, 1961 –
THE KEY – English 20-1
ISBN: 978-1-77044-421-8

1. English – Juvenile Literature. I. Title

Published by
Castle Rock Research Corp.
2000 First & Jasper
10065 Jasper Avenue
Edmonton, AB T5J 3B1

10 9 8 7 6 5

Dedicated to the memory of Dr. V. S. Rao

THE *KEY* – ENGLISH 20-1

THE KEY consists of the following sections:

KEY Tips for Being Successful at School gives examples of study and review strategies. It includes information about learning styles, study schedules, and note taking for test preparation.

Class Focus includes a unit on each area of the curriculum. Units are divided into sections, each focusing on one of the specific expectations, or main ideas, that students must learn about in that unit. Examples, definitions, and visuals help to explain each main idea. Practice questions on the main ideas are also included. At the end of each unit is a test on the important ideas covered. The practice questions and unit tests help students identify areas they know and those they need to study more. They can also be used as preparation for tests and quizzes. Each unit is prefaced by a ***Table of Correlations***, which correlates questions in the unit (and in the practice tests at the end of the book) to the specific curriculum expectations. Answers and solutions are found at the end of each unit.

KEY Strategies for Success on Tests helps students get ready for tests. It shows students different types of questions they might see, word clues to look for when reading them, and hints for answering them.

Practice Tests includes one to three tests based on the entire course. They are very similar to the format and level of difficulty that students may encounter on final tests. In some regions, these tests may be reprinted versions of official tests, or reflect the same difficulty levels and formats as official versions. This gives students the chance to practice using real-world examples. Answers and complete solutions are provided at the end of the section.

For the complete curriculum document (including specific expectations along with examples and sample problems), visit http://education.alberta.ca/teachers/program.aspx.

THE KEY *Study Guides* are available for many courses. Check www.castlerockresearch.com for a complete listing of books available for your area.

For information about any of our resources or services, please call Castle Rock Research at 780.448.9619 or visit our website at http://www.castlerockresearch.com.

At Castle Rock Research, we strive to produce an error-free resource. If you should find an error, please contact us so that future editions can be corrected..

TABLE OF CONTENTS

KEY Tips for Being Successful at School

KEY TIPS FOR BEING SUCCESSFUL AT SCHOOL

KEY FACTORS CONTRIBUTING TO SCHOOL SUCCESS

In addition to learning the content of your courses, there are some other things that you can do to help you do your best at school. You can try some of the following strategies:

- **Keep a positive attitude**: Always reflect on what you can already do and what you already know.
- **Be prepared to learn**: Have the necessary pencils, pens, notebooks, and other required materials for participating in class ready.
- **Complete all of your assignments**: Do your best to finish all of your assignments. Even if you know the material well, practice will reinforce your knowledge. If an assignment or question is difficult for you, work through it as far as you can so that your teacher can see exactly where you are having difficulty.
- **Set small goals for yourself when you are learning new material**: For example, when learning the parts of speech, do not try to learn everything in one night. Work on only one part or section each study session. When you have memorized one particular part of speech and understand it, move on to another one. Continue this process until you have memorized and learned all the parts of speech.
- **Review your classroom work regularly at home**: Review to make sure you understand the material you learned in class.

- **Ask your teacher for help**: Your teacher will help you if you do not understand something or if you are having a difficult time completing your assignments.
- **Get plenty of rest and exercise**: Concentrating in class is hard work. It is important to be well-rested and have time to relax and socialize with your friends. This helps you keep a positive attitude about your schoolwork.
- **Eat healthy meals**: A balanced diet keeps you healthy and gives you the energy you need for studying at school and at home.

How to Find Your Learning Style

Every student learns differently. The manner in which you learn best is called your learning style. By knowing your learning style, you can increase your success at school. Most students use a combination of learning styles. Do you know what type of learner you are? Read the following descriptions. Which of these common learning styles do you use most often?

- Do you need to say things out loud? You may learn best by saying, hearing, and seeing words. You are probably really good at memorizing things such as dates, places, names, and facts. You may need to write down the steps in a process, a formula, or the actions that lead up to a significant event, and then say them out loud.
- Do you need to read or see things? You may learn best by looking at and working with pictures. You are probably really good at puzzles, imagining things, and reading maps and charts. You may need to use strategies like mind mapping and webbing to organize your information and study notes.
- Do you need to draw or write things down? You may learn best by touching, moving, and figuring things out using manipulatives. You are probably really good at physical activities and learning through movement. You may need to draw your finger over a diagram to remember it, tap out the steps needed to solve a problem, or feel yourself writing or typing a formula.

SCHEDULING STUDY TIME

You should review your class notes regularly to ensure that you have a clear understanding of all the new material you learned. Reviewing your lessons on a regular basis helps you to learn and remember ideas and concepts. It also reduces the quantity of material that you need to study prior to a test. Establishing a study schedule will help you to make the best use of your time.

- Regardless of the type of study schedule you use, you may want to consider the following suggestions to maximize your study time and effort:
- Organize your work so that you begin with the most challenging material first.
- Divide the subject's content into small, manageable chunks.
- Alternate regularly between your different subjects and types of study activities in order to maintain your interest and motivation.
- Make a daily list with headings like "Must Do," "Should Do," and "Could Do."
- Begin each study session by quickly reviewing what you studied the day before.
- Maintain your usual routine of eating, sleeping, and exercising to help you concentrate better for extended periods of time.

Creating Study Notes

Mind-Mapping or Webbing

Use the key words, ideas, or concepts from your class notes to create a mind map or web, which is a diagram or visual representation of the given information. A mind map or web is sometimes referred to as a knowledge map. Use the following steps to create a mind map or web:

1. Write the key word, concept, theory, or formula in the centre of your page.
2. Write down related facts, ideas, events, and information, and link them to the central concept with lines.
3. Use coloured markers, underlining, or symbols to emphasize things such as relationships, timelines, and important information.

The following mind map is an example of one that could help you develop an essay:

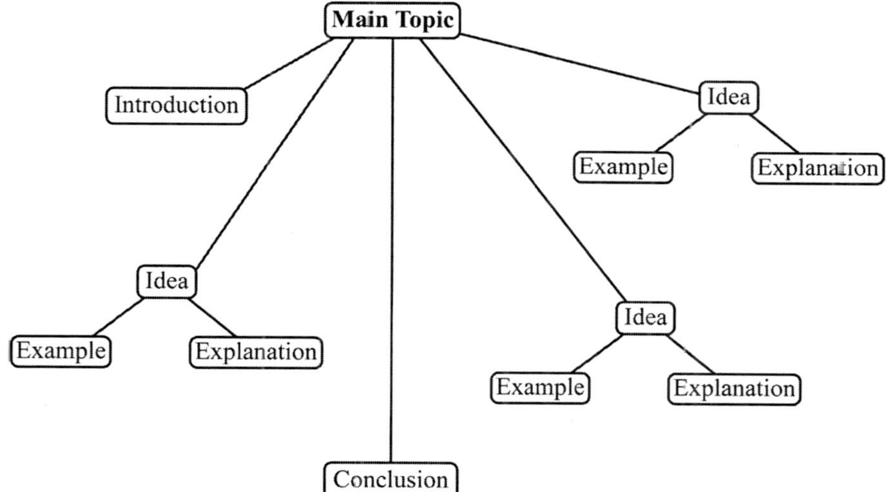

INDEX CARDS

To use index cards while studying, follow these steps:

1. Write a key word or question on one side of an index card.
2. On the reverse side, write the definition of the word, answer to the question, or any other important information that you want to remember.

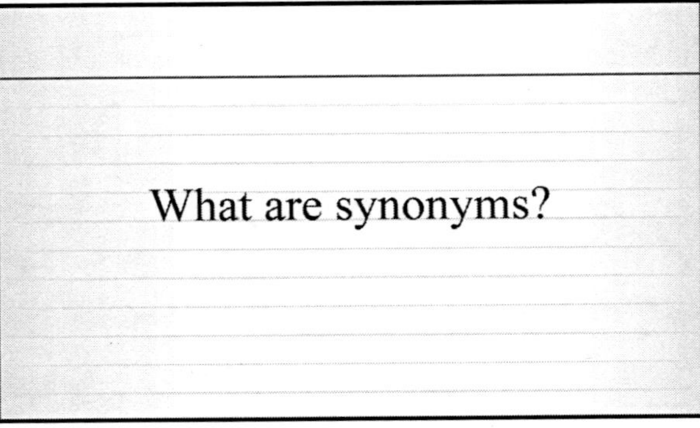

What are synonyms?

Synonyms are words that have the same or almost the same meaning.

For example, "coarse" is a synonym for "rough"

SYMBOLS AND STICKY NOTES—IDENTIFYING IMPORTANT INFORMATION

Use symbols to mark your class notes. For example, an exclamation mark (!) might be used to point out something that must be learned well because it is a very important idea. A question mark (?) may highlight something you are not certain about, and a diamond (◊) or asterisk (*) could highlight interesting information that you want to remember. Sticky notes are useful in the following situations:

- Use sticky notes when you are not allowed to put marks in books.
- Use sticky notes to mark a page in a book that contains an important diagram, formula, explanation, or other information.
- Use sticky notes to mark important facts in research books.

Memorization Techniques

The following techniques can help you when you need to memorize something:

- **Association** relates new learning to something you already know. For example, to remember the spelling difference between dessert and desert, recall that the word *sand* has only one *s*. So, because there is sand in a desert, the word *desert* has only one *s*.
- **Mnemonic** devices are sentences that you create to remember a list or group of items. For example, the first letter of each word in the phrase "**E**very **G**ood **B**oy **D**eserves **F**udge" helps you to remember the names of the lines on the treble-clef staff (E, G, B, D, and F) in music.
- **Acronyms** are words that are formed from the first letters or parts of the words in a group. For example, RADAR is actually an acronym for Radio Detecting and Ranging, and MASH is an acronym for Mobile Army Surgical Hospital. HOMES helps you to remember the names of the five Great Lakes (Huron, Ontario, Michigan, Erie, and Superior).
- **Visualizing** requires you to use your mind's eye to "see" a chart, list, map, diagram, or sentence as it is in your textbook or notes, on the chalkboard or computer screen, or in a display.
- **Initialisms** are abbreviations that are formed from the first letters or parts of the words in a group. Unlike acronyms, an initialism cannot be pronounced as a word itself. For example, BEDMAS is an initialism for the order of operations in math (Brackets, Exponents, Divide, Multiply, Add, Subtract).

KEY Strategies for Reviewing

Reviewing textbook material, class notes, and handouts should be an ongoing activity. Spending time reviewing becomes more critical when you are preparing for a test. You may find some of the following review strategies useful when studying during your scheduled study time:

- Before reading a selection, preview it by noting the headings, charts, graphs, and chapter questions.
- Before reviewing a unit, note the headings, charts, graphs, and chapter questions.
- Highlight key concepts, vocabulary, definitions, and formulas.
- Skim the paragraph, and note the key words, phrases, and information.
- Carefully read over each step in a procedure.
- Draw a picture or diagram to help make the concept clearer.

KEY STRATEGIES FOR SUCCESS: A CHECKLIST

Reviewing is a huge part of doing well at school and preparing for tests. Here is a checklist for you to keep track of how many suggested strategies for success you are using. Read each question, and put a check mark (✓) in the correct column. Look at the questions where you have checked the "No" column. Think about how you might try using some of these strategies to help you do your best at school.

***KEY* Strategies for Success**	**Yes**	**No**
Do you attend school regularly?		
Do you know your personal learning style—how you learn best?		
Do you spend 15 to 30 minutes a day reviewing your notes?		
Do you study in a quiet place at home?		
Do you clearly mark the most important ideas in your study notes?		
Do you use sticky notes to mark texts and research books?		
Do you practise answering multiple-choice and written-response questions?		
Do you ask your teacher for help when you need it?		
Are you maintaining a healthy diet and sleep routine?		
Are you participating in regular physical activity?		

Reading

READING

2.1.1a describe the text creator's purpose, and analyze the target audience

2.1.1b describe how societal forces can influence the production of texts

PURPOSE

Understanding a writer's purposes is one of the first steps in effective reading. Identifying these purposes gives readers critical information about the writer's decisions regarding content, structure, and even the design of their document.

Every writer begins with a purpose for writing. It may be as simple as completing an assignment as required or it may be to develop his or her writing skills. A writer's purpose might be to convince others to adopt a particular point of view about an issue, or the writer might want to voice a protest against a situation.

Although it may not seem so at first glance, the acts of reading and writing can be viewed as very social activities. Writing almost always addresses an audience, thus creating a social circle of communication that creates its own context of reader expectations and the writer's experiences. A writer wants to convey a message to a reader and urge the reader to consider the message—and possibly, to contemplate and respond to it. Texts are shaped by many things, such as:

- practical purposes like the need to describe or instruct
- response to societal forces
- entertainment
- persuasion

A writer's purpose demands an ongoing interaction between the reader's thoughts and a text. Questions should be formulated, images of descriptions should be conjured, and analysis of the meaning of the text should all be a natural part of the reading process.

EXTENDING UNDERSTANDING OF TEXTS

One of the ways you can enjoy texts is through the experience of the emotions they inspire within you. You can deepen your understanding of the technical aspects of a text and appreciate the level of expertise that is required to create a compelling piece of writing. At the same time, your responses to what you read tell you something about yourself. You might find yourself supporting characters you typically would not support or resisting those with whom you would typically identify. This movement in and out of the text, from the craft of the writer to the interpretation of the reader, gives an exciting variety to the range of meanings in any one text.

To better understand what you read, you should connect, compare, and contrast.

Connect: As you read different things, look for connections between the ideas, themes, and issues that are presented in the writing. First of all, are there connections to other pieces of writing that you have read? Is the subject the same? Do the writers feel the same way about it? Even when two pieces of writing seem to be about different subjects, you can often find connections.

Compare: When you compare pieces of writing, you think about how they are similar to each other. Perhaps they are very different in style, but they give the same basic information. When you compare, similarities are your focus.

Contrast: When you contrast pieces of writing, you think about how they are different from each another. Perhaps the writers give the same information, but the way they go about it is very different. When you contrast, differences are your focus.

Social, Political, and Historical Perspective

Social norms and values evolve and change through time. When reading a text, it is important to it keep in mind the social, political, and historical perspectives of the time in which the text was written and of the time in which the text is set. There are often many different perspectives from the people within any given society, depending on their social status. Authors sometimes write using these different perspectives to present readers with the realities of the lives of people from different social standings in order to provide a more detailed and accurate context for their work.

It is also important to consider the political setting of both the text and the author. Writers will often choose a particular political setting to shed light on that time period and the realities of that political era. Other times, writers are influenced by their own current political setting and will write to depict the realities of that political setting. The political context of a text, both of the writer and of the setting, will greatly influence the information presented.

Historical perspective is a very important aspect of a story and its setting. It provides an emotional and philosophical background for the characters, who are usually guided in their actions and choices by the customs, traditions, and beliefs that dominate their society. These conflicts may drive the actual plot of the story. Historical perspective can show a reader how aspects of history affect people and how history can repeat itself. Often, historical works show a reader how little has changed over time.

Review the following two documents in light of their social, political, and historical contexts.

The Issue: Working Conditions and Issues that Led to Change

CHARLES DICKENS—CHRONICLER OF HIS TIMES

Charles Dickens, one of the great English novelists of the nineteenth century, was a keen observer of life in his times. Dickens often drew on his own experiences to write his books about life in England during the Industrial Revolution. Born of a poor father who spent time in prison for debt, Dickens knew what poverty was like. He worked at age 12 in a London factory, pasting labels on shoe polish bottles. Later, he worked as a newspaper reporter, and gained fame as a novelist. Dickens had great energy.
He wrote, went to the theatre, toured as a dramatic reader, and busied himself with many charities. He would often walk for hours to wear off his nervous energy. This is perhaps how he came to know the streets and alleys of London better than most people of his time.

Many of Charles Dickens's books describe life in British industrial cities. In his book *Hard Times*, he describes life in Coketown:

It was a town of red brick, inhabited by people equally like one another, who all went in and out at the same hours, with the same sound upon the same pavements, to do the same work, and to whom every day was the same as yesterday and tomorrow, and every year the counterpart of the last and the next.

This item provides some background on the English writer who described the working conditions of the nineteenth century in several novels such as *Oliver Twist, Great Expectations*, and *David Copperfield*. You could become better informed about some of these working conditions by examining the "Mill

Rules" in the following document.

RULES
TO BE OBSERVED
By the Hands Employed in
THIS MILL.

RULE

1. All the Overlookers shall be on the premises first and last.
2. Any Person coming too late shall be fined as follows:—for 5 minutes 2d, 10 minutes 4d, and 15 minutes 6d, &c.
3. For any Bobbins found on the floor 1d for each Bobbin.
5. For Waste on the floor 2d.
6. For any Oil wasted or spilled on the floor 2d each offence, besides paying for the value of the Oil.
7. For any broken Bobbins, they shall be paid for according to their value, and if there is any difficulty in ascertaining the guilty party, the same shall be paid for by the whole using such Bobbins.
8. Any person neglecting to Oil at the proper times shall be fined 2d.
9. Any person leaving their Work and found Talking with any of the other workpeople shall be fined 2d for each offence.
10. For every Oath or insolent language, 3d for the first offence and if repeated they shall be dismissed.
11. The Machinery shall be swept and cleaned down every meal time.
12. All persons in our employ shall serve Four Weeks' Notice before leaving their employ; but L. WHITAKER & SONS shall and will turn any person off without notice being given.
16. The Masters would recommend that all their workpeople Wash themselves every morning, but they shall Wash themselves at least twice every week, Monday morning and Thursday morning; and any found not washed will be fined 3d for each offence.
18. Any persons found smoking on the premises will be instantly dismissed.
19. Any person found away from their usual place of work, except for necessary purposes, or Talking with any one out of their own Alley will be fined 2d for each offence.
21. Any person wilfully damaging this Notice will be dismissed.

The Overlookers are strictly enjoined to attend to these Rules, and they will be responsible to the Masters for the Workpeople observing them.

WATER-FOOT MILL, NEAR HASLINGDEN.
September, 1851.

J. Read, Printer, and Bookbinder, Haslingden

You can synthesize two general ideas from this document:

- workers were harshly treated in the nineteenth century
- it is evident that the workers had no rights and were subservient to their employers

After reading the above documents, you will have a better understanding of the social, political, and historical contexts when reading a novel written by Charles Dickens, or a text from that time period.

2.1.1c explain the relationship between text and context in terms of how elements in an environment can affect the way in which a text is created

Context and Background

The context of a text includes background information, knowledge, ideas—anything that adds to the understanding of a text. Writers frequently draw on the experiences of their own lives when they write. It makes sense, then, that finding out more about the time during which a writer lived or the issues that surrounded a writer's life will give you added insight into the themes and main ideas of a text.

Context provides perspective. A better understanding of the context of even a single word can help you to better understand an entire text. You might be reading the lyrics to a ballad and be puzzled by a verse such as the following one.

> It's out with the jiggers the first of the spring,
> And over the gunnel you can hear the line ring;
> Perhaps lose a jigger, get froze with the cold,
> And that's the first starting of going in the hole,
> And it's hard, hard times.

At this point, you might want to slow down the pace of your reading and analyze the piece in smaller pieces. Also, you might want to view the verse with respect to the entire piece. Looking at the rest of the ballad, you will find that the speaker is a Newfoundland fisherman, so you might infer that the unfamiliar vocabulary refers to tools or terminology linked to a fisherman's life. Readers know that it is a necessary element for catching fish and that to "lose a jigger" represents a loss of income. The reader is told that the speaker works as soon in the season as he can, under great hardship, fighting the elements as he goes. If you research the time during which the ballad was penned, it will become clear that it was written during the Great Depression in Newfoundland, so the "hard times" refer to the terrible hardships experienced by workers (fishermen or otherwise) during those difficult years. Taking the entire passage into consideration, knowing the era during which it was written, pinpointing the area from which it originates—all of these bits of information that contribute to context, help you to arrive at a better understanding, even if the initial words caused you some confusion.

Look at the entire poem from which the verse in question was taken.

> **HARD, HARD TIMES**
>
> So now I'm intending to sing you a song,
> About the poor people how they get along.
> They start in the spring and they work till the fall,
> And when they clew up they've nothing at all,
> And it's hard, hard times.
>
> Poor fishermen, we been out all the day.
> Come home in the evening full sail up the bay.
> There's Kate in the corner with a wink and a nod,
> Saying, "Jimmy or Johnny, have you got any cod?"
> And it's hard, hard times.

It's out with the jiggers the first of the spring,
And over the gunnel you can hear the line ring;
Perhaps lose a jigger, get froze with the cold,
And that's the first starting of going in the hole,
And it's hard, hard times.

When so much is caught it's put out for to dry,
'Twill take all your time for to brush off the flies;
They'll buzz all around and make trouble for you,
Then out comes the sun and it all splits in two,
And it's hard, hard times.

First comes the merchant to see your supply,
Saying, "The fine side of fishing you'll have by and by."
Seven dollars for large, six-fifty for small.
Pick out your West Indie, you've nothing at all,
And it's hard, hard times.

And then comes the carpenter to build you a house;
He'll build it so snug you can scarce find a mouse.
There's a hole in the roof, and the rain it do pour,
The chimney do smoke, and it's open the door,
And it's hard, hard times.

The baker has loaves, grow smaller each week.
The same for the butcher that weighs up your meat.
The weights they fly up and the scales they fly down,
And when it's all over you're short half a pound,
And it's hard, hard times.

Then come the doctor, the worst of them all,
Saying, "What's been the matter with you all the fall?"
He says he will cure you of all your disease.
When your money he's got, you can die if you please,
And it's hard, hard times.

The best thing to do is to work with a will,
For when it's all over you're hauled on the hill.
Hauled up on the hill, put down in the cold,
And when it's all over you're still in the hole,
And it's hard, hard times.

—*by* William Emberley

Observe how the poet provides details and experiences to lend realism to his tale and to help the listener understand the plight of the people that are the central focus of his ballad. If a writer sets his or her story in a particular time and place, he or she will often refer to details that were part of the reality for that setting. Poverty would have been a reality for the fishermen and their families living in Newfoundland at the time of the Great Depression. When a writer refers to details of the world he or she is creating in order to make that world more realistic, the writer is using a technique called verisimilitude. For example, if a writer wanted to employ verisimilitude in a novel set in Canada in 2008, he or she might mention Prime Minister Harper, the war in Afghanistan, or the economic recession.

Consider the poem "The Blind Men and the Elephant." This poem shows in just a few stanzas why making an assumption too quickly about anything is a mistake.

THE BLIND MEN AND THE ELEPHANT

It was six men of Hindostan,
To learning much inclined,
Who went to see the elephant,
(Though all of them were blind):
That each by observation
Might satisfy his mind.

The *first* approached the Elephant,
And happening to fall
Against his broad and sturdy side,
At once began to bawl:
"Bless me, it seems the Elephant
Is very like a wall."

The *second*, feeling of his tusk,
Cried, "Ho! What have we here
So very round and smooth and sharp?
To me 'tis mighty clear
This wonder of an Elephant
Is very like a spear."

The *third* approached the animal,
And happening to take
The squirming trunk within his hands,
Then boldly up and spake:
"I see," quoth he, "the Elephant
Is very like a snake."

The *fourth* stretched out his eager hand
And felt about the knee,
"What most this mighty beast is like
Is mighty plain," quoth he;
"'Tis clear enough the Elephant
Is very like a tree."

The *fifth* who chanced to touch the ear
Said, "Even the blindest man
Can tell what this resembles most;
Deny the fact who can,
This marvel of an Elephant
Is very like a fan."

> The *sixth* no sooner had begun
> About the beast to grope,
> Than, seizing on the swinging tail
> That fell within his scope,
> "I see," cried he, "the Elephant
> Is very like a rope."
>
> And so these men of Hindostan
> Disputed loud and long,
> Each in his own opinion
> Exceeding stiff and strong,
> Though *each was partly* in the right
> *And all were in the wrong.*
>
> —*by* John Godfrey Saxe

The poem shows that looking at only one part of an issue allows you to form a very mistaken opinion on a subject. People often choose to only look at one part of an issue. The best way to avoid making biased opinions is to try and find as many viewpoints and as much information as possible about any given issue. Analyzing all sides of a text or of an issue will help you form rational, balanced opinions.

Analyzing a text is a complex process. Finding meaning in a text often means relating that text to your life or to information you have already read, and examining smaller parts of a text. One of the great things about literature is that one text can mean different things to different people. It is important to form opinions that are informed when you analyze a text. This section of your *KEY* has shown you how using a variety of methods to analyze a text can ensure that the meaning you find in a text is balanced and enriching.

2.1.1d identify the impact that personal context—experience, prior knowledge—has on constructing meaning from a text

Using What You Read Every Day

Books are powerful: they have the ability to change your thoughts and actions. When you read a book, you are adding the information and experiences of a writer to your body of knowledge. The information you receive from reading does not stay inside the pages of books; it becomes a part of how you interact with the world. After you read a book on pollution, for example, you are likely to begin to look at everyday things differently. If you see someone throwing out a pop can into the garbage rather than the recycling bin, the information you learned in that book will spring to your mind. Activities that might not have bothered you before, such as littering or driving a car, may seem more negative now that you have read that book.

The knowledge that books give allows you to experience the world with a new perspective.

The ultimate goal of most writers, whether they write to inform, explain, persuade, or entertain, is to have their readers connect with and understand what they have written in a personal way. When you make connections in text, you are remembering or internalizing what you read. You make connections by:

- accessing prior knowledge that can help you understand new material
- expressing a new insight or way of looking at an issue or topic by reading a related story, poem, or article
- feeling empathy with a character because of a similar problem or personal experience in your own life
- remembering a movie, play, or other novel that has a related plot or theme to what you are reading

Broaden Your Literary Context

Nearly every form of communication requires context. Until the last century, anyone writing in the English-speaking world could assume an audience had at least some knowledge of the Bible, Shakespeare's plays, Greek and Roman mythology, some poetry, and some classic works of prose like *Pilgrim's Progress*, as well as a basic knowledge of history.

If you want to do as well as possible in your study of English, and especially if you will be going on to university, experience in reading a wide variety of texts is necessary. Each new text you read offers a new perspective and widens your overall knowledge of literature. The more general knowledge you have, the better.

Predicting and Generating Questions

To aid understanding, try to connect yourself with the text. Are there personal experiences in play that influence how you view it?

Connect the words on the page to what you already know. For example, if you are interested in forensics, reading an article on crime investigation is easy because you already have a framework for reading, understanding, and analyzing the language that is used in such an article. When you read any text, think about what you already know about the subject and connect it with what you are reading.

Try to predict what you will learn or what will happen before you begin reading. Using your background knowledge and clues from the text, you can form hypotheses (predictions) as you read. You should be able to support your predictions with facts from the text. Before you begin reading, create questions that will help focus and guide your reading.

The following steps form an example of how you can predict what will be in a text:

1. Before you start reading, ask "I wonder..." questions.

2. Predict what the story will be about, perhaps based on its title.

3. If there are headings or chapter titles, think about what ideas or subjects are being touched upon before reading further.

4. Use any information provided in the text (i.e., about the writer, the preface, the introduction, etc.) to help you predict what information you will be reading or what the story will be about.

The following are types of questions you can ask yourself to guide your reading before you begin:

1. Ask yourself what you already know about the topic of the text or the context of the story.
2. Prepare a written or mental list of questions about what you want to learn and understand from the reading.

An excellent example of the importance of context is seen in almost any of the political cartoons that appear in major daily newspapers all over the world. A reader can read the caption, but without the help of the context of the graphic (which often lends important insight into the historical setting) the caption makes little sense.

In this example, with the aid of the picture, you can infer that the cartoon refers to a victory that has been achieved after a long struggle. The characters in the cartoon indicate that the struggle involves both men and women and that equality has now been elevated to the point where it has been recognized by parliament.

Personal Criticism of Literature

What you enjoy reading is important. Knowing why you enjoy what you read is also important. The reason that you like some texts and dislike others is somewhat elusive and hard to define. What you like has to do with the details of your identity and personal tastes. However, as a critical reader and thinker, you should be able to explain why you feel a certain way about a piece of literature.

In order to illustrate this, take a look at a few stanzas from "The Highwayman" by Alfred Noyes. Why is this poem memorable and appealing? Think about that question as you read the concluding lines to the tragic love story of a beautiful young woman who sacrifices her life in order to warn her outlaw lover that he is riding into a trap.

Example

Tlot-tlot, in the frosty silence! Tlot-tlot in the echoing night!
Nearer he came and nearer! Her face was like a light!
Her eyes grew wide for a moment; she drew one last deep breath,
Then her finger moved in the moonlight,
    Her musket shattered the moonlight,
Shattered her breast in the moonlight and warned him—with her death.
He turned; he spurred to the West; he did not know who stood
Bowed, with her head o'er the musket, drenched with her own red blood!
Not till the dawn he heard it, his face grew grey to hear
How Bess, the landlord's daughter,
    The landlord's black-eyed daughter,
Had watched for her love in the moonlight, and died in the darkness there.

Back, he spurred like a madman, shrieking a curse to the sky,
With the white road smoking behind him and his rapier brandished high!
Blood-red were his spurs in the golden noon; wine-red was his velvet coat,
When they shot him down on the highway,
    Down like a dog on the highway,
And he lay in his blood on the highway, with the bunch of lace at his throat.

And still of a winter's night, they say, when the wind is in the trees,
When the moon is a ghostly galleon tossed upon cloudy seas,
When the road is a ribbon of moonlight over the purple moor,
A highwayman comes riding—
    Riding—riding—
A highwayman comes riding, up to the old inn-door.

Over the cobbles he clatters and clangs in the dark inn-yard;
He taps with his whip on the shutters, but all is locked and barred;
He whistles a tune to the window, and who should be waiting there
But the landlord's black-eyed daughter,
    Bess, the landlord's daughter,
Plaiting a dark red love-knot into her long black hair.

—*by* Alfred Noyes

Here is one student's explanation of why she finds this poem appealing. After reading it, think about what you might agree or disagree with.

Example

I like this poem because of the rhythm—the rhythm is like the beating of a horse's hooves and it gives the poem a lovely atmosphere. The descriptions are very good. They give polish to the poem. I also really like the wording—the specific words, like the rhythm, add atmosphere. It is written in a kind of bold, romantic style that makes the story it is telling more vivid. The poem is well-written—the poem is written in a very sensitive way. The tension is built up very well.

Remember, the purpose of context is to help you better understand what you read. Any strategy that becomes an automatic part of your reading contributes to your success in school and in life and allows you to pursue academic goals with confidence.

2.1.2a use a variety of strategies to comprehend literature and other texts (for example, reading passages out loud, forming questions, making predictions, using context to determine the connotative meanings of words, using graphic organizers and making annotations,) and develop strategies for close reading of literature in order to understand contextual elements (for example, understanding subtext)

Reading and Viewing with a Purpose

As a student in Grade 11, you will be reading a variety of texts and viewing an assortment of materials with your teacher and class, and also on your own. Literature will be set in any number of places, from your home province and country to around the world. Literature is also set in an array of time periods from the past to the present to the future, told from many different perspectives, and representing all cultures. Whether prose or poetry, movies, art, or websites, from Canada or abroad, it is vital that you understand what you are reading and viewing.

Information and Persuasive Texts

As a high school student, you will also be reading a variety of texts, including articles and reports for information and reference; magazines, newspapers, textbooks, biographies and autobiographies for enjoyment and information; print and electronic reference material; opinion-based material and student-generated material. All of this information and texts will be presented in a variety of forms and complexities, and you can use the information and strategies presented in this ***KEY*** to help your comprehend and enjoy these materials.

Visual Texts

As a student in the twenty-first century, you are well versed in the visual arts. Broadcast media, such as television and advertising, play a major role in people's lives today, so it is very important to understand the ideas and forms of media to ensure that you fully comprehend the complex information and media strategies. Film, video, photographs, art, visual print media, and visual texts all offer unique and interesting opportunities for you to understand the components of visual media, how it is meant to affect you, and how you can analyze it for a deeper understanding.

Comprehension Strategies for Pre-Reading and Viewing

Reading comprehension strategies help you to make sense of what you read by focusing on the task and purpose for reading by using your prior knowledge and by making predictions and creating questions. The following strategies highlight how being a thoughtful reader and taking your time as you read is important. The following section provides some specific reading strategies, explanations, and examples that show you how to use these strategies for reading prose, poetry, and visual texts. These strategies are also easily adapted for comprehension of visual texts such as websites, graphic novels, film and video, photographs, art, etc., as you are still able to determine your purpose, access prior knowledge, make predictions, and generate questions of material that you are viewing rather than reading.

A Purpose for Reading

What you do before you start to read can add to your reading experience. One of the most important steps to take before reading is to establish your purpose. The reason you are reading a text can help you decide how to read it. Are you reading to research information for an essay, to answer questions for an assignment, for enjoyment, or to locate the phone number, hours of operation, and address of a new clothing store? How you go about reading for any of these different tasks will change with your purpose.

When you have a purpose for reading, you can keep a closer eye on your progress. You know when to stop and turn around when something is not quite right. Sometimes, you need to revisit your purpose, and at other times, your purpose changes.

The following are some questions to ask before reading a piece of text.

Before Reading

- Are there headings, charts, graphs, vocabulary, or questions that I can preview?
- What is my purpose for reading?
- What will I be doing with the information I read?
- What do I already know about the topic?
- What reading strategies should I use to read this text?
- How is the text organized?
- What questions do I have before reading this text?
- Can I turn headings or subheadings into questions?

Selecting a Reading Rate

Before you begin to read, you should select a reading rate. Your reading rate will vary according to the form of the text, the level of difficulty of the text, and whether you are previewing, skimming, scanning, rereading, rechecking a fact, or reading for enjoyment. For example, if you are skimming a text for information, you will read more quickly than if you are researching a particular topic.

Previewing

Previewing means taking a brief overview or glance at the parts of the text that stand out to you. When previewing, take a look at the reading selection and think about what stands out. Are there headings or titles? Are there graphs or charts? Are there any pictures? Are there captions that describe the pictures? If the passage has any of these things, make a little note in your mind to pay close attention to them as you read.

It is an excellent idea to preview a new text, such as a textbook, before you receive any reading assignments. You can learn helpful information about a course and its content before you even begin.

Here are some possible previewing activities to try with textbooks or any book.

- Look at the publication date. Is it important that this particular text is current?
- Look over the table of contents. How is it organized?
- Does the text have a glossary?
- Is there an index?
- Leaf through the text to check the graphics: pictures, diagrams, charts, maps, and so on. How will these aid your learning?
- Skim through at least one chapter:
  - How is it organized?
  - Are vocabulary terms listed at the beginning?
  - Are the subheadings in a larger, bolded font?
  - Are key words bolded?
  - Are there questions or comments in side bars to help you understand the text as you read?
  - Is there an overview paragraph at the beginning of the chapter?
  - Is the chapter summarized at the end?
  - Is there a chapter review?
  - Does the text include an answer key?

Using Prior Knowledge

Build on your background knowledge and experiences to help you understand any text you read. Take your time reading and use what you already know about something to make the text you are reading clearer. To do this, make connections between what you know and what you read by asking yourself the following questions:

- Does this story remind me of any other stories or texts?
- What do I already know about the topic I am reading about?
- Is there something in this text that is similar to something I already know?

Comprehension Strategies to Use While Reading and Viewing

Clarifying Meaning

While you are reading, it is important to continue to refine the predictions, questions, visualizations, and connections that you created in the pre-reading process so that you are able to monitor and fully understand the text. Here are some questions to ask yourself while reading a piece of text:

During Reading

- Am I meeting the purpose I set out for reading?
- Am I making sense of what I am reading?
- Do I understand what I am reading?
- Do I have a clear visual image in my mind's eye?
- Is what I am reading what I expected?
- Are some parts different or similar to my predictions?
- What is the main idea of the text so far?
- What kind of graphic organizer would I use to begin organizing the ideas?
- What did I visualize in my mind about these ideas while I was reading?
- Is the information in the text similar to other passages that I have read?

In cases where you are not permitted to mark the text itself, you can put symbols or reading comments on sticky notes that can be removed later.

Thoughtful Reading

A thoughtful reading involves the following strategies:

- Activating background knowledge by making connections between new and known information
- Questioning the text to clarify and deepen understanding
- Drawing inferences using background knowledge and clues from the text
- Determining importance in order to distinguish details from the main ideas
- Monitoring comprehension to ensure meaning is being constructed
- Rereading to employ fix-up strategies to repair any confusion
- Using sensory imagery to deepen and enhance comprehension
- Synthesizing to create new thinking

Monitoring for Meaning

Monitoring for meaning refers to checking your understanding of the material that you read. Think about whether or not the text makes sense to you, and think about the broader meaning of the story. Keep in mind that it is perfectly acceptable to have difficulty with or to be confused about some part of a text. Monitoring for meaning means to think about what you understand as well as what you do not understand.

To practice monitoring for meaning, you can ask yourself the following questions as you read:

- Do I understand what I just read?
- What is happening in the story?
- How do the important ideas and details relate to each other?

When you are finished reading, think about any questions you still have. These questions can help you pinpoint parts of the text you may have had trouble with.

- Think about the broader meaning of the text by considering the following questions.
- Who are the characters?
- When does the story take place?
- Where does it take place? What is the conflict?
- Why did the author write the text?

Visualizing

Visualizing is a process in which what you are reading can be like watching a movie. Writers convey information with words. As you read, you can use these words to create pictures in your mind that show what is happening in the text. Usually, visualizing is something that happens naturally for the reader. Through visualization, you can create images of the characters, settings, and events of a story. This can help you remember information more easily than by words alone, and it can deepen your understanding of the text.

To practice visualizing while reading, try the following techniques:

- Pause frequently and describe any pictures in your mind.
- After reading a passage, draw a picture of what you see in your mind.
- Work backward. This could include looking at a wordless picture book and creating a story to match the pictures.

Using Textual Cues to Locate Information

Two ways of using textual cues to locate information are scanning and skimming. Both scanning and skimming involve selective reading to locate specific impressions or information.

Scanning involves looking for specific words related to the information you are seeking. Scanning is not reading; it is searching. For example, you may be asked to read a passage and then answer the following question:

The writer explains that the smallest bone in the body is found in the

A. ear

B. foot

C. skull

D. hand

You could scan the passage for the word *smallest* to check your answer to the question. This technique is also very useful for scrolling through books or the Internet for research.

Following are some situations in which scanning would be effective:

- Looking over a test to assess the number and types of questions
- Looking over a story to assess the length, level of difficulty, introduction, and ending
- Looking over a table of contents of a new text
- Looking over newspaper headlines to see where certain sections or articles are located

Some textbooks have subheadings, notes under diagrams and pictures, or notes in the margins. These notes and subheadings often help to give readers a better understanding of the text by summarizing the information. When reading an expository text, it is useful to be able to summarize the writer's message as you read.

Look at the following article, "Journey Inside," about how blood flows from the heart, around the body, and back to the heart. As you read, try to summarize each paragraph and look for context clues that will help you to understand the vocabulary words, which are bolded.

JOURNEY INSIDE

Look closely at the inside of your wrist and forearm. Can you see any veins? If not, clench your fist and look again. Those bluish veins are carrying blood to your heart. The story of that journey to the heart and back again through your arteries is a little one-minute miracle. Before you continue, write two questions that you would like the article to answer about how blood travels through your body.

Let us follow a drop of blood on a trip around the body. We will start at the tip of a finger, in a **capillary**, the smallest kind of blood vessel. The channel is very narrow here—so narrow that the red blood cells floating along in our drop of blood have to bend and squeeze to slip through.

But after a while the channel begins to broaden. Now the drop of blood is flowing through a little vein called a **venule** (ven′–yool). On and on the blood flows, as the channel grows even wider. It has passed from the tiny venule into a larger vein

Then, suddenly, there is something that looks like a funnel. The drop of blood flows on through. This funnel is a **valve** in the vein; there will be a number of them on the way. These valves help keep the blood flowing along so that it will not slip backward.

On the blood flows, through widening channels of the veins. Then, suddenly, the drop of blood seems to be plunging down into a giant cave. This is an **auricle**, a chamber of the heart. The mighty walls of the cave seem to close down upon the blood in the chamber. But just in time, the floor of the chamber (which is really a valve) opens up wide and the drop of blood goes plunging through, into an even larger and deeper cave. This is a **ventricle**. Now the walls of the second cave close in and the blood is whisked upward through still another valve and out into another channel. This is the **pulmonary artery**, and the blood is now on its way to the lungs.

In the lungs, the blood flows through a network of tiny capillaries, very close to the surface of the many small air pockets of the lungs. The walls of the capillaries are so thin that **gas molecules** can pass freely in and out. It is here in the lungs that the important exchange of gases takes place.

The blood flowing into the lungs is dark, laden with the waste product, **carbon dioxide**, which it has picked up from the cells of the body. This carbon dioxide passes out into the air pockets and is breathed out of the lungs. **Oxygen** that has been breathed into the lungs passes from the air pockets into the capillaries, and the blood flowing out of the lungs is bright and red. Scientists say that it is oxygenated—it has picked up a load of oxygen, which will soon be taken around to the cells of the body.

But first the blood must pass through the heart again. Just as before, the capillaries widen into veins. But the trip this time is much shorter than the journey from a fingertip, and the blood enters the heart from the opposite side. In it flows, down it falls, into an auricle, through a valve, into a ventricle, and out again, into a very wide artery called the **aorta** (ay-or′–ta).

The blood is a raging river now. The red blood cells bounce violently about through the rapids, bumping against other blood cells and against the walls of the artery. As the blood rushes along, the channels get narrower and narrower, as the arteries branch again and again into smaller and smaller blood vessels. These many branches lead to various parts of the body. Some go to the legs, others to the heart, and still others to organs such as the stomach and the liver

But the drop of blood we are following happens to take the branches that lead back to the fingertip where we began to follow its journey. The whole trip took less than a minute!

By scanning, you can see that the passage is about how blood travels through the body.

Here is a summary of the paragraphs of "Journey Inside."

Paragraph 1 – Blood's journey begins in the capillary

Paragraph 2 – Blood travels through little veins (venules) to larger veins

Paragraph 3 – Blood must pass through little valves and keep flowing forward

Paragraph 4 – Blood plunges from one giant cave in the heart (auricle) into another (ventricle) and out into the pulmonary artery to the lungs

Skimming involves quickly looking over all the parts of a text. You are skimming a text when you look at pictures, headings, and bold text without reading the whole piece. This is a useful strategy before and after reading a text in detail. It is especially helpful in reading newspaper articles, textbooks, and web pages. Skimming just part of a story or report to find information that you need will save time.

Skimming is extremely useful for searching the Internet. Skimming through your search results helps you to choose which sites to view. Once you get to a site, skimming can help you to decide if it is what you were looking for. Good skimming skills can save you a lot of time on the Internet.

Skimming a chapter of your textbook before you begin to read it will help you to grasp more of the content and comprehend the organizational parts of the chapter. Here are some tips and strategies for skimming a chapter in a textbook:

- Before reading a chapter, preview it by noting headlines, charts, graphs, and chapter questions.
- Turn each heading and subheading into a question before you begin your reading.
- Read the complete introduction to identify key information that is addressed in the chapter.
- Read the first sentence of each paragraph for the main idea.
- Skim each paragraph, noting key words, phrases, and information.
- Read the last sentence of each paragraph.
- Read the complete conclusion to summarize each chapter's contents.
- Answer the questions you created.
- Answer the chapter questions.

Determining Meanings and Uses of Words Based on Context

Using Context Clues to Substitute a Different Word

When you are having trouble understanding a word, try looking at the context clues in the surrounding words of the sentence. Often, there will be other words in the sentence that you understand and that add to the meaning of the sentence. There may also be other words that you are struggling with. Once you have an idea of the context of the word, try substituting a different word into the sentence to see if it makes sense. If the new word agrees with the meaning of the sentence, chances are the word you were struggling with means something similar to the new word you substituted.

Example

- Glancing *dispassionately* at his list of instructions, Gordon, with a casual shrug of his shoulders, took his time leaving the office.

Figure it out: the context, especially the words glancing and casual, suggests that Gordon does not care. Try substituting carelessly or indifferently for dispassionately. Do they work?

Example

- In her white furs, emerald jewelry, and shimmering silver gown, the countess made her *ostentatious* entrance into the Grand Ballroom as the strains of the first waltz wafted from the orchestra pit.

Figure it out: the context of jewels, expensive clothing, and the Grand Ballroom suggest possible substitutions such as *showy* or *extravagant* for ostentatious. Do these substitutions make sense?

Substituting might not give you the exact definition of a word, but it will get you close. Use the words you know to help you with the words you do not know. Use a dictionary to confirm that your guess is correct. The dictionary will give you a precise answer, but guessing and substituting are important stages of understanding the meaning of a word.

Using Context Clues to Comprehend Words

When you are reading a text, you can often clarify the meaning of an unfamiliar word in one of the following ways.

- Find the definition in the text.
  - In Japan, the most popular good luck charm is the Daruma-San. This is an egg-shaped doll with a fierce face and blank eyes.
  - Many foods spoil quickly because of microorganisms. Microorganisms are bacteria that are too small to be seen with the naked eye.

Sometimes, the word will be bolded with the definition provided at the bottom of the page or in the glossary at the back of the book.

- Look for examples in the text. Often, an example is introduced by the phrases *for example* or *for instance*.
  - A pickle, for instance, is a fermented food.

You can conclude from this example that *pickled* and *fermented* are synonyms.

Look for a restatement of the word or phrase. Often, this restatement follows *or* or *which is*

- My maternal grandfather, or my grandfather on my mother's side, lived to be 101.
- Pemmican, which is a pounded paste of dried meat, melted fat, and berries, was a staple of the diet of First Nations people.

- A term may also be restated as an appositive without a cueing word or phrase.
  - Softball, a form of baseball played with a larger and softer ball, is becoming more popular.
  - India braces each year for the monsoons, seasonal winds from the Indian Ocean that bring heavy rains.
- Look for contrasts. If you notice pairs of contrasts, try to predict the meaning of the unfamiliar word from the other word in the pair.
  - The sauerkraut was not bland, but sour and acidic. (*bland* must be neutral)
  - How could an experience be both gratifying and frustrating at the same time? (*gratifying* must be similar to rewarding)
  - Anson stared at the bubbling mixture. Would it be toxic or harmless? (*toxic* must mean harmful or poisonous)
- Find comparisons. Words such as *like*, *similar to*, or *as if* give clues to meaning.
  - A lagoon is like a pond.
  - A lagoon is similar to a pond.
  - Jeremy's face look frightened, as if he had seen a ghost.

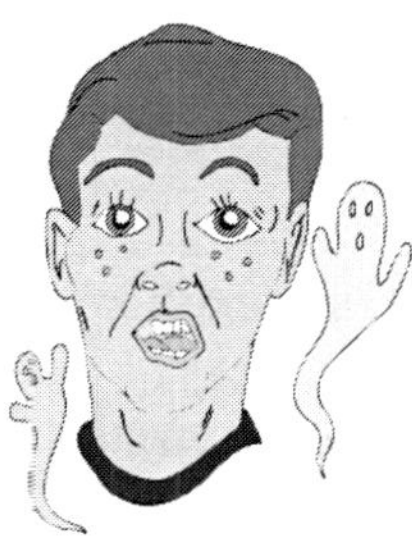

Multiple-Meaning Words

Words can have more than one meaning, and sometimes these meanings are quite different from each other. The word *break*, for instance, has multiple uses: break the glass, coffee break, "Give me a break," break some news, break the silence, etc.

Homographs or *multiple-meaning words* are words that share the same spelling but have different meanings. Sometimes, the words are pronounced differently, but when you read them, you can determine their meaning from the context.

Example

- *well* (noun) – a hole drilled into the ground
- *well* (adverb) – in good health

I was feeling well enough to help my father drill a new *well.*

Example

- *sound* (adjective) – untroubled, strong, secure, sensible, free from injury
- *sound* (noun) – something heard as noise or musical tones
- *sound* (verb) – to carefully find out someone's thoughts or feelings
- *sound* (noun) – a narrow passage of water

I was awoken from a sound sleep by the *sound* of the distant drums from across *Puget Sound.*

These sentences demonstrate that you can usually figure out the meaning of a word that has more than one possible meaning when you see the word in context.

Coined Words

Etymology is the study of word origins. It is fascinating to discover how and where words originated. Because English is a living language, it is continually changing and growing. New words are always being added to the lexicon (English dictionary).

Coined words are catchphrases or sayings that evolve and then become commonly used. Because they are so commonly used, they tend to be perceived as trite and clichéd. Shakespeare is probably the best-known writer for coining phrases that have become very familiar. Following are some examples of a few words Shakespeare coined or made up: *fashionable*, *dauntless*, *vulnerable*, *unearthly*, and *embrace*.

Shakespeare also coined some well-known phrases, such as *eaten out of house and home*, *pomp and circumstance*, and *neither rhyme nor reason*. Since Shakespeare coined words and phrases in the 16th and 17th centuries, they are no longer really considered coined words. Coined words and phrases should generally be avoided in your writing. Rather, you should choose a more concise and colourful vocabulary that your reader will be sure to understand. However, if you do use them deliberately, do so sparingly.

Dialects in Literature

Dialect refers to a particular manner of speech within a language. Words spoken in a dialect can have their own pronunciations. Various dialects even use different words and phrases than the main language. Many people in Quebec, for example, speak a dialect of French that is different from the French that is spoken in France. Dialect is usually a product of the speaker's cultural or regional background. Dialects can be so specific to a region that it can be difficult for others to understand.

For example, Cockney is a dialect that is used by people native to south London. The musical *My Fair Lady,* based on the play *Pygmalion* by George Bernard Shaw, provides a wealth of examples of the Cockney dialect from its main character, Eliza Doolittle. In an opening scene of the musical, Professor Higgins, a linguistics professor, is hiding behind a nearby pillar, copying every word she says. He is intrigued by how different Eliza's dialect is from formal English. Eliza is heard to remark "I say, capt'n', n'baw ya flahr orf a pore gel," which Higgins translates into formal English as "I say, captain, now buy yourself a flower off a poor girl."

Writers generally use dialect to make their characters more believable according to the setting in which the story takes place. Sometimes, writers will even spell words according to how they sound in a certain dialect.

Roots, Prefixes, and Suffixes

Many scholars think that in prehistoric Europe, there may have been a common language, which is now referred to as proto-Indo-European. However, as people moved around over many hundreds of years seeking food and grazing lands, they became isolated from each other and, as a result, developed their own languages.

The three main branches of the Indo-European language family that have most influenced the development of English are the Germanic, Italic, and Hellenic languages.

The Germanic language branch had the greatest influence on the English language, but Italian, Latin, French, Spanish, and Greek have all contributed to the development of the English language. To this day, the English language continues to change and grow as it absorbs new words and phrases.

Many English prefixes and suffixes are derived from Greek and Latin. These words become altered and can often lead to new words being invented.

A *prefix* is defined as one or more syllables added to the beginning of a root word to form a new word. Here are a few examples of prefixes derived from Greek and Latin.

Latin Prefix	Meaning	Example Word
ante-	before	anterior, antemeridian (a.m.)
ben-, bon-	good, well	benefit, bonanza
bi-	two	bicycle, binary
mal-	bad, ill	malfunction, malnutrition
migr-	to move, travel	migrate, migration
Greek Prefix	**Meaning**	**Example Word**
anti-	against	anticlimactic
auto-	self	automatic, automobile
hemi-	half	hemisphere, hemicycle
tele-	far off	telephone, telepathic
poly-	many	polygon, polygraph

Suffixes have the special job of changing the root word to another part of speech; for example, a verb, a noun, an adjective, or an adverb. Here are a few examples of Latin and Greek suffixes with their purposes.

Latin Suffix	Role of the Suffix	Example Word
-age	forms a noun	belongs to (storage)
-ance	forms a noun	state of being (appearance)
-ible, -able	forms an adjective	capable of being (possible)
-ive	forms an adjective	belonging to/quality of (attractive)
-ly	forms an adverb	like/to the extent of (happily)
-ate	forms a verb	to make (alienate)
-fy	forms a verb	to make (simplify)
Greek Suffix	**Role of the Suffix**	**Example Word**
-y	forms an abstract noun	state of (e.g., happy)
-ism	forms a noun	act/condition
-ic	forms an adjective	having the nature of (e.g., pathetic)

As you can see, there are more Latin suffixes than there are Greek. As the English language developed, many prefixes, suffixes, and root words from both Latin and Greek were joined together and the resulting English word is derived from both languages.

Adding a prefix to a root word changes its meaning. For example, the prefixes *pre-*, *post-*, and *ante-* all change the time frame of a root word. *Pre-* and *ante-* both mean "before," while *post-* means "after." Look at the following root words and how their meanings change when a prefix is added.

Root	Meaning	Prefix + Root	New Meaning
Condition	State of person or a thing	*Pre*condition	Something necessary for a result to occur
View	Act of seeing or looking	*Pre*view	An advance showing
Chamber	A room, especially a bedroom	*Ante*chamber	A waiting room
Script	Handwriting	*Post*script	A note added to a letter that has already been signed

A suffix also adds meaning to a root word or changes it slightly.

The suffixes *-ic, -tic, -ical,* and *-al* mean "having to do with." When one of these suffixes is added to a root word, the new word takes a different form, including a different spelling. Look at how a suffix affects a root word. Notice also how the spelling of each word is altered and how each root is changed from a noun to an adjective.

Root	Meaning	Root + Suffix	New Meaning
Economy	Financial system	Econom*ic*	To do with the economy
Drama	Plays and theatrical art	Dramat*ic*	Overtly expressive or emotional
Analyse	Examine carefully	Analyt*ical*	Logical or reasoning
Structure	A building or other constructed object	Structur*al*	Part of a structure

Root words from Greek and Latin can sometimes appear to be prefixes and suffixes, but they are actually the roots or main parts of the words. Here are some examples of Greek and Latin root words.

Root	Origin	Meaning	Derivations
bio	Greek	life	*bio*graphy
lab	Latin	to work	*lab*our
phone	Greek	voice, sound	*phono*graph
port	Latin	to carry	*port*able

If you take the time to learn the meanings of commonly used prefixes, suffixes, and root words, you can better identify the meanings of words that use them. This knowledge allows you to break unfamiliar words into meaningful chunks that can be decoded or figured out.

Look at the following examples to help you understand this concept. Remember that prefixes (pre = before) are placed before the root word and suffixes (suf = under) are placed after the root word.

- ***atheist*** = *a-the-ist* = *a* (without), *theo* (God), *ist* (one who) = one who does not believe in God
- ***incredible*** = *in-cred-i-ble* = in (not), *credibilis* (deserving of belief) = seems to be impossible or unbelievable
- ***circumnavigation*** = *circum*-navigate-ion = *circum* (around), *navigate* (to travel by ship), *ation* (state of) = the act of travelling around the world

Most of the time when you read text, you do not have to rely on a dictionary or thesaurus to understand most of the words. These tools should be a last resort. You will generally have good vocabulary comprehension if you watch for context clues. Context clues come from the familiar words around the unfamiliar words.

Frequently Used Foreign Words

English is a language of borrowed words. As you have already seen, the majority of English words have been derived from Greek, Latin, or Old English origins; however, as the English language has spread throughout the world, through travel, trade, and settlement, many other cultures have also contributed words to the English language.

A sampling of familiar foreign words has been provided, along with their culture of origin. Most of these words have been so completely adopted that you use them as everyday words without even thinking about their origins.

African		Dutch		French	
• banana	• jazz	• ahoy	• cruiser	• abhor	•competition
• banjo	• jive	• apartheid	• deck	• able	• force
• bongo	• jukebox	• boss	• dock	• academy	• machine
• coffee	• tango	• bow	• drive	• account	• police
• chimpanzee	• trek	• bundle	• etch	• adolescence	• publicity
• gumbo	• zebra	• buoy	• easel	• adopt	• role
		• clove	• freight	• a la carte	• routine
		• cookie	• gas	• art	• table
		• crimp	• golf		

German		Hawaiian		Indian (Hindi)	
• frankfurter	• sauerkraut	• hula	• luau	• bangle•	guru
• hamburger	• strudel	• kahuna	• aloha	• bandana	• karma
• kindergarten	• wiener			• bungalow	• loot
• pretzel	• wurst (liverwurst)			• caravan	• pajamas
				• chai (tea)	• path
				• cheetah	• punch
				• cot	• shampoo
				• cushy	• verandah

Irish		Italian		Japanese	
• bog	• crag	• arcadei	• carpet	• bonsaii	•karate
• bother	• dig	• artisan	• cartoon	• futon	• ninja
• boycott	• drum	• balcony	• conversation	• haiku	• samurai
• brogue	• galore			• judo	• sumo
• clan				• karaoke	• origami

Indigenous (American—Algonquin, Mikmaq, etc.)		**Persian**		**Russian**	
• caribou	• muskrat	• angel	• bronze	• babushka	• parka
• chipmunk	• muskeg	• arsenic	• carafe	• cosmonaut	• ruble
• hickory	• opossum	• azure	• carcass	• mammoth	• sable
• husky	• pecan	• bazaarr	• cash		
• moccasin	• toboggan	• beige	• caviar		
• moose		• borax			

Spanish		**Yiddish**	
• adobe	• armadillo	• bagel	• kosher
• adios	• armada	• chutzpah	• lox
• albatross	• artichoke	• glitch	• nosh (food)
• albino	• avocado	• kibitz	• schmuck (foolish person)
• alcove	• barbeque	• klutz	
• alligator	• bonanza		
• amigo	• breeze		
• apricot	• buckaroo		
• barracuda			

Determining Meaning of Unknown Words and Phrases

Understanding Unfamiliar Words

What should you do when you encounter an unfamiliar word as you are reading?

When you read, you automatically decode words. *Decoding* means identifying or understanding meaning. As you read a passage, the familiar words are quite easy to decode because the meaning you know fits appropriately into the sentence or context. If your automatic decoding does not work for a particular word, or if the word is unfamiliar, some of the decoding strategies described below may help you to understand the word as it is being used in the passage. Understanding the words you read improves your reading comprehension.

Decoding

Read the whole sentence to see if you can guess the meaning of the unknown word. Does your guess make sense, or do the other words in the sentence give you a clue to what the unknown word might be?

- Look for root words. For example, the root word of *simplify* is *simple*.
- Look for compound words. Compound words are made up of two parts; for example, *some* and *thing* becomes *something*.
- Look for word families or chunks within the word. For example, *infatuate* can be broken into easy chunks like *in-fat-u-ate*.
- Sound out the word.
- If possible, look the word up in a dictionary.

If you are unable to figure out the word, skip the word and try to understand what is being said in the sentence without the word.

Figure it out:

Knowing what part of speech a word is and then recognizing its syntax or word order in a sentence pattern can help you to decode a word's meaning. First of all, look at the form of the following words used for different parts of speech:

Verb	Noun	Adjective	Adverb
beautify depend	beauty dependent	beautiful dependable	beautifully dependably

Now, look at how these words might be used in sentences:

The students *beautified* the field behind their new school by planting trees and shrubs.

Figure it out: Beautified is a verb, and the suffix *–ified* usually refers to the changing or acting upon of something. The word must mean the students made the grounds more beautiful by planting trees.

You will be a *dependent* until you turn 18.

Figure it out: Dependent is a noun. You know the meaning of the verb *depend*, so *dependent* must mean a person who relies on adults for their care because he or she is not self-sufficient.

Sounding Words Out Phonetically

Another strategy you can use to decode unfamiliar words is to sound words out phonetically by breaking them into smaller parts or syllables. Often, a word will have syllables that are prefixes roots, and suffixes. Breaking down a word into its smaller parts of meaning is a good strategy to find the meaning of that word.

The following example is taken from a poem "The Prelude," by William Wordsworth. Wordsworth is describing the joy and freedom associated with outdoor skating. Because the language of the poem may be unfamiliar to you, some of the strategies described earlier in this section will help you understand the more difficult words in the poem, some of which have been underlined to be decoded for meaning after the poem has been read. While you are reading, try to guess what the meaning of each underlined word is from the context of the poem as well as by using the strategies you have learned about prefixes, suffixes, and root words.

"SKATING" FROM "THE PRELUDE"

—All shod with steel,

We hiss'd along the polish'd ice, in games

Confederate, imitative of the chace

And woodland pleasures, the resounding horn,

The Pack loud bellowing, and the hunted hare.

So through the darkness and the cold we flew,

And not a voice was idle; with the din,

Meanwhile, the precipices rang aloud,

The leafless trees, and every icy crag

Tinkled like iron, while the distant hills

Into the tumult sent an alien sound

Of melancholy, not unnoticed, while the stars

Eastward, were sparkling clear, and in the west

The orange sky of evening died away.

—by William Wordsworth

Word Meanings in "Skating"

Confederate: The word *confederate* is used here as an adjective describing the noun games. *Con-* as a prefix means with, while you might associate *federation* with a group of states or provinces united under one government. Put all that together, and "games confederate" would mean ice games in which all or most of the skaters joined.

Chace: When you read this word in the context of the adjective *imitative* along with the whole propositional phrase "of the chace" and read the next two lines, you could understand that the poet is referring to *chase*, which was an English foxhunt. The skaters are involved in a chase or probably a form of tag on ice.

Resounding and bellowing: These words are being used as adjectives ("resounding horn," "Pack loud bellowing"). When you go back to "imitative of," understand the root words *imitate*, *sound*, and *bellow*, and think about the meaning of the prefix *re*-, you should arrive at the meaning. The skaters are sounding pretend horns as they chase each other over the ice, and baying or barking loudly like a pack of hunting dogs.

Now, try to think of definitions of the next six words that were underlined in the poem using the clues and questions in the following section.

Din: What does "not a voice was idle" imply about the meaning of *din*? What word could you substitute here?

Precipices: What part of speech is this? How is "icy crag" similar to this word? What do the verbs *rang* and *tinkled* tell you about "precipices" and "icy crags"?

Tumult: Could this be substituted with another underlined word used earlier?

Alien: What part of speech is this? What is the meaning of *alien* used as a noun? What would it mean, then, as used to describe "sound"?

Melancholy: In the whole phrase, "alien sound / Of melancholy," what must be meant by "melancholy"? What word suggests it is quite different from the noisy sounds coming from the skaters?

Unnoticed: What is meant by the root word *notice*? What does the prefix un- do to the meaning of the word? What does placing the word *not* before the word do to the meaning?

Exploring Word Families Using Graphics

The discipline that searches for the origins of words is called *etymology*. Basic word derivation information is provided in any good dictionary. If you check the front section of the dictionary, you will find an abbreviation key that will explain abbreviations used in the derivation portion of the entry.

Example

Gk = Greek

It = Italian

Related words or word families (from the same root) can also be explored as a strategy for expanding your vocabulary. You could use a graphic organizer to track and expand a word, as illustrated in the example that follows.

Word derivation shown in dictionary:

master [L. *magister*: akin to L. magnus great –] 1. a male teacher 2. a person holding an academic degree higher than a bachelor's but lower than a doctor's.

Word family derivation shown in graphic diagram:

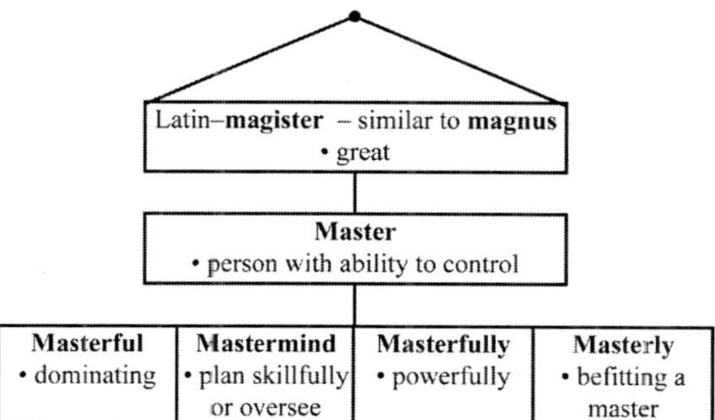

You may use these decoding strategies more consciously at first. Over time, though, you may find that these strategies become a more internal part of how you read, and you may find that you use these strategies quickly without thinking about them too much. You will find that these decoding strategies will begin to become second nature as your vocabulary and reading comprehension improves.

2.1.2b describe how supporting ideas and supporting details strengthen a text's controlling idea

Find the Controlling Idea

Determining what is important in a text is particularly useful for non-fiction and informational texts. You can save time by distinguishing between what is vital information in a text and what may be less important. By identifying important ideas and themes, you can set aside less important information.

To practice determining what information is most important in a text, try the following techniques:

- While reading, look for clues in the format of the text that might indicate importance. Pay attention to the first and last lines of a paragraph, the title, any headings or subheadings, captions, framed text (text with a box drawn around it), quotation marks, font size, and font style (underlined text, italicized text, bold text).
- Pay particular attention to pictures, illustrations, charts, and diagrams; they may provide you with important information.
- As you read, focus on remembering information that appears to be "must-know" information.
- After reading, think about what was the most important information you learned.

Determining the Relationship between the Controlling Idea and Supporting Ideas

If you are having trouble understanding something you are reading, different strategies can help. As you use these strategies, they will become more and more familiar to you, and in time, you will probably use them without even realizing it. The following list describes some strategies that can help your reading comprehension.

- **Reread:** sometimes, a second reading is all that it takes. If you cannot make a picture in your mind or you do not understand what you have just read, try reading it again.
- **Skip ahead:** sometimes, you need to move on. If you do not understand something you have just read, skip ahead and continue reading. There may be information later on that helps you to understand the section that you are having trouble with. You can always go back and reread difficult sections later.
- **Context clues:** use familiar words surrounding an unfamiliar word to help you determine the unfamiliar word's meaning.
- **Picture clues:** use information from pictures to help make sense of what you have read.
- **Ask for help:** ask a teacher, parent, classmate, or sibling for help when you have tried your own strategies and still do not understand something.

Summarizing and Paraphrasing

While you are reading, it is often helpful to take notes or record information for future use. Summarizing is used to put the main point or points into your own words and give a broad overview of the information. Paraphrasing is used to condense the information from a passage. Whether summarizing or paraphrasing, you must properly attribute the original source.

When reading literature, you would then be able to summarize the piece for future reference. When reading a textbook or other informational source, you may need to record and paraphrase the information for later use. Be sure to always record the appropriate information so that you may attribute the source correctly.

Summarizing

There are many efficient methods for summarizing and recording information. Methods that work well for recording information are logical notes, summaries, and graphical organizers such as charts. Imagine that you have come across the article below, "Signs of Eruption," while researching information for a report on volcanoes. Read through the article, and then look at how you might organize its key information using these methods.

Logical Notes

The word "logical" simply means makes good sense. Logical notes put main ideas and supporting details into sensible order and clear patterns so that you can understand them more easily. This also makes them easier to use in your assignments. Because this particular volcano developed over a period of time, a chronological order makes sense for recording some notes. You might also prefer a cause-and-effect pattern of notes, because the eruption of Mount St. Helens was a natural catastrophe with clear causes and devastating results. Examine the two types of notes that follow. Do they seem to include all of the key information from the article?

SIGNS OF ERUPTION

Over the past 500 years, Mount St. Helens in Washington has erupted numerous times. There were never any warning signs or ways to detect when it would happen again.

This all changed in the early 1980s when scientists believed they had found clues that Mount St. Helens was going to erupt again. They were right. On May 18, 1980, Mount St. Helens erupted violently causing vast damage. Why did this happen? Scientists now know the volcano erupted because of the movement of tectonic plates. The undersea Juan de Fuca plate is slowly sliding under the North American continental plate. The process creates molten rock, which is what provided Mount St. Helens with its incredible power.

How did scientists detect that another volcanic eruption was coming? There were three major clues. The first clue came when small earthquakes that trembled under the volcano became bigger and happened more often. The second clue was a different type of earthquake that showed up on scientific instruments on April 1, 1980. This was the sound of creeping magma and several small eruptions of steam and ash. The third clue was a large bulge that developed on the north face of the volcano. Scientists realized that this bulge was filling with magma. Because of these clues, they believed that Mount St. Helens would soon erupt violently.

On the morning of May 18, an earthquake knocked the bulge off of the north face. The volcano was now a pressure cooker without a lid to prevent it from blowing. The magma expanded and a gigantic blast occurred. The eruption destroyed trees for up to 28 kilometres around and sent nearly 500 million tones of ash into the atmosphere which fell to Earth up to several hundred kilmetres away.

The eruption killed 57 people, along with thousands of forest animals and fish. It also did devastating damage to valuable property and crops.

Only one benefit came out to the destructive eruption: the ash that Mount St. Helens poured along the Pacific Coast made it some of the richest agricultural land in the world.

a) Timeline Mount St. Helens

- 1480–1980 – Mt. St. Helens erupts several times
- ongoing – Juan de Fuca plate is shifting under North American plate, creating molten rock called magma
- April 1, 1980 – new type of quake shows on instruments
  - creeping magma sounds
  - mini-eruptions of ash, steam
  - bulge pushes against north face of mountain as magma builds
- May 18, 1980 – earthquake cracks bulge open
  - huge blast of gases and steam
  - entire forests levelled nearly 28 kilometres away
  - 500 million tons of ash create cloud around the globe
  - 57 people die
  - millions of animals, trees destroyed
  - property, crops flattened or buried under ash
- 1980–2000 and beyond – ash transformed into some of the best agricultural land in world

b) Cause-and-Effect Notes

A Natural Disaster – Eruption of Mount St. Helens

Cause	Effect
• Undersea plates shift	• Molten rock is created • Small earthquakes • Larger, more frequent earthquakes • New quake April 1, 1980 • Bulge created by magma in north face of mountain • Large earthquake on May 18 blows out bulge • Massive volcano eruption

Mount St. Helens erupts on morning of May 18, 1980

- Gases and steam in magma expand
- 500 million tons of ash blow high into stratosphere
- Cloud of ash circles Earth
- 57 people, millions of animals die
- Forests 28 kilometres away levelled
- Property, crops destroyed
- Farmers lose millions
- Ash converts to rich soil over next few decades

A KWL Chart can also help you to organize your thoughts so that you stay focused and on topic. The K represents *Know*, as in what you know already; the W represents *Want to Know*, as in what more you want to know as a result of reading a text; and, the L represents *Learned*, as in what you learned by reading the text.

Topic ____________________

What I Know	What I Want to Know	What I Learned

2.1.2c describe the relationship among plot, setting, character, atmosphere and theme when studying a narrative

Plot, Setting, Character, Atmosphere and Theme

The elements of plot, setting, atmosphere, and character combine almost inextricably in a connective web to establish the theme of a piece of literature. A narrative or a play usually involves a character with some problem or conflict, and thus the plot naturally revolves around this problem. The manner in which this central problem is resolved can often become the theme of a piece. Similarly, the setting or the atmosphere of the piece contributes to the plot and how the characters behave. Shakespeare's *Macbeth* offers an excellent example of how the abovementioned components operate together to enhance the themes of corrupt ambition and paradox.

Plot

Plot is not merely a string of events—it is the causal relationships between the events and the characters that experience them; therefore, plot cannot be isolated from character. Characters do things for reasons, and those reasons form an indispensable element of plot. Obviously, which character did what to whom is the basis of this component of the story—the "why" for the things that happen.

The plot draws the reader into the characters' lives and helps the reader understand the choices that the characters make. In *Macbeth*, for example, Lady Macbeth and her husband commit treachery and murder Duncan so that Macbeth can achieve the power they both lust for. The guilt and remorse that plague them both after having committed this terrible deed give rise to the further violence and betrayal that defines the play.

Character

Character refers to the qualities assigned to the individual figures in the plot. Consider why a writer might give particular qualities to a character or characters. Consider, too, how character can be affected through plot. What if a loyal, devoted soldier were suddenly faced with the possibility of great power and wealth? This might serve as a basis for the man's development into a much more remarkable, dynamic character. Such is the case with Macbeth.

Lady Macbeth's ambition for her husband is even stronger than his own. This character trait is what makes it possible for her to goad him into committing murder. The unfolding plot of his descent into treachery and violence at her bidding shows how ambition and greed can alter even a man who was once honest and loyal.

Setting

Setting refers to the environment in which the actions of a story occur. The time period, the location, the time of day, the season, and the weather, the type of room or building—all of these elements can reflect on the story's plot, atmosphere, and even the character.

The dark, wintery, remote area of medieval Scotland and a shadowy castle at night is a fitting setting for the events that occur in *Macbeth.* Political unrest is the catalyst for the murders; the motivation is ambition for power. Macbeth and his wife commit their evil deeds under cover of the darkness so that they will not be discovered. Even the scenes with the witches are carefully set to encourage the audience to accept the sorcery and prophecies of Macbeth's doom.

Atmosphere

Closely bound to setting is the atmosphere of a narrative. By providing a suitable setting for the action of the plot to take place, the writer can achieve the necessary mood or atmosphere. Of course the atmosphere affects the characters and consequently their actions, thus linking it tightly to character and plot.

In *Macbeth* the atmosphere creates an important image in the mind of the audience, and more importantly, the instinct to respond in a biased way to the events in the play. When the witches appear, the audience suspects (rightly so) that something bad will happen.

The plot of *Macbeth* revolves around disorder and chaos, and the atmosphere of dark, brooding castle is a plausible setting for such actions—the eclipse, the owl killing the falcon, the assertion by the witches of "fair is foul and foul is fair" all contribute to a brooding, menacing atmosphere. Here, actions can be initiated and characters can be moved to foul deeds and confusion.

2.1.2d compare the personality traits, roles, relationships, motivations, attitudes, values and archetypal qualities, when appropriate, of characters developed/persons presented in literature and other texts

The characters in a story provide you with figures you can try to relate to. Their attitudes and values, their motivations, and their relationships with each other provide the basis for the piece of literature. Character is the element of a text that ties all the other elements of plot, setting, and theme together.

Because character is so closely linked to other elements, skilful character analysis provides an effective tool for understanding a piece of literature.

Analyzing a Character

Here are some questions to consider when you examine a character. They are accompanied by some examples related to the novel *Of Mice and Men* by John Steinbeck.

- What is the character's motivation?
  - Think of George and his attempt to protect Lennie while striving to fulfill their dream of a ranch of their own
- What does the character think and feel?
- What is the character's effect on other characters?
- What are the items associated with the character? What do they mean?
- Lennie's mouse is a symbol of both his love for small things and also of his uncontrolled strength
- What does the character look like physically?
  - Lennie is enormous—often described with words associated with an animal (hands like paws)
  - George: small, quick, restless eyes, and sharp strong features
- What do other characters (or the narrator) say about the character? What is the historical time period or context of the character? Are there external forces that influence, challenge or motivate the character?

All characters in a story have a purpose. Ask yourself if the character is a major or minor character in the story's plot.

Minor Characters

If the character is minor, what is his or her function in the story?

For example, in John Steinbeck's *Of Mice and Men*, Curly's wife is a minor character. Steinbeck does not even give her a name. However, she plays a vital role in the story, serving as the catalyst for Lennie's demise and the destruction of his and George's " dream." Often, the archetypal qualities of a character represent the challenge or conflict that the major characters must struggle to overcome.

Major Characters

If the character is major, determine whether he or she is the protagonist or antagonist. The answer to this question gives rise to the type of conflict in the story: Man vs. Man, Man vs. Society, Man vs. Himself, Man vs. Nature. It is also important to note whether or not the character is static or dynamic.

In *Of Mice and Men*, George is protagonist of the story. His character blends gruffness with loyalty and devotion to Lennie, his friend. Through this character, the conflict of Man vs. Society in the story is defined: George struggles to protect Lennie from the persecution of a society defined by rules and judgement. Through George's actions and relationships with other characters, the reader is urged to consider the views of society and contemplate the themes of power, loneliness, and loyalty. George's progression from a man who sometimes teased Lennie for fun to a friend who sacrifices his dream to the point of killing Lennie to save him from the cruelty of others indicates that he is a dynamic character. Examining this progression gives you a deeper understanding of theme.

Lennie is a major character, but he is less dynamic than George. Nevertheless, these unchanging characteristics help the reader to understand the futility of George's quest to include Lennie in his "dream" and to care for and protect him.

Archetypes or Stereotypes

Archetypes or stereotypes are employed as a type of shorthand for storytelling, because they are instantly familiar. In *Of Mice and Men*, Steinbeck employs the recognizable archetypal characters of the small, quick, clever man (George) and the lumbering kind-hearted giant (Lennie). When the plot throws these men together with the archetypical temptress (Curly's wife), the outcome is predictably disastrous. These archetypal qualities go a long way in defining the character for the reader.

2.1.2f interpret figurative language, symbol and allusions; recognize imagery; and explain how imagery contributes to atmosphere, characterization and theme in a text

Figurative Language

When you read a piece of literature, it is important to bear in mind that the sound of a word can be as important as its meaning. Literature employs a broad range of figurative language, symbolism, and imagery in order to help the reader look through the obvious meaning and content of a piece to infer an implied meaning. Symbols and imagery tend to appeal more to the senses than to reason and intelligence. In this manner, they add just as much to the effect of a piece as do the words themselves.

On an examination, you should be prepared to recognize not only different figures of speech, but also to identify their meaning, as well as their appeal, within the piece of literature. More than anything, figures of speech embellish style. Some paint a picture, others describe proportion, and some compare and contrast to add clarity and interest.

Figurative language uses imagery and figures of speech to convey an idea, a feeling, or a concept. Figurative language is the opposite of literal language. Literal language describes something just as it is, as in the following sentences:

- He was unfriendly to his guests.
- I was angry
- She was very beautiful.

Figurative language expresses things in a nonliteral way, by creating imagery and affecting the senses of the reader, as in these examples:

- He gave his guests a chilly reception.
- Smoke was coming out of my ears.
- She took my breath away.

A writer paints a picture in the mind of the readers by appealing to their senses of smell, taste, touch, sight, and hearing. For example, this sentence should paint a picture in your mind:

- "The wind whistled through the dancing leaves of copper and gold as the storm howled its fury in glow of twilight"

Examples of figures of speech include metaphor, hyperbole, simile, paradox, personification, and irony.

Figurative language is used in prose (stories, articles) as well as in poetry. Pay close attention to the underlined phrases in the following paragraph:

> Out in the bay, treacherous currents sizzle and leap among the underlying rocks with the relentless (1) purpose of a hungry dragon. Which unsuspecting ship will be (2) on the menu today? (3) Like a spoiled child, the waves demand (4) their favorite meal, the creaking timbers of a vessel too weak to escape the (5) cruel, crunching (6) jaws of the ravenously hungry sea.

The figurative and metaphorical uses of words in the paragraph are explained below:

1. "purpose of a hungry dragon" is a metaphor that compares the sea with a dragon.
2. "on the menu" is a metaphor that compares the sea with a restaurant.
3. "Like a spoiled child" is a simile that compares the sea with a child in the middle of a temper tantrum.
4. "Their favorite meal" is a metaphor that compares the waves with customers ordering food at a restaurant.
5. "cruel, crunching" is an alliteration, which is the repetition of the beginning consonant sound.
6. "jaws" is a metaphor that compares the frightening waves with the jaws of a monster dragon.

Allusion

Allusion is another way in which a writer can create images or create connections in the reader's mind. Allusion is a reference to something or someone in history or literature that helps to create a mental image in the reader's mind. Allusions are almost universally recognized, so the strong images and ideas they conjure up can add immeasurably to the theme or message of a piece simply by their mention. Common allusions are biblical allusions, literary allusions (for example allusions to Shakespeare), and mythological allusions.

Through allusion, a writer can say much more than is expressed in the words themselves.

Consider these examples:

- Allusion to the Greek warrior Achilles, or the expression "Achilles' heel" immediately suggests a fatal weakness in a character.
- Suggesting that a character is a "Romeo" conjures up the image of a passionate lover.
- Calling a character "a Scrooge" refers to his or her greed
- The mention of "Judas" or of "the kiss of death" helps the reader to imagine duplicity and betrayal.

2.1.2g analyze visual and aural elements, and explain how they contribute to the meaning of texts

Analyzing Texts

Sometimes, students say that analyzing a text is what ruins it for them or that it is like dissecting a frog in a biology class: after you are finished dissecting the poor creature, there is nothing left of the original living, breathing frog. But it is possible to analyze a text and not ruin it completely for yourself by keeping in mind what you are really doing. Analysis is not like dissecting a frog; rather, it is a way to return to a text you have really enjoyed and ask yourself some technical questions about what makes it enjoyable. Here, analysis refers primarily to the craft of composition, the art of fine writing. In order to find ways to talk about the finer points of a text you have enjoyed, you will need some special terms. As you become a better reader, you will want to become more skilled at analyzing texts while continuing to enjoy them for your own personal reasons.

Analytical skills develop as you explore and assess ideas, themes, concepts, and arguments while reading.

Analyzing imagery

Imagery is the use of vivid language to describe objects, actions, or ideas. The imagery used to convey sights and even sounds helps a writer to create the mood in a piece of writing. Layering these images over the message in the work enhances the effect on the reader. Often, the sounds evoked by the words mirrors the emotion of the work. The following poem by Archibald Lampman contains excellent examples of both visual as well as aural imagery.

Note the consistent use of the "s" and "t" sounds in the poem, evoking the sounds of the wind in the storm. The poem contains dark, low vowels, evident in such words as "swallows," "muttering," "storm," "rolling," "thunder," and "column." These words sound menacing and ominous, calling to mind the dark, rumbling sky preceding a storm.

At the same time, Lampman includes many high pitched "ee" and "i" sounds in the poem ("flight," "sky," and "twilight"). These sounds give the poem a sense of eeriness.

A THUNDERSTORM

A moment the wild swallows like a flight
Of withered gust-caught leaves, serenely high,
Toss in the windrack up the muttering sky.
The leaves hang still. Above the weird twilight,
The hurrying centres of the storm unite
And spreading with huge trunk and rolling fringe,
Each wheeled upon its own tremendous hinge,
Tower darkening on. And now from heaven's height,
With the long roar of elm-trees swept and swayed,
And pelted waters, on the vanished plain
Plunges the blast. Behind the wild white flash
That splits abroad the pealing thunder-crash,
Over bleared fields and gardens disarrayed,
Column on column comes the drenching rain.

—*by Archibald Lampman*

2.1.3a reflect on and describe strategies used to engage prior knowledge as a means of assisting comprehension of new text' and select, monitor and modify strategies as needed

Connections

Predicting and Questioning: Using Prior Knowledge in Interpretation

As you are reading, try to predict what you will learn or what will happen next. Continue to use your background knowledge and clues from the text to form predictions as you read. You should be able to support your predictions with facts from the text. You should also be able to use your prior knowledge to ask questions and to make connections.

To use prior knowledge means to build on your background knowledge to understand something new or unfamiliar. Background knowledge consists of an individual's existing understanding and past experiences. When you read, you will better understand what the writer is saying if you use your background knowledge. Readers who actively think about the text and use their background knowledge in their reading will have a better understanding of what they have read will than readers who do not make these associations.

Try to make connections between what you already know and what you are reading. Ask yourself the following questions as you read:

- Does this text remind me of anything?
- What do I already know about the topic of this text?
- Does this text remind me of anything else I have read?
- Is there something in this text that is like something I already know?

Inferences and Conclusions

Inferring

Inferring is a part of everyday life. When you wake up, you make inferences, or assumptions, about what is going to happen throughout the day. You brush your teeth, get dressed, and perform other morning tasks because you infer that you are going to school. Suppose that, in the middle of breakfast, you learn that it is a snow day and school is cancelled. Now, you immediately start thinking of what else to do and make inferences about your options for the day. Reading is the same way. When you open up a book, you immediately make assumptions about the text based on what kind of book it is, if you know other books by the writer, how the cover of the book looks, etc. You will make different inferences about a textbook than you will about a novel or an instructional manual.

Explicit and Implicit Ideas

Explicit ideas are clear statements that are directly stated in the text. An explicit idea states the meaning, as shown in the following example:

The temperature yesterday dropped to –27°C.

Implicit ideas, which are also known as inferences, are suggested, implied, or inferred. An implicit idea is not directly stated: You needed a warm jacket, hat, and gloves if you went outside yesterday.

In texts, conclusions and predictions are usually presented through implicit ideas or inferences, and often themes must be inferred by the reader because they are rarely directly stated.

The inferences you make are based on your life experiences and what you have already read and understand. Your background knowledge and the information in the text create meaning beyond what is directly stated in the text. The inferences that you draw may include conclusions, predictions, and new ideas.

To practice inferring while reading, ask yourself the following questions:

- What do I think this story/text is about?
  - How did I know that?
- How do I think the character feels?
- Why did I think that would happen?
  - How did I know that?
- What is the writer actually saying?
- What is the writer leading me to believe?

Read the following article about the origin of pretzels. Make inferences that can be supported by explicit ideas in the text.

FORTUNATE ACCIDENTS CAN LEAD TO THE BEST INVENTIONS

Some inventions are the consequence of an idea followed by trial and error (like Edison and the light bulb) or of a flash of inspiration. Other inventions are born through fortunate accidents.

Some of the greatest inventions in history have been made because of fortunate accidents. Take the microwave oven, for example. Percy Spencer, the inventor of the microwave, was motivated to join the Navy in the area of wireless telegraphy (radar) because as a child in 1912 he had been deeply inspired by the valor of the Titanic's wireless operator. When his Navy service ended, Spencer got a job with the Raytheon Company as an engineer. Raytheon specialized in defense contracts and commercial electronics.

Spencer's job at Raytheon involved working with magnetrons that generated microwave radio signals, which are the core of radar. Spencer was looking at ways to increase the production of magnetron tubes because of WWII. One of his tubes had a hole in it and he wondered what effect this might have. He had a chocolate bar in his pocket while he was running experiments with the leaking device. Lo and behold, the chocolate bar melted. He then brought in a bag of popcorn, which popped all over the lab. He also tried the experiment on an egg, which exploded because it was still in its shell. Spencer came to realize that the microwave could be used to cook food.

Raytheon sold the first commercial microwave in 1947. It weighed 750 pounds and was nearly six feet tall. Obviously, this was not a microwave for a personal home. It was used in restaurants, rail cars, and on large ships. It wasn't until 1955 that the first domestic microwave was for sale, and it was still too big for the average kitchen. Plus, it cost $1300 – nearly as much as an automobile in those days. In 1967 Japan manufactured a smaller magnetron and hence a smaller microwave. It sold for $495 and the world's love affair with the microwave began in earnest. Now, it would not be a stretch to say that more than 99% of the homes in North America have a microwave in the kitchen.

Here are some explicit ideas from the text:

- Percy Spencer invented the microwave.
- The company Raytheon specializes in defense contracts and commercial electronics.
- Raytheon sold the first commercial microwave in 1947.
- The first commercial microwave weighed 750 pounds.
- The first smaller microwave sold for $495.

The following explicit statements lead to the inference that while popular ideas or discoveries often begin by accident, they can then spread over a large area:

- "he wondered what effect this might have"
- "Lo and behold, the chocolate bar melted"
- "more than 99% of the homes in North America have a microwave in the kitchen"

Inferences allow different readers to arrive at various conclusions and interpretations of the same text. The following two interpretations of this text are both logical and valid, even though they are different:

- Even though the microwave was invented by "accident", it caught on quickly throughout the world.
- It took a long time for the general public to see the benefits of having a microwave in their own homes.

Conclusions

As you read, ask questions and make inferences that allow you to draw conclusions about what you are reading. Draw conclusions about the writer's purpose, what the characters learned and felt, why events happened as they did, and what the writer was trying to express

2.1.3c use metacognitive strategies to understand how knowledge of rhetorical devices, textual elements and structures used in previously studied texts contributes to understanding new texts.

METACOGNITION

The word *metacognition* refers to thinking about how you think; this process includes thinking about how you learn. As you discover and think about strategies that work best with your individual learning style, you will become a more confident and productive learner. It is important to think about your learning and to ask yourself questions about how it works for you. Do you work better in groups or on your own? Do you memorize things visually? What kind of reading do you like to do best? The more time you spend analyzing how you think, the better able you will be to pinpoint the areas where you excel and the areas where you have trouble.

The following section of the ***KEY*** gives you many examples and guidelines on understanding metacognition. The examples are designed to show how an individual student performs metacognition activities. Keep in mind that the way you think and learn is unique, so different methods may appeal to you more than others. Learning what appeals to you is also a part of metacognition.

Setting Goals

One of the keys to improving your English skills is to set personal goals for language growth. You may wish to use the following rubric that identifies some of the major English skills in order to identify your strengths and areas for growth. Reviewing assignments and assessment rubrics from your current or past English courses will help you to assess your strengths and the areas that need improvement.

Skill	Yes	Needs Improvement	Most Effective for Me
I read regularly			
I predict and ask questions while reading, discuss unfamiliar concepts with others			
I take note of words I am not sure of and use context or references to find meanings			
I go back to reread passages to clarify meaning			
I use visualizing and graphic organizers as aids to analyzing text and planning for communicating ideas			
I connect what I am reading to what I know about and to other texts I have read			
I understand symbols, archetypes, and literary devices and use them to enhance understanding of texts			
I use ideas in texts to better understand and communicate understandings of myself and the world around me			
I know how to effectively introduce and conclude topics in writing or oral presentations			
I connect all ideas to a controlling idea			
I fully support ideas with explanations and examples			
I identify when ideas are not communicated clearly			
I use a variety of sentences and precise diction for effect			
I find and correct errors in spelling, usage, and punctuation			
I understand oral instructions			
I listen carefully, build on the ideas of others, and ask questions to help others clarify ideas			
I am comfortable making formal presentations			
I use my voice effectively—volume, rate, tone, and pacing to communicate effectively and convey emotion			

Skill	Yes	Needs Improvement	Most Effective for Me
I use eye contact and gestures for emphasis			
I use charts, graphs, and visual aids to contribute to presentations			
I know how to find resources, effectively record information, and correctly reference sources			

Using the Checklist

Put check marks in the "Most Effective for Me" column next to the five strategies in the checklist that work best for you.

- Write a number beside each check mark showing how effective the strategy is for you (1 is most effective, 5 is least effective).
- Think of logical reasons for the order you have chosen.
- Discuss and compare your top five most effective strategies with a peer.
- Collaborate to identify the top five strategies from you and your peer, and describe the best uses for each strategy.
- List five ways that you and your peers can become better readers.

Reading Metacognition Checklist

The following questions are examples of what you can ask to use metacognition to examine your learning

- What is the best way to approach this learning task?
- At this point, how well do I understand information, concepts, and characters?
- How can I maintain my motivation to complete what I have started?
- Am I using the best tools for this learning task?

The following checklist shows different strategies that you can use to get the most out of your reading. More importantly, it helps you to think about how you approach various reading tasks. You could use this checklist several times during the school year to help you understand or change your approach.

Thinking About My Reading Strategies	Most Effective for Me	Use Most Often	Use Sometimes	Should Try
Before Reading I *preview* (look over exams, texts, stories, articles, and assignments) to determine: What is involved in this text? What is my purpose for reading? How should I approach this? How should I read (speed, etc.) this text?				

Thinking About My Reading Strategies	Most Effective for Me	Use Most Often	Use Sometimes	Should Try
I think about my *prior knowledge*—what I already know that might be relevant to the topic or task in front of me.				
I *visualize* or try to picture the characters, setting, what I hope to find out, etc.				
While Reading I *check back* to verify a definition, information about a character, etc.				
I use *vocabulary strategies*, such as context clues, root words, prefixes, and suffixes, to understand unfamiliar words and phrases.				
I make point form notes or *graphic organizers* when I need to remember plots, key ideas, etc.				
I pause while reading and *predict* what I think will happen next in the story.				
I *tag text* with sticky notes or mark parts I find confusing, so I can ask about them later.				
I use a *highlighter*—when I am allowed—to mark the text (notes, handouts, etc.) for key phrases and important ideas.				
I write *notes*, *questions*, and *comments* in margins if I am allowed, or on sticky notes. Sometimes, I use these later on to clarify information.				
I ask questions to *monitor my understanding* of what I read: • Does this make sense to me? • What exactly is the writer saying? • What is the narrator's point of view? • Do I agree? Why or why not?				
When the text does not state something directly, I make *inferences* and draw *conclusions* from my reading.				
I deliberately use *skimming* and *scanning* skills when appropriate, for example, when I need to locate a specific answer or idea in the text.				

Thinking About My Reading Strategies	Most Effective for Me	Use Most Often	Use Sometimes	Should Try
I *adjust my reading rate* as needed, slowing down for detailed information, etc.				
I pay *attention* to diagrams, pictures, charts, and graphs—anything that may help me make more sense of the text.				
After Reading I *summarize*, using notes or a graphic organizer.				
I write my thoughts, questions, and reactions in a *personal response journal.*				

2.2.1a identify a variety of text forms, including communications forms and literary forms (letters, memoranda, poems, narratives and dramatizations); and describe the relationships of form to purpose and content

Form and Genre

Genre sometimes means any classification of texts by form, style, or subject matter. However, a more careful definition distinguishes between form and genre.

Form describes structure.

Examples of Forms	Characteristics
Letter	Generally begins with an inside address and date; uses conventional greetings and closings like *Dear*______ and *Yours sincerely*
Memorandum	Often brief and addressed to a limited group such as the employees of a company; limited to essential information
Short story	20 000 words or less; usually few characters, one main character; a single plot
Novella	20 000 to 50 000 words; a shorter version of a novel
Novel	Over 50 000 words; usually 90 000 to 100 000 or more; may contain many characters and multiple plots within the main story
Screenplay	Contains mainly dialogue and directions for the action; special rules for margins and font size give a standard length of approximately one page to one minute of screen-time

Genre describes content or subject matter.

Genres contain certain characteristic elements. A western usually includes a gunfight. Science fiction often includes imaginary scientific developments like interstellar spaceships. A romance is always complicated with misunderstandings and difficulties.

Forms and genres are combined in various ways. For example, an *epistolary novel*, a novel told through letters, is a combination of two forms. Such a novel could be written in any genre and genres can be combined. A science fiction story might also be a romance, and an historical novel might also be a detective story. Also, elements of one genre are sometimes used in different genres.

There are many possible combinations of form and genre. The following chart shows a few of the more common examples.

<table>
<tr><th colspan="3">Examples of Forms</th><th>Examples of Genres</th></tr>
<tr><td rowspan="3">Fiction</td><td>poetry</td><td>metrical
free verse
sonnet</td><td>epic
ballad
lyric</td></tr>
<tr><td rowspan="2">prose</td><td>play
musical
motion picture
Shakespearean
modern</td><td>tragedy
comedy</td></tr>
<tr><td>novel
novella
short story</td><td>historical
detective
fantasy
science fiction
realistic</td></tr>
<tr><td rowspan="9">Non-fiction</td><td rowspan="9"></td><td>history</td><td>political
social
military</td></tr>
<tr><td>biography
autobiography
memoir</td><td></td></tr>
<tr><td>documentary film</td><td></td></tr>
<tr><td>essay</td><td>expository
persuasive
research</td></tr>
<tr><td>letter</td><td>personal
business
letter to the editor</td></tr>
<tr><td>diary</td><td></td></tr>
<tr><td>references</td><td>encyclopedia
dictionary
thesaurus
atlas</td></tr>
<tr><td>textbook
manual</td><td></td></tr>
</table>

The choice of form depends on the writer's purpose and on the expected audience.

Some forms of writing, such as non-fiction, give specific, accurate, and real-life details. Other forms may use more vivid and intense language (think of poetry), and still others rely heavily on dialogue (such as plays or television scripts).

The following table gives you a brief outline of different types of literature, their sub-categories, and descriptions of each. By looking at this table and the poetry example, you will get an idea of how texts are similar and different in what they have to say and how their information is presented.

Genre or Type of Literature	Description
Fiction	**Products of writers' imaginations**
Short story	• 3 000 to 4 000 words that can be read in one sitting
Mystery	• contains a puzzle or a riddle that needs to be solved
Historical fiction	• fictitious characters participating in events that actually occurred
Fantasy	• imaginative fiction with strange, fanciful creatures and settings
Science fiction	• alien characters, often in a futuristic story
Murder mystery	• a murder occurs that needs to be solved
"Realistic" fiction	• stories that appear to be very real or true to life
Non-fiction	**Writing that is based on facts or reality**
Biography	• the life story of a specific person, written by someone else
Autobiography	• a biography of a person told or written by himself or herself
General non-fiction	• any writing about true situations rather than about imaginary events and/or characters
Poetry	**Structure, characteristics, and use of language are different than prose**
Ballads, epics	• narrative poems often passed down through the years; "story poems"
Lyric poem	• usually short; usually expresses the poet's feelings
Limerick	• silly, humorous five-line poem with a distinct rhyming and rhythmic pattern
Haiku	• originated in Japan; poem of 17 syllables usually about an aspect of nature
Sonnet	• a 14-line poem with a regular rhythm and rhyme scheme
Free verse	• free poetry that does not follow any of the characteristics of traditional poetry

Plays	**Stories that are meant to be acted out; dialogue is the most important aspect of a play** There are many varieties of plays, just like there are varieties of stories.
Other fiction • Fairy tales • Legends • Folk tales • Myths • Fables	

Text Forms

Text is intended to communicate ideas. Text, as you know, comes in a variety of forms that are designed to suit the ideas that a writer wants to communicate. Literary forms of text are published works that are usually in the form of poetry or prose.

Text appears in many different forms. The following chart shows three categories of text and gives some examples of each. More detail is provided in the following sections about the items with asterisks beside them.

Literary Text Forms	Informational Text Forms	Graphic Text Forms
* poem	history	* advertisement
* play	biography	poster
musical	autobiography	cartoon
screenplay	memoir	comic book
* short story	newspaper article	* graphic novel
novella	* essay	graphic organizer
* novel	* letter	
	diary	
	journal	
	* reference	
	text book	
	manual	
	* consumer document	
	* workplace document	
	* public document	
	* memorandum	

Functions of Texts

Literary Text Forms

As you know, literary texts exist in many different forms. The form of a text gives you an idea of the type of ideas you should be looking for. For example, if you wanted to present facts about a current events issue that interested you, you probably would not choose the form of a poem to write about it. Chances are good that you would choose to write an essay or give an oral presentation. Poems and novels are usually more expressive, whereas essays tend to be more factual or objective. Here are some definitions and descriptions of different literary text forms that you have encountered in class.

Poems

Poetry can be created in a number of forms that follow pattern guidelines, such as limericks, epics, ballads, odes, and sonnets. What a poet wants to write about and how he or she wants to write it often determines the structure or form of the poem.

A sonnet is a poem of 14 lines, following a set rhyme scheme and a logical structure. Some sonnets are written as an octave (8 lines) followed by a sestet (6 lines), while others are written as 12 lines followed by a couplet. The following example is the octet/sestet combination.

Example

ON HIS BLINDNESS

When I consider how my light is spent
    E're half my days, in this dark world and wide,
    And that one Talent which is death to hide,
    Lodg'd with me useless, though my Soul more bent
To serve therewith my Maker, and present
    My true account, lest he returning, chide;
    'Doth God exact day-labour, light deny'd?'
    I fondly ask; But Patience, to prevent
That murmur, soon replies: 'God doth not need
    Either man's work or his own gifts, who best
    Bear his milde yoak, they serve him best, his State
Is Kingly. Thousands at his bidding speed
    And post o'er Land and Ocean, without rest:
    They also serve who only stand and waite.'

—*by John Milton*

An ode is a lyric poem expressing admiring or enthusiastic emotion. The following example uses vivid imagery to express a love and admiration for the beauty of autumn.

Example

TO AUTUMN

Season of mists and mellow fruitfulness!
Close bosom-friend of the maturing sun;
Conspiring with him how to load and bless
With fruit the vines that round the thatch-eaves run;
To bend with apples the moss'd cottage-trees,
And fill all fruit with ripeness to the core;
To swell the gourd, and plump the hazel shells
With a sweet kernel; to set budding more,
And still more, later flowers for the bees,
Until they think warm days will never cease,
For summer has o'er-brimm'd their clammy cells.

—*by* John Keats

This excerpt is the first of three parts of the poem. Traditional odes often follow the structural pattern of poems written in ancient Greek and Latin. The first part of the ode is called the *strophe*, and it is followed by the *antistrophe* and the *epode*. You might notice, as well, the interesting rhyme scheme: ABABCDEDCCE.

Plays

A play is a story that is meant to be acted. Dialogue is a huge part of a play, but how a set looks and how actors look and move during a play are also important. Plays have different forms, which usually affect their length. A one-act play is usually under an hour long, whereas a full five-act play, such as *Hamlet*, can take as long as three or four hours to enact.

Short Stories

A short story is a story of 20 000 words or less, usually with a limited number of characters, one main character, and a plot without subplots.

These plot elements can be quite easily outlined in a plot diagram.

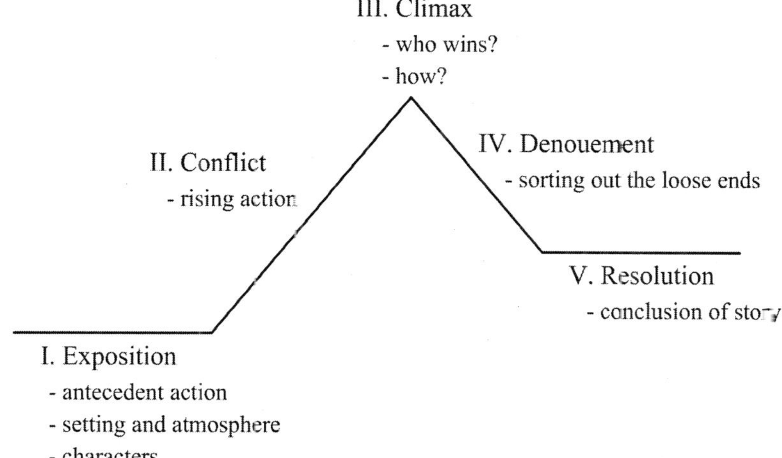

Either the plot headings or the plot diagram can be used to outline the events that occur in a short story. Short stories can be further categorized according to different forms, such as detective, fantasy, or science fiction.

Novels

While a novella (20 000 to 50 000 words) is longer than a short story, a novel (90 000 to 100 000 or more words) is generally much longer and may contain many characters and multiple plots. Some novels, such as the three novels that comprise Tolkien's *Lord of the Rings* trilogy, have so many characters and intertwined subplots that readers may have to keep backtracking just to keep track of the main plot and the characters. Novels come in many forms, such as historical, detective, romance, horror, and so on. Some novels are a combination of forms, like a historical romance or an epistolary novel, which is a story told through a series of letters.

Non-Fiction Elements—Informational Text Forms

Informational texts are non-fiction, which means that they are based on reality or facts, although they may also contain some of the writer's opinions. Informational texts are generally presented in a prose style of writing, which means in sentences and paragraphs. It is important to be careful with non-fiction or informational texts because they are not always written without bias. Non-fiction can have a writer's slant just as fiction can.

Essays

Essays consist of a thesis, body, and conclusion. An essay attempts to communicate an opinion or idea. Different forms of essays include expository, persuasive, and research essays.

Letters

Letters generally begin with an inside address and date and use conventional greetings and closings such as "Dear ____" and "Yours Sincerely." Letters may be personal and informal (friendly letter) or formal (business letter). Each has a slightly different format. It is common for opinion essays to appear in a newspaper as letters to the editor.

Reference Books

Reference books contain specific, non-fiction information. Examples of reference books are encyclopedias, dictionaries, thesauruses, atlases, and almanacs.

Consumer Documents

A consumer document provides important information about products and services. These documents take different forms, such as consumer reports, warranties, recall announcements, and advertisements.

Workplace Documents

Most workplaces have specially designed documents suited to that particular workplace. These include application forms, contracts, safety policies, dress codes, emergency procedures, Internet use rules, and email policies.

Public Documents

Public document are often provided through a government office or agency. They often contain information that supports public safety and welfare. Examples of public documents are clean air legistation, safe water and highways acts, littering laws, driver's handbooks, and library policies.

Memorandums

A memorandum is often brief and is addressed to a limited group such as the employees of a company. It is limited to essential information and is frequently sent in the form of an inter-office email.

Graphic Text Forms

Graphic text forms rely heavily on drawings and illustrations or on showing information using graphic organizers such as charts or plot diagrams. There are various forms of graphic text. Some forms are legitimate means of conveying art or entertainment, and other forms are used primarily for organizing statistics or other information. Using visual aids to convey meaning in addition to providing text gives a work more depth and can often explain information in a way that text alone cannot.

Advertisements

Text advertisements are mostly found in newspapers and magazines and posted in public places such as buses and on billboards. The Internet is, as you know, full of advertisements that range from pop-up ads to ads that are built into the design of a website. Companies even pay search engines so that their company website will show up on the first page of a person's search.

Graphic Novels

Graphic novels are also known as picture novels. A graphic novel is a full-length novel in which the action and characters have been drawn by an artist to complement the narrative text, which is framed in captions and word balloons similar to those in a regular comic book. A comic book really differs from a graphic novel only in length.

Graphic novels, in one form or another, have been around since the 1940s. They are not really a new or recent trend. At that time, a series of stories from classical literature was published in a comic book format called *Classics Illustrated,* with well-known titles such as *Robinson Crusoe* and *Treasure Island.* The intention was to entice young readers to read literature that they might be reluctant to read in full-length novel form.

By 1975, graphic novels were gaining broader acceptance as a genre. In 1986, a graphic novel called *Maus* by Art Spiegelman won the Pulitzer Prize for the category of Letters, Drama, or Music. You may have read a graphic novel such as *5 Shots* by Jemir Johnson or *Diary of a Wimpy Kid* written by Jeff Kinney. A selection of graphic novels can be found at your school or local library.

2.2.1b describe audience factors that may have influenced a text creator's choice of form and medium (for example, age, gender and culture of the audience)

Using Vocabulary Appropriate to Audience and Purpose

Formal and Informal Language

The choice of words in a text determines whether the writing is formal or informal. It is important to decide first whether the language in a particular piece of writing is to be informal or formal. Usually, this decision is made based on who the intended reader is.

Formal writing uses words and expressions that are chosen carefully to avoid slang and contractions. In general, formal writing should follow the rules of grammar. Formal writing uses proper English and should be used in schoolwork. Formal writing is also necessary in job applications and resumes, letters of thanks for scholarships and awards, and any other situation in which you want to show that your intelligence and time have been applied.

Informal writing uses contractions and is more relaxed in terms of word choice and grammatical rules. Informal writing, especially that in journals or friendly letters, allows for the use colloquial expressions or slang. In an informal narrative that includes dialogue, characters talk to each other informally as well. For example, the sentence "My buddies bought the coolest clothes on the weekend" contains colloquial or slang words and has a casual tone.

When you read a text, you can determine whether the language is formal or informal in the same way that you would create or recognize it in your own writing. Most textbooks are written in a formal style because they are addressed to a general audience that includes educators, parents, and students.

Online Language

As members of today's generation, young people are, for the most part, very computer literate. Having grown up in the "Age of Technology," they take computers for granted and have difficulty comprehending how anyone could find computer technology frustrating, challenging, or intimidating. Many teenagers even have their own blog sites.

Like other groups, bloggers are developing their own catalogue of jargon. Here are some examples.

Blog—a form of writing that consists of a single column of chronological text, generally with a sidebar that is regularly updated. Most blogs are unprofessional sites maintained by a single writer

Blogosphere—a network of websites

Fisk—to use a blog site to criticize a news article or segment

Barking moonbat—an extremist or fanatic

Blog mute—someone who only blogs on occasion

Bloggerel—opinions that are repeated so frequently that they become trivial and annoying

In all forms of online writing, shorthand is frequently used. *Leetspeak* is often used to indicate emotions or actions that would take a lot of time to type out conventionally. For example, rather than saying "I'm laughing out loud" or trying to indicate laughter by typing out "haha," most people online just type "lol." This makes online conversation faster and more similar to real-time conversation. Leetspeak has become built in to how people communicate online. It is also easily adapted to text messaging from the small keypad of a cellphone. It is strongly discouraged, however, in any formal writing for school or work.

Online lingo has become an integral part of computerized communication. It has become so important, in fact, that there are free websites allowing users to translate regular English to chat room lingo, and vice versa. Even if you are not a blogger, you most likely chat online in some form. Chat lingo is becoming more popular as more forms of online chatting are created. Chat lingo adapts easily to text messaging from the small keypad of a cell phone. Here are some examples.

CUL8R = See you later

LOL = Laughing out loud

THX = Thanks

HOWRU = How are you doing?

Messages that are sent via the computer also incorporate visual jargon where symbols are used to visually represent the message. Consider the following examples.

:) = happy

: (= angry

;) = winking

Slang

Slang words are often used by a certain group of people, such as teenagers. Slang differs from jargon in the sense that slang is regarded as very casual language, whereas jargon is usually used by professionals to discuss something specific. Slang expressions tend to come and go. For example, in the 1950s, a "hot rod" referred to a powerful car, while today the term is used very rarely and may not be used to refer to a car. Slang, like online language, may be used in dialogue, but should be avoided in all but the most informal of uses.

2.2.1c explain how a variety of organizational patterns and structural features contribute to purpose and content

Text Features

Organizational Features of Books

Informative books are organized with features meant to help you find information quickly. After you have read a book, these features can also help you recall or find the information that you need again. Here are some features with which you should be familiar.

A **title page** tells you the topic of the book and its writer or editor.

The **table of contents** is found at the front of a book, usually just after the title page. It lists the book's chapters or divisions in order from first to last. The starting page number of each chapter is also given.

You can skim a table of contents from top to bottom to find out where a particular chapter begins and how long it is.

Example

Chapter 1 – Under the Sea...........................1
Chapter 2 – Fish, Fish, Fish!...............................17
Chapter 3 – Why We Like Diving....................28
Chapter 4 – Underwater Machines....................36

A **preface or foreword** is an introduction that sometimes includes helpful or positive features of the book.

The **visual layout** of a book refers to how the book is put together, whether it contains pictures and diagrams, etc.

The **appendix** is a section found at the back of some information books. It contains extra information to help you understand the material such as notes, charts, maps, or diagrams.

An **index** is an alphabetical list of the important topics in an information book. It tells you which pages have information on each topic.

A **glossary** is often found at the back of a non-fiction book. It lists and explains the meanings of words in the book that are important or that you may not already know. While reading a book with a glossary, you can quickly check the meaning of a word without getting out a dictionary.

Chapter organizers are arranged according to the order of the content. Organizing and presenting material using many different styles can help you learn difficult material. These features also help you navigate through a chapter. This is especially useful if you want to read only certain kinds of material from each chapter as you study for an exam.

Text Features

Font refers to a set of images (glyphs) representing the characters from a particular character set in a particular typeface. The words "font" and "typeface" are not interchangeable. Font refers to the size of the characters and the design of the characters, for example, 10-point Cambria or 12-point Arial.

When texts are being written, the font style, the layout of the text, and the spacing are all taken into consideration in order to enhance meaning and strengthen the impact of the text on the reader.

Visuals as a Text Feature

When you read cartoons, you are also interpreting the visual clues that convey meaning. The cartoon characters' facial expressions and body language contribute to meaning as much as the text in dialogue and thought balloons. When you read a caption under a picture in your social studies text and connect it to the picture, you are better able to understand the meaning of the picture. You can easily recognize the value of visuals in science books, math texts, and manuals. Diagrams make complex systems or processes easier to understand, whether you are trying to solve a problem or figuring out the functions on your new cell phone.

Visuals enhance communication and convey meaning within text. Whether you are researching a topic or reading in a textbook, do not underestimate the power of any visuals that are included.

Text Layout Used to Enhance Meaning

The manner in which text is laid out or presented on a page can add to and change the meaning of the text itself. Concrete poetry is an example of how text layout affects meaning. Concrete poetry, sometimes called shape poetry, uses configurations of words that are related to the subject of the poem. In the following example, only 18 words are used to reflect on the topic of sunset. The poet's message becomes more powerful as the action of sunset is read in the poem as descending from the sky. The young man's attitude of sinking down, follows the words of the poem downward in the direction of probable failure.

Sunset

the

sun

has

set

on

you

and

I

too

many lies

have weighed

down your high

noon position

Using such dramatic visual features is usually most appropriate in poetry assignments, but visual tools can be used in less obvious ways in other texts as well. Newspapers, which will be discussed in the following part of this section of the ***KEY***, use many visual tools to keep readers interested.

Specialized Text Features

Certain texts, such as newspapers, have design features that are related to their purpose. Many daily newspapers are designed for rapid reading for people on the go. Large newspapers come in sections so that readers can quickly find the topics that they are more interested in first. The front page presents an index, similar to a table of contents, of the main sections and daily features, such as the entertainment section, classifieds, and letters to the editor. It also shows an overview of the weather and the newsworthy stories of the day. As you examine the structure of the following news article, you will see how the stories themselves are presented in a format that makes the key facts from the news quickly accessible to the readers.

Structure of a News Article

A news article usually consists of a headline, a byline, a dateline, and a body. Writing a news article is very different than writing a narrative. Generally, a narrative will build up to the climax, or most important part, of the story. A news article, on the other hand, begins with the most important information and then proceeds to less important information, leaving the least important to the end. The structure of a news article can be likened to an inverted pyramid. A news article begins with a lead paragraph that contains the most significant information in the story and then continues through the middle paragraphs to the concluding paragraph of the article. The following information is an overview of each part of a news article.

Headline

The headline is the title of the news article. It is a very brief summary of the news article. The headline must grab the reader's attention by using exciting and vivid words. It often contains a noun and a verb. All important words are capitalized, and there is usually no punctuation at the end of the title.

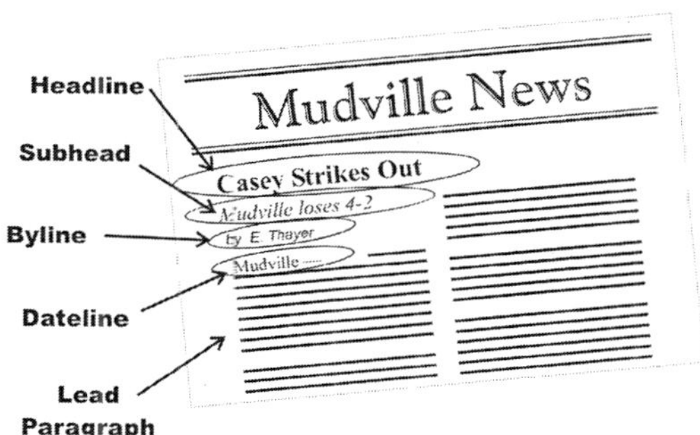

Subhead

Sometimes, a subhead, or secondary title, appears immediately after the headline. A subhead provides additional information about the story, but not all stories have a subhead.

Byline

The byline is positioned after the subhead. As the name suggests, it indicates who has written the article. Often times, the byline will just state the news source rather than an individual journalist. Reuters and The Associated Press are examples of news sources that are commonly found in news articles.

Dateline

The dateline usually appears at the beginning of an article. It is included at the start of the lead paragraph. It tells the reader where the story happened. It does not tell the date. Often, the byline and the dateline appear in the same line of text.

Lead Paragraph

The beginning of a news article is called the lead, and it introduces the subject of the article. The most important ideas of the article are included in the lead. A good lead usually answers the questions who, what, when, where, why, and how.

Who the subject of the article. The article could be about a person, place, idea, event, or object—basically anything about which an article can be written.

What the action of the article—what has happened or what is currently happening.

When the time frame of the article. Did the action take place last night, last week, or over the course of a month?

Where the place the action is happening.

Why explains the "what," or the action, of the article.

How describes the sequence of events or actions that occurred.

The 5 Ws and How are usually covered in the first one or two sentences. The rest of the first paragraph may include additional details or important information. The first sentence of the lead, in particular, is very important. It must hook readers and encourage them to continue reading. In most news articles, the first sentence gives answers to as many of the 5 Ws and How as possible, in as few words as possible. The first sentence should provide a good lead-in to the rest of the paragraph and article.

Answer the following questions about the sample front page of the fictional newspaper provided. Try to answer the questions before looking at the answers that follow the sample. They will help to clarify and highlight some of the text features that are unique to newspapers.

Questions and answers about the front page of the *Mudville News*

Question: What are some text features that you recognize on the front page of this newspaper?

Answer: Some text features are the headlines, bylines (Meg Miller, Mario Chase), datelines (Mudville, Lake Simcoe), lead sentences that are good "hooks" and provide key information, boxed text with main sections, and features listed.

Question: What might be the purposes behind the different text fonts and sizes used on this page?

Answer: The largest font is used for the main headline about the police chief. The other two headlines have slightly smaller fonts but are still prominently positioned on the front page. The bylines and datelines are in block letters for easy recognition of the reporter and location of the story. The contents list is in small font because there is not much room for it, but it is set apart with a boxed-in frame so readers can find it easily.

Question: How do the photograph and caption draw attention to a key story?

Answer: The photograph is large and dominates the front page because it is also the only picture. The caption draws attention to the story about the medals immediately below the photo.

Question: What features help readers to navigate through this newspaper?

Answer: The features that help readers navigate through the paper are the text box entitled "Inside This Edition," the section follow-up locators by the last sentence of continued stories, and the section locator for an article of interest to the business community ("Franchise Thriving Overseas F3 Business").

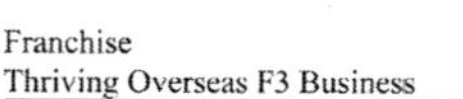
Franchise
Thriving Overseas F3 Business

Podium Premiums
Medals Money in the Bank
for Athletes C7 Sports

GREATER MUDVILLE EDITION   TUESDAY, NOVEMBER 20, 2007

MUDVILLE NEWS

www.mudvillenews.com   Mudville's Newspaper Since 1910   Cloudy, High 11 Low 4

Police Chief Resigns Over Game Rampage

Meg Miller
Mudville Staff Writer
Mudville

Citing "personal stresses", local Police Chief Ronald Mudslinger announced his resignation in a press release issued late last evening. "The force needs external leadership," he stated. "The fact that Casey is my grandson is not a factor in my decision."

See CHIEF RESIGNS / A2

A Mudville Hero

INSIDE THIS EDITION

A/ News	D/ Entertainment
B/ Around Town	E/ Classified
C/ Sports	F/ Business

Births	E3	Doctors In	B4
Comics	D2	Horoscope	D3
Sudoku	D6	Obituaries	B3

Michael Marlo, 14, wears the bronze medal for bravery he was awarded Monday by the Royal Canadian Humane Association. Michael fended off a coyote which attacked his younger sister during a hike.

Medals Recognize Selfless Courage

Morley Poon
Mudville Staff Writer
MUDVILLE

Even the police officers and tough journalists were close to tears. Seventeen Ontario citizens were honoured Monday, for acts of courage that risked their own safety to help others.

See MEDALS A3

Coffee, Anyone?

Mario Chase
Can WEST NEWS service
LAKE SIMCOE

The regulars gaped in surprise as an inquisitive deer recently followed an unsuspecting patron through the door of a downtown coffee shop. It could be argued that the deer was equally surprised. He did not linger for coffee, but hastily backed toward the door, which was thrust open for him by a quick-thinking customer.

Fish and wildlife officials were summoned, and the wayward deer is once again munching grass in the woods outside of town.

2.2.2a explain how rhetorical devices and stylistic techniques used in print and nonprint texts create clarity, coherence and emphasis

Word Choice and Personal Style

Writing style refers to how writers use words and sentences to present ideas. When writers choose their words carefully so that sentences are precise and vary in length and structure, the writing becomes clearer, livelier, and more enjoyable.

General Word	More Specific or Descriptive Words
Fear (noun)	terror, trepidation, panic, nervousness, horror, cowardice
Tidy (adjective)	orderly, fastidious, clean, neat, smart, well-groomed
Ask (verb)	inquire, request, probe, interrogate, challenge, question, query

Look at some of the specific and vivid words in an excerpt from Edgar Allan Poe's short story "The Tell-Tale Heart." Specific phrases of particularly vivid word choice are underlined.

> It is impossible to say how first the idea entered my brain; but once conceived, it haunted me day and night. Object there was none. Passion there was none. I loved the old man. He had never wronged me. He had never given me insult. For his gold I had no desire. I think it was his eye! Yes, it was this!
> One of his eyes resembled that of a vulture—a pale blue eye, with a film over it. Whenever it fell upon me, my blood ran cold; and so by degrees—very gradually—I made up my mind to take the life of the old man, and thus rid myself of the eye forever.
>
> Now this is the point. You fancy me mad. Madmen know nothing. But you should have seen me. You should have seen how wisely I proceeded—with what caution—with what foresight—with what dissimulation I went to work! I was never kinder to the old man than during the whole week before I killed him.

A Writer's Unique Style

Some well-known writers have imprinted their writing with personal style preferences. These style choices are usually consistent with a writer's work but are different from the style choices of other writers. If you become familiar with these style choices, often you can recognize who the writer of a work is just by examining the writing style.

For example, Charles Dickens, author of *A Christmas Carol*, *Oliver Twist*, *A Tale of Two Cities*, and many other books, is well known for writing long, descriptive sentences and passages. Dickens often describes his characters in meticulous detail, in both appearance and manner.

Guy de Maupassant, credited with the earliest examples of the short story genre, liked to present human nature in stories such as "The Piece of String" and "The Diamond Necklace." In these stories, the plot seemed to be secondary to his well-drawn character studies. The characters portrayed by this author, like Maitre Hauchecorne and Madam Loisel, are memorable mainly because of the character flaws that lead to great misfortune in their lives.

Style Overview

Read the following essay. As you read the prose, ask yourself the following questions: What is the effect or mood created by this passage? What is the tone or attitude of the writer? Would the effect be enhanced or diminished if different words were used? Think about how you will answer these questions as you read the passage. These questions will help you examine elements of style.

Memories and Mindsets

I grew up in a small suburban town in California. Our house was a three-bedroom bungalow with a nice yard. My sister and I each had our own room, and we even had a pool for a number of years. They called it a "bedroom community" in those days. We walked to school and played outside hour after hour. Our parents were not afraid of perverts, child molesters, or serial killers in those days. We didn't even have to wear seatbelts in the car. The major fear seemed to be swimming after eating. All the mothers went on and on about it, setting timers and making numerous reminders.

Most of the mothers stayed home. I realize now, with the hindsight of an adult's perspective, that they were bored and dissatisfied. Some drank. Some were on Valium, which was the Prozac of the 70s. As we got older, the pervasive goals became clear. Girls aspired to go to community college, or sometimes even university, where they would meet their future husbands. The ambition went no further than this. The purpose of the education was not for self-development, nor for career building. It was simply to meet one's future spouse. Or, it was "just in case" one ended up divorced or dumped by the husband.

One of my girlfriends, Linda, who I admired to no end because she was a few years older, had an excellent figure, and always had the latest and coolest clothes and shoes, never escaped the stifling lack of imagination. She married her high school sweetheart right after graduating from high school. He, of course, had played on the football team, and she, of course, had been a cheerleader. He turned out to be abusive, and after years of putting up with it, Linda had to move home to live with her parents because with a high school education what were her job prospects?

There were so many great things about my childhood in a small town that I shall never forget. There was safety and freedom and prolonged innocence. However, looking back, I am glad to have moved away and had a taste of the wider world. I travelled and was educated and have lived in other places. My eyes were opened to all the other choices available to women. I wish I could have offered my children a place as free from care and as safe to grow up in, but the world has changed and so, thankfully, have the options.

What words would you use to describe the author's writing style? What would you say the tone and the mood of this text are? Try to write a description of how this text is written. This type of analysis will make aspects of form and style more obvious to you.

Sentence Variety

Successful writers use a variety of sentence types: questions, commands, exclamations, or statements. They also vary sentence beginnings and sentence lengths because these help to create interesting word rhythms and an enjoyable reading experience.

Look at how Edgar Allan Poe has constructed his sentences at the beginning of "The Tell-Tale Heart."

> True!—Nervous—very, very dreadfully nervous I had been and am; but why *will* you say that I am mad? The disease has sharpened my senses—not destroyed—not dulled them. Above all was the sense of hearing acute. I heard all things in the heaven and in the earth. I heard many things in hell. How, then, am I mad? Hearken! And observe how healthily—how calmly I can tell you the whole story.

By using the word "true" as an exclamation, he alerts the reader to the fact that he is about to claim something. Then, through the question "why will you say that I am mad?" the reader is being addressed in a direct way and is being asked by the narrator to think about his character. The question draws the reader into thinking more actively about the character of the narrator.

2.2.2b explain how various textual elements and stylistic techniques contribute to the creation of atmosphere, tone and voice (for example, qualification and interrupted movement)

Identifying Stylistic Techniques

Elements of Style

Language and syntax are used by writers in creative ways to manipulate mood, tone, suspense, and other elements of a text. You have probably noticed how short, staccato sentences in the middle of a narrative denote rapid action. Through the use of specific language and syntax, a writer can create the desired response in readers.

Use of Style to Create Tone and Mood

A writer's style of writing and tone help to create the mood of a given work. As you read more, you will be able to recognize how style, tone, and mood all work together to have an effect on the text.

Tone

A writer's tone is the overall attitude that he or she has toward what is written. Tone is established by the writer's word choice, or diction. Tone conveys the writer's attitude toward the story or characters.
It sets the mood of the writing; it must always be appropriate to the purpose and audience. The tone of a story can be, for example, serious, light-hearted, sad, emotional, formal, or informal. Because writers cannot use a speaker's tone of voice, they create their tone through the choice and arrangement of words, punctuation, sentence length, and so on.

Look again at this excerpt from Poe's "The Tell-Tale Heart" to see how the serious tone allows the reader to see the narrator's insanity. The more the narrator talks about how serious and unemotional his decision to murder the old man for seemingly no real reason, the better able the reader is to understand that the narrator is not in his right mind.

From "The Tell-Tale Heart"

True!—Nervous—very, very dreadfully nervous I had been and am; but why *will* you say that I am mad? The disease has sharpened my senses—not destroyed—not dulled them. Above all was the sense of hearing acute. I heard all things in the heaven and in the earth. I heard many things in hell. How, then, am I mad? Hearken! And observe how healthily—how calmly I can tell you the whole story.

It is impossible to say how first the idea entered my brain; but once conceived, it haunted me day and night. Object there was none. Passion there was none. I loved the old man. He had never wronged me. He had never given me insult. For his gold I had no desire. I think it was his eye! Yes, it was this! One of his eyes resembled that of a vulture—a pale blue eye, with a film over it. Whenever it fell upon me, my blood ran cold; and so by degrees—very gradually—I made up my mind to take the life of the old man, and thus rid myself of the eye forever.

Poe's tone is seen in his attitude toward the narrator in the story. The narrator uses eccentric, strange, and defensive language, which reveals that the writer perceives the character to have those characteristics.

Mood

While tone describes the writer's attitude toward the story, mood is the atmosphere of a piece of writing that is felt by the reader. Mood is not often explicitly stated; rather, writers carefully choose their words, phrases, and images in order to lead their readers to feel the mood they wish to create. In the following passage, readers can tell that the narrator is frustrated and angry as a result of the writer's use of repetition, the word choices and punctuation, and the use of sarcasm.

GARBAGE

Garbage! Garbage! Garbage! Why is there so much garbage and waste? Do people think it will disappear on its own? I work hard to recycle and reuse, yet garbage heaps up on us all the time! There is no end to it!

The mood of a story can be angry, sad, frightening, suspenseful, enthusiastic, scary, etc. You can use a variety of words to describe mood. The famous opening line of the novel *Paul Clifford*, "It was a dark and stormy night," does not contain enough description to establish a mood of, say, fear and terror. To create this kind of mood, you would need to add more creative descriptions.

In the following paragraph the author creates a mood of eeriness, suspense, and loneliness. As a reader, you wonder what is going to happen, and you can feel the narrator's loneliness and sadness.

The storm advances with chaos and purpose combined. There is a noise to the wind like a vast machine. Are there voices in the wind, screaming? Or, is it just a trick of the furious gale as it struts among the buildings and signs and trees? A large tree rips free of its moorings and topples over. One hundred years of growing undone in one capricious moment. The rain, having fallen for hours, loosened the tree's roots and its co-conspirator, the wind, pushed it down like a playground bully.

In this passage, it is the writer's style of writing—the short, simple sentences and the tone that is established through the choice of words such as "vast machine," "furious gale," and "pushed it down like a playground bully"—that creates the mood you experience as you read.

In summary, tone and mood are closely related, but they are separate aspects of style. Tone is the writer's apparent attitude toward his or her subject, characters, or readers. The writer's tone, depending on aspects such as subject matter, use of formal or informal language, and characterization, may come across to you, the reader, as serious, light, cynical, sympathetic, indifferent, or passionate.

Mood, on the other hand, describes the atmosphere that the reader feels while reading a text. Ideally, mood should be transmitted so that you feel connected to an atmosphere that is morbid, optimistic, sinister, thoughtful, suspenseful, romantic, and so on.

Point of View or Perspective

Point of view or perspective is the lens through which the writer writes a text. The process used by a writer writing a story is similar to that of a person using a camera to shoot a video. A person shooting a video decides where to stand and what to capture. A writer chooses what kind of character is going to tell a story and how the story is going to be told. The two most common points of view that writers use are first person and third person.

First Person

In writing done from the first person point of view, the writer chooses one of the characters in the story to tell about the events of the story. The pronouns *I*, *me*, *my*, *mine*, *we*, and *us* are used. When a first person point of view is used, the reader usually knows only what the person who is telling the story thinks and feels. The following passage is written in first person.

Example

I was terrified. After all, there were only three straws left. I would crumple into a heap of misery if I picked the short one. I can't imagine being stuck with all of the cabins' chores for a week. Devon and Maggie's laundry? No thanks!

"Come on, Katie," Trisha snapped, "Don't dawdle. It's your turn to pick." Trish was probably only irritated because she was last to draw and was getting nervous herself. I figure that since I never win draws or contests that maybe my luck is getting saved up for this very moment in time. Yeah, right.

As you can see from the example, the reader has access to the narrator's thoughts and feelings, but not to the thoughts and feelings of any of the other characters. The narrator guesses as to what other characters might be feeling, but in the first person point of view, the reader is limited to the narrator's inner thoughts and observations.

Third Person

Stories written from a third person point of view are told from the viewpoint of a narrator. The pronouns *he, she, his, her, they, and their* are used. When third person point of view is used, you can sometimes learn a great deal about the story because the narrator tells you what is happening in many different places and from any number of points of views. Often, a third person narrator can access the thoughts and emotions of all of the characters in a work.

In the following excerpt you can feel some of the suspense Trisha experiences as she and her fear face each other because it is written in the third person.

Example

> Trisha was only here on a dare. It wouldn't be the first time her big mouth had gotten her into trouble. She turned to look at her friends standing on the sidewalk in front of the abandoned house. Her own weight shifting on the rotten wood of the front porch made it sound like someone was inside.
> She whipped her head back towards the front door and for no reason that she could have articulated, Trisha knocked on the door. *Like, DUH, as if someone will answer!* She stifled a nervous giggle, pushed open the door and stepped into the front hall of the dilapidated house. The floorboards were diabolical ventriloquists sending the sounds of her footsteps all over the place. Some sounded like they were creaking straight ahead and down the front hall at least fifteen feet away; others sounded like they were coming from one side or the other. None of the sounds seemed to originate from beneath her feet. She had never felt this spooked before.

The point of view that a writer chooses affects the text and how readers will feel about the characters. Perspective or point of view can be more precisely defined in the following definitions:

Limited

First person narration (I, we) is usually limited because the narrator is usually personally involved in the story, often as a main character. The narrator's perspective is limited to what he or she sees and knows as he or she interact with other characters and with situations in the story.

Omniscient

"Omni" means "all," and "science" means "knowing." An "all-knowing" or omniscient point of view is usually third person (he, she, they) narration. It allows the narrator to show a much broader perspective because the narrator is outside of the story. The narrator can therefore express the circumstances and motivations of all the characters.

Subjective and Objective Viewpoints

Subjective

A subjective point of view can be directly affected by a personal or emotional bias. For instance, if you received a poor mark on a math test, your mother might have a subjective view of that mark because she knows that you were not feeling well the night before the test. Sometimes, first person narration can be quite subjective because it is so personal.

Objective

An objective point of view reports the facts of a situation without emotional overtones or bias. Newspaper reporters, for example, should report the news objectively, without inserting their own opinion.

Evocative Language and Mood

Now that you have reviewed a number of elements of style that enhance or clarify texts, you can consider examples from literature. The following examples show elements of style as they relate to actual text.

The first paragraph of Charles Dickens' novel *A Tale of Two Cities* contains a fine example of this use of evocative language. The side-by-side phrases are known as juxtaposition, crafted by the witer to create a mood of tension between two countries (England and France), two approaches to change, and two contrasting characters.

Example

from **A TALE OF TWO CITIES**

It was the best of times, it was the worst of times, it was the age of wisdom, it was the age of foolishness, it was the epoch of belief, it was the epoch of incredulity, it was the season of Light, it was the season of Darkness, it was the spring of hope, it was the winter of despair, we had everything before us, we had nothing before us, we were all going direct to Heaven, we were all going direct the other way—in short, the period was so far like the present period, that some of its noisiest authorities insisted on its being received, for good or for evil, in the superlative degree of comparison only.

There were a king with a large jaw and a queen with a plain face, on the throne of England; there were a king with a large jaw and a queen with a fair face, on the throne of France. In both countries it was clearer than crystal to the lords of the State preserves of loaves and fishes, that things in general were settled for ever.

The persistent use of comparison and contrast serves to describe the emotional moods of the two countries of Britain and France. The "king with a large jaw" and "queen with a plain face" were King George III and his queen, Charlotte Sophia, while the other pair referred to Louise XVI and Marie Antoinette of France. The French royals, as it turned out, were destined to lose their heads to the guillotine during the French Revolution. During the same period in England, the British royals kept their heads, both literally and figuratively, because most of the dissent was resolved, not in the streets, but in the House of Parliament. The language used by the writer is memorable, evocative, and crafted to create one of the most well-known opening passages in literature.

Incongruity

When something is said to be incongruous in a given text, it means that the words that are used are inconsistent with a character in a given situation. Here is an excerpt that illustrates the use of incongruous language to provide humour.

TO THE FIRING SQUAD

"Now, gents look lively," Captain Smith said with a simpering smile. "You want to make a good showing of it, now, don't you?" he continued. "You there, stand up straight. And you, stop looking so glum. Let's remember our audience, shall we?"

The men were finally lined up to Captain Smith's liking. "Fire," he ordered.

The language in the above excerpt is incongruous because it is far too polite and formal for the situation. A real captain would more likely be yelling at his soldiers and not concerning himself with the soldiers' appearance or being careful with their feelings in commanding them.

Repetition in Song Lyrics

Music and lyrics have an important relationship. They influence each other and add to the emotional effect that is created in a song. The repetition of words and phrases is another example of deliberate word choice, usually for dramatic effect, for emphasis, or to make a phrase more memorable. Consider, for example, repeated choruses and refrains in songs—you may not remember all of the words of a song but can usually join in on the chorus. In many popular songs, the focus is on the beat and musical texture of the song, so there may only be a few lines of lyrics.

Word Meaning in Poetry

This application of a couple of style elements can be seen in the following short poem by Robert Frost.

NOTHING GOLD CAN STAY

Nature's first green is gold,
Her hardest hue to hold.
Her early leaf's a flower;
But only so an hour.
Then leaf subsides to leaf.
So Eden sank to grief,
So dawn goes down to day.
Nothing gold can stay.

You can see that the word "gold" has been used three times in this poem: in the title, in the first line, and in the last line. A word being mentioned so many times in such a short work should be a signal to you that this word is probably an important key to understanding the poem.

The poet is referring to how the "first green," or youth of nature, is gold but is also the "hardest to hold." Gold is a soft, precious metal, which means that it is highly valued and many people desire it. Gold often indicates the top level of something, such as the gold medal at a sporting event. The poet is saying that possessions and achievements may be golden, and people may strive to have them, but they will fade in time. The "first green" of youth may be something that people long for even after they age.

Visual and Artistic Devices

There are many ways to enhance writing using visual and artistic devices. The creative use of fonts and text features can emphasize key elements. Poets will sometimes use text features to create certain moods. Textbooks often contain these devices to highlight important terms and definitions. Graphics are also used to better illustrate important information. Visuals can also be used to demonstrate figurative language.

It is worth noting that sometimes repeated words or phrases can make lyrics annoying to music fans, who may criticize a song for being superficial. While some people listen to music for a catchy beat or melody, others value songs for having good lyrics. When lyrics in songs are too repetitive or lack meaning, many listeners will criticize or simply choose not to listen to those songs. Some songs focus more on the music rather than the lyrics of a song. In this same way, some listeners care more about the music than the lyrics, or vice versa. Either way, the lyrics of a song can be understood and analyzed as poetry.

2.2.2c analyze the use of irony and satire to create effects in print and nonprint texts (for example, dramatic irony to create suspense, verbal irony to create humour, and satire to evoke response)

IRONY AS AN EFFECTIVE TECHNIQUE

Irony is an excellent tool that a writer can use to intensify the reader's involvement in literature. Skillful use of irony means that the writer can suggest more than what is said through just the actual meaning of the words. Both reader and writer know that what is written or said is not actually what is meant. In this manner, many levels of meaning can be overlaid on one text. Subtle use of irony often keeps the reader wondering what is meant, thus increasing the level of engagement in the text. When the irony is understood and appreciated, it leaves the reader with a sense of satisfaction that the irony was understood. Thus, it creates a kind of shared understanding between writer and reader.

Irony can be obvious and simple, like the snide or sarcastic tone that suggests an insult delivered in the form of a compliment:

- "Wherever did you find such an interesting dress?"
- "Aren't you the smart one?"

Similarly, irony can refer to a twist of fate, like when it rains on the day you have just washed your car.

However literary irony is a great deal more subtle. The reader must examine and consider the text closely in order to find and appreciate the irony. Identifying and explaining irony in an essay is a good way of improving your mark.

There are three main types of irony: dramatic, verbal, and situational. The following explanations will draw on examples of irony in Shakespeare's *Macbeth*, a tragedy known for its intricate and skillful use of irony to achieve its powerful effect on an audience.

Dramatic Irony

Dramatic irony occurs when the reader has a greater knowledge than the characters have themselves. The audience knows more about their situation or their future than they do. When used well, it makes readers want to tell the character what he or she is not aware of. It creates suspense and involvement, heightening readers' level of interest in the text or play. Good examples of dramatic irony can be found in Shakespeare's *Macbeth*. In fact, the dramatic irony begins in the opening lines of the play:

First Witch:	When shall we three meet again
	In thunder, lightning, or in rain?
Second Witch:	When the hurlyburly's done,
	When the battle's lost and won.
Third Witch	That will be ere the set of sun.
First Witch:	Where the place?
Second Witch:	Upon the heath.
Third Witch:	There to meet with Macbeth.
First Witch:	I come, graymalkin!
Second Witch:	Paddock calls.
Third Witch:	Anon!
All:	Fair is foul, and foul is fair:
	Hover through the fog and filthy air.

Overhearing this conversation between the witches and their prediction imparts knowledge to the reader that Macbeth will meet with them, even before Macbeth knows it himself. The reader may suspect that there may be dark side to Macbeth's character because Shakespeare has allowed us a glimpse of what is to come. Their prediction that "fair is foul and foul is fair" sets the tone and theme for all of the events of this tragedy.

However, a short while later in the play, Duncan and his soldiers comment on Macbeth, and we see that the people around Macbeth believe him to be noble and honorable. The sergeant speaks of him highly with the ironic words:

> For brave Macbeth—well he deserves that name—
> Disdaining fortune, with his brandish'd steel,
> Which smoked with bloody execution,

Even Duncan himself calls Macbeth "valiant cousin!" and "worthy gentleman!"

When you take both of these situations into consideration, you see that Macbeth will be involved in something ominous, but also that none of the people around him imagine or consider that it could be so. This excellent use of dramatic irony achieves suspense and captures the reader's full engagement in the play. As you will see, Macbeth plots to kill Duncan, all the while pretending loyalty. When his true deceit and treacherous nature is revealed, the reader feels a certain satisfaction of having understood what many characters in the play did not. In this manner, the play becomes much more mysterious and far more exciting. The reader's sense of *knowing what the characters do not helps* the reader to see the hidden meaning in what characters say.

For example, when Macbeth and Banquo return from the battlefield in Act 1, Scene 3, Macbeth says of the day, "So foul and fair a day I have not seen." Taken as such, it has one meaning, but if the reader recalls the prediction of the witches, it takes on a whole new significance and has the effect of heightening the suspense significantly.

In Act 2, Scene 3, the porter at the gate of the castle wonders what it would be like to be porter at the gates of hell.

> Here's a knocking indeed! If a
> man were porter of hell-gate, he should have
> old turning the key.

These lines are an excellent example of dramatic irony, because, as the reader knows, the treachery committed within the castle's gates will soon be discovered. Thus it could be said that the porter does indeed guard the gates of hell, considering the evil deeds that have been committed in the castle that he guards.

Verbal Irony

In this type of irony, the intended meaning of the words is different from what the words appear to express. Thus, a character will say one thing, but mean something different. One of the best-know examples of verbal irony can be found in Act 2, Scene 3 of the play, when Lennox comments to Macbeth about the dreadful things he heard in the night:

> The night has been unruly: where we lay,
> Our chimneys were blown down; and, as they say,
> Lamentings heard i' the air; strange screams of death,
> And prophesying with accents terrible

When Macbeth responds with the words "'Twas a rough night," it might appear (as it does to Lennox) that he is simply agreeing with him. The audience knows, however, that a treacherous plot has been hatched by Macbeth and that his words harbour a meaning unknown to Lennox but understood by the audience.

Situational Irony

The difference between what is expected to happen and what actually does happen is called situational irony. A good example of situational irony from the play is when Macbeth visits the witches and views the apparitions that foretell his fate at the beginning of Act 4. Through his association with the dark and sinister sisters, Macbeth believes he is collecting knowledge that will give him power and advantage. Among the predictions is the one made by the second apparition.

> Be bloody, bold, and resolute; laugh to scorn
> The power of man, for none of woman born
> Shall harm Macbeth.

Macbeth's thirst for power combined with this prophesy that no man born of a woman shall ever harm him imbues him a sense of invincibility, because he confidently (but falsely) assumes that all men must be born of women. Macbeth arrogantly quotes the prophecy later:

> Bring me no more reports; let them fly all:
> Till Birnam wood remove to Dunsinane,
> I cannot taint with fear. What's the boy Malcolm?
> Was he not born of woman? The spirits that know
> All mortal consequences have pronounced me thus:
> 'Fear not, Macbeth; no man that's born of woman
> Shall e'er have power upon thee.'

When Macbeth is killed by Macduff, the reader sees the irony of the prediction. During the fight, which will end tragically for Macbeth in the final act of the play, he is still arrogant. He brags to Macduff:

> Thou losest labour:
> As easy mayst thou the intrenchant air
> With thy keen sword impress as make me bleed:
> Let fall thy blade on vulnerable crests;
> I bear a charmed life, which must not yield,
> To one of woman born.

However, Macduff retorts:

> Despair thy charm;
> And let the angel whom thou still hast served
> Tell thee, Macduff was from his mother's womb
> Untimely ripp'd.

Macduff, who was born by caesarean section, was not technically "born"—an ironic twist of fate.

One of the main themes of the play, the paradox of "Fair is foul and foul is fair," spoken in the first act by the witches is also ironic. Throughout the play, it is proven again and again that things are not what they seem, that words contain more meaning than is first assumed, and that life holds a fate different to the one first assumed. This brilliant use of all manners of irony by Shakespeare defines the play's power, fascination, and lasting appeal.

2.2.2d describe the effects of musical devices, figures of speech and sensory details in print and nonprint texts (for example, alliteration used to create emphasis, metaphor used to evoke images, and sensory details used to evoke pathos)

Musical Devices

Alliteration: The opening consonant sound is repeated in two or more words. Alliteration draws attention to a phrase and is often used for emphasis. It is the figure of speech that helps people to remember such expressions as

- "the bigger, the better"
- "fast and furious"

Consonance: Consonance is very similar to alliteration, but with consonance, the consonant sounds are placed differently. Alliteration refers to the repeated consonant sound found at the beginning of the words. If the repeated consonant sound is anywhere else, it is consonance. Observe the "ng" sound in the following line from "The Conqueror Worm" by Edgar Allan Poe:

- "An angel throng, bewinged, bedight
  In veils, and drowned in tears,

Assonance: the repetition of a vowel sound within words. It is useful in the "near rhyme" or "imperfect rhyme," where, although a word may not rhyme exactly, the sound is pleasing to a listener. Assonance helps to create and strengthen the mood a writer seeks to establish. Consider, for example, the manner in which the "o" sounds in the following lines of Poe's poem help to create a mood of doom and despair.

- "And much of Madness, and more of Sin
  And Horror the soul of the plot.

Onomatopoeia: This is a technique where the words used imitate the sounds associated with the objects or actions they refer to. *Purr, quack, screech* and *thump* sound like the sounds they describe. Onomatopoeia is used mainly because it is difficult to describe sounds. These words are a useful device in adding aural imagery and, therefore, interest and dimension to a piece of writing. The following line of Poe's poem contains good examples:

- "Mutter and mumble low"

Word placement and sentence order can also be used to emphasize and suggest ideas or themes.

Repetition: When writers use repetition, they repeat a sound, syllable, word, phrase, line, stanza, or metrical pattern. This technique acts as a basic unifying device, giving the line structure and emphasis. The following poem by Gwendolyn Brooks contains an excellent example. Observe the effect of the word "we" at the beginning and ends of the lines. It provides the poem with a crucial rhythm, evoking the graffiti-like expression of the youth of the ghetto, as well as establishing the simple tone of the boys whose voices are heard in the poem.

We Real Cool

THE POOL PLAYERS
SEVEN AT THE GOLDEN SHOVEL

We real cool. We
Left school. We

Lurk late. We
Strike straight. We

Sing sin. We
Thin gin. We

Jazz June. We
Die soon.

FIGURATIVE LANGUAGE

Figurative language employs "figures of speech"—techniques that are based on saying or describing something, using expressions other than the literal meaning of the words. In this manner, figurative speech creates images. The writer helps the reader imagine something through the use of unusual comparisons or by adding effect and interest, and thus make things clearer.

Figures of speech are used for effect and sometimes to convey information. Here are some examples of figures of speech.

Symbolism: the use of something concrete to represent an abstract belief, feeling, idea, or attitude. For example, a red rose is often used to symbolize love. Even certain colours can symbolize abstract ideas, for example, black often symbolizes death.

Personification: the attribution of human qualities or actions to something that is not human. Animals, inanimate objects, and ideas can all be personified.

- "The wind howled and vented its rage on the bowing trees and the supplicating forest."

Simile: a comparison that uses the words like or as.

- "My throat felt as dry as dust."
- "The dewdrops glittered like diamonds."

Hyperbole: deliberate exaggeration that is use to make a point, but not to deceive.

- "She ran as fast as the wind."
- "I'm so hungry, I could eat a horse."
- "The air was so clear, you could see for miles."

Metaphor: This technique makes use of a comparison of two things without using the words "like" or "as." An efficient way of conveying an image or idea to your reader, the metaphor can be understood as the substitution of one idea or object with another in order to assist understanding. Calling a person an "star" or a "bull in a china shop" are examples of common metaphors. Here are two other examples.

- "time is a thief"
- "love is a battlefield"

Oxymoron: a two- or three-word phrase that contains opposite words or ideas.

- "exact estimate"
- "minor crisis"

Synecdoche: the naming of one part of something to stand for the whole thing, or of a whole thing to stand for a part. A common example is the name of a country standing for a team or a group of players:

- "Brazil won the soccer championship" (instead of "The Brazilian team won the championship").

Another common expression exemplifying the synecdoche is the statement,

- "The pen is mightier than the sword" (instead of "Words can achieve more than fighting and bloodshed can achieve").

Idiom: an expression that means something other than what it actually says; it is often associated with colloquialisms and proverbs.

"It's raining cats and dogs!"

Paradox: an extended oxymoron that appears to have contradictory ideas.

- "War is peace."
  "Freedom is slavery."
  "Ignorance is strength."
  (George Orwell, 1984)

Metonymy: the use of something associated with a second thing to stand for that second thing. The association can be arbitrary, as long as it is widely understood.

"It's good to see some *new faces* around the boardroom table."
"The *suits in the bank* don't care about the *ordinary Joe.*"

Metonymy is often visual and is commonly used in film. For example, falling calendar pages are a visual representation of the passage of time and the wheels of a train engine represent progress and exploration.

Imagery: words or phrases that appeal to the senses and help the reader imagine sights, sounds, smells, tastes, and touch.

- "Oh Juliet, your love burns my skin."
- "The light wings of her lashes brushed my cheek."
- "A deep chill crept up his spine."

The following examples demonstrate the appeal of literary devices.

Effects of Literary Devices

When you read poetry, you expect to find figurative language, to help you see, hear, taste, touch—to experience—literature through your senses. Consider the following example.

THE CONQUEROR WORM

LO! 't is a gala night
Within the lonesome latter years!
An angel throng, bewinged, bedight
In veils, and drowned in tears,
Sit in a theatre, to see
A play of hopes and fears,
While the orchestra breathes fitfully
The music of the spheres.

Mimes, in the form of God on high,
Mutter and mumble low,
And hither and thither fly—
Mere puppets they, who come and go
At bidding of vast formless things
That shift the scenery to and fro,
Flapping from out their Condor wings
Invisible Woe!

That motley drama!—oh, be sure
It shall not be forgot!
With its Phantom chased for evermore,
By a crowd that seize it not,
Through a circle that ever returneth in
To the self-same spot,
And much of Madness, and more of Sin
And Horror the soul of the plot.

But see, amid the mimic rout,
A crawling shape intrude!
A blood-red thing that writhes from out
The scenic solitude!
It writhes!—it writhes!—with mortal pangs
The mimes become its food,
And the angels sob at vermin fangs
In human gore imbued.

Out—out are the lights—out all!
And over each quivering form,
The curtain, a funeral pall,
Comes down with the rush of a storm,
And the angels, all pallid and wan,
Uprising, unveiling, affirm
That the play is the tragedy "Man,"
And its hero the Conqueror Worm.

—by Edgar Allan Poe

2.2.2e explain the contribution of motif and symbol to controlling idea and theme

Symbolism

Symbolism is used to enhance a theme, suggest a mood, or create an effect. Symbolism occurs when a writer uses an object, a situation, or an action to suggest another meaning. A writer might use a tiger to symbolize strength or fierceness. Another writer might use a lamb to suggest peace and gentleness. Symbols usually occur throughout a story. Generally, if an image or word is used three times or more in a story, there is a good chance that it is important enough to be a symbol in the story.

"The Most Dangerous Game" is a well-known short story by Richard Connell. The story involves the blood sport of trophy hunting, which has deteriorated into full-blown brutality. In the story, the reader is drawn into a sinister plot where the hunter who proposed the contest is actually pursuing his rival as prey. In the story, smoking is used to symbolically to reveal enhanced levels of meaning.

In "The Most Dangerous Game," smoking seems to be a symbol of power. At the beginning of the story, the protagonist, Rainsford, is a confident and powerful man who speaks as a successful hunter while smoking his pipe. While on the boat, "He leaped upon the rail and balanced himself there, to get greater elevation; his pipe, striking a rope, was knocked from his mouth. He lunged for it; a short, hoarse cry came from his lips as he realized he had reached too far and had lost his balance." His loss of his pipe symbolizes his loss of power: he is no longer the hunter.

Once on the island, Zaroff, who wants to hunt and kill Rainsford, has all the power over his prey. He smokes "black cigarettes," and his smoking represents his authority as the dominant hunter. When Zaroff is close to finding Rainsford's hiding spot in the jungle, Zaroff "straightened up and took from his case one of his black cigarettes; its pungent incense-like smoke floated up to Rainsford's nostrils." Zaroff's smoking indicates that he is in control and is dominant over Rainsford at this point in the story.

In "The Most Dangerous Game," Rainsford begins as an accomplished hunter and becomes the prey of another hunter. Smoking symbolizes the power and authority of hunting. Rainsford possesses this power at the beginning of the story, and Zaroff possesses the power throughout the hunt, although Rainsford ultimately triumphs over Zaroff at the end of the story. Smoking shows a position of dominance and power. The hunter dominates, and this dominant position seems to carry a specific mark of civilization, which in the case of "The Most Dangerous Game," is symbolized through smoking.

Symbolism can be complicated or simple. There is a certain amount of creativity in trying to figure out if something is a symbol or not. After reading through a story, try and think of the images and ideas that stood out to you. This can be a good start to discovering symbols in a text.

Symbolism plays a key role in other forms of media text, particularly films and advertising. In the long-running television drama series *Touched by an Angel,* one regular character is a young man dressed in black. He is the "Angel of Death."

The following list provides a number of symbols that are commonly found in literature. Knowledge of these universal symbols can help you find more meaning in the literature that you encounter, regardless of the type (genre) or cultural source of the literature.

Common Symbols in Literature

Water – fertility, life-giving, rebirth, purification, and redemption

Stagnant or polluted water – corruption, evil

Fire – destruction, purification, passion, death

Earth – baseness, fertility

Air/wind – spirits, freedom, inspiration

Sun – wisdom and vision, power, life-giving, regeneration

Sunrise – birth, rebirth, joy, hope

Sunset – death, old age

Mountains – obstacles, achievement, aspirations, awe, glory

Storms – death, evil, inner turmoil

Roads, ships, trains, railroads, etc. – journeys, changes

Fork in the road/crossroads – choices, decisions

Doors/gates/arches – escape, opportunities, utopias, fantasy worlds, freedom

Bridges – transitions, crossing over

Walls/fences/hedges – barriers, dividing lines, prisons

Windows – freedom, longing, imprisonment

Mirrors – illusion, unreality, passage to other worlds

Birds/sky – freedom

Circle – wholeness, unity

Gardens – Eden, paradise, innocence, fertility

Desert – spiritual aridity, death, hopelessness, sterility

Lamb – innocence, Christ

Sheep – conformity

Black – evil, death, despair

White – innocence, good, redemption

Red – war, anger, blood, vengeance, love, passion

Green – growth, renewal, life, nature, envy

Yellow – sun, happiness, cowardice, betrayal

2.2.2g analyze persuasive techniques used in a variety of print and nonprint texts

Techniques that Persuade

Writers resort to many techniques to win their readers over to seeing their point of view or to convince them of an image or a message. Becoming familiar with them can add to your understanding of a text and can also strengthen your own writing.

Here are some techniques used by writers to persuade readers.

Hyperbole: This technique is fun to use and usually has a great effect on the reader. Hyperbole involves exaggeration for emphasis. Especially when a writer wants to persuade or convince a reader, it is tempting (and sometimes effective) to employ hyperbole. This technique is very common in both spoken, as well as written English, especially in the media. The word "hype" comes from the term "hyperbole"—exaggeration.

- "There was a lot of media hype about the latest movie."

Here are two examples of hyperbole as a persuasive technique.

- The Roughriders slaughtered the Bluebombers!
- Watching him fumble that play was torture.

Diction (Word Choice): The choice of words can influence a reader's perception of an issue or an occurrence. Consider the difference between the description of someone as "obese" and and that of someone "carrying a few extra pounds." Is an oil spill an "incident" or an "accident"? What is the difference between a "poor choice" and a "mistake"? Choice of diction contributes to the establishment of a writer's voice or tone.

The audience that a writer wishes to address determines his or her choice of words . In addition, an audience will respond in very different ways to alternate word choices. Consider the following sentences.

- "The mayor selected a lady to help him with the project"
- "The mayor designated a woman to collaborate on the project."

What differences do you perceive between the two sentences? Might they convey a different attitude or underlying tone?

Rhetorical Question: Sometimes, a writer will ask a question to which no answer is required. The writer implies that the answer is obvious; the reader has no choice but to agree with the writer's point.

This technique is often used in a speech. Of course, the audience has no opportunity to answer, but the speaker's goal is to engage them and urge or persuade them to consider what they would answer if they could.

- "So what **IS** the best solution?"
- "Can we allow this travesty to continue?"

Sometimes, the purpose of a rhetorical question is to assert a point that the speaker is unwilling to make in an outright statement.

- "Isn't that the sweetest thing?"
- "Don't you think they should reconsider?"

Emotional Appeal: Writers appeal to a wide variety of emotions such as joy, anger or fear in order to persuade their readers. Some critics maintain that our popular culture is a culture of fear, for example. Appealing to our sense of safety, then, is an example of emotional appeal:

- "Inoculate your children if you do not want them to fall prey to disease."
- "If you care about Earth at all, you will not support this political party."

Appeal to the readers' emotions contributes in a major way to swaying them to accept the speaker's point of view. Advertisers make liberal use of the images of happy couples or families to promote their product. Appealing to people's desire for contentment and happiness through the suggestion that a particular product will help them to achieve such contentment and happiness is a common technique.

Repetition: Although overly repetitive writing is in danger of appearing tiresome, it can strengthen a writer's message. A word, a phrase, or an entire sentence might be repeated for emphasis. Examine the following excerpt from Edgar Allen Poe's poem, "The Bells."

Oh, the **bells, bells, bells!**
What a tale their terror tells
Of Despair!
How they **clang, and clash, and roar!**
What a horror they outpour
On the bosom of the palpitating air!
Yet the ear it fully knows,
By the **twanging,**
And the **clanging,**
How the danger ebbs and flows:
Yet the ear distinctly tells,
In the jangling,
And the wrangling,
How the danger sinks and swells,
By the sinking or the swelling in the anger of the bells
Of the bells
Of the **bells, bells, bells, bells,**
Bells, bells, bells
In the clamor and the clangor of the bells!

The repetition of both the words themselves (the bells, bells, bells, bells), as well as the structures of such words as "twanging" and "clanging" or word pairs like "and clash, and roar," contributes much to the power and flow of the poem. The repetition also strengthens the image of madness conveyed by the speaker. The reader of this poem does not have to stretch to be persuaded that the speaker is slowly going mad.

Similarly, a TV ad might feature a speaker who repeats a certain phrase many times

Two days only! Amazing deals! No money down! Discount Dan's!!
Though it may seem annoying, the repetition serves to make the commercial memorable, which is just the desired effect.

Parallelism: When a writer creates a "balanced" sentence by re-using the same word structure, he or she has achieved parallelism. The strength behind this technique is that parallel structure creates rhythm and cadence. The repeated word structure encourages the listener to expect consistency, thus adding emphasis to whatever points are made. Because the elements seem equal in emphasis, the strength of one point is transferred to the next one:

> "Let every nation know, whether it wishes us well or ill, that we shall pay any price, bear any burden, meet any hardship, support any friend, oppose any foe to assure the survival and the success of liberty."
>
> — *John F. Kennedy, Inaugural Address*

2.3.1a identify and consider personal, moral, ethical and cultural perspectives when studying literature and other texts; and reflect on and monitor who perspectives change as a result of interpretation and discussion

2.3.1b respond personally and analytically to ideas developed in works of literature and other texts; and analyze the ways in which ideas are reflected in personal cultural opinions, values, beliefs and perspectives

Good literature offers the reader more than a good story. Often, it presents readers with the opportunity to consider values, perspectives, and world views in a way that encourages careful thought and interpretation. Good literature makes readers think about the ideas it presents and how these ideas might relate to the real world.

Moral, Ethical and Cultural Perspectives

Values are based on the beliefs and principles that influence your *perspective*, on the experiences of your life, and on the issues you encounter. Values shape your world view, which influences your judgements, the way you feel toward and treat others, and the motivations that govern your actions.

In literature, world views are revealed through narration, description, and character motivation. Characters in literature and poetry often become a voice for values, perspectives, and world views. Stories and poems offer perspectives and world views for exploration, interpretation, and comparison. As a reader, you are invited to join the discussion, analyze descriptions and voice what you perceive in the text, and agree or disagree with the writer or characters.

Joy Kogawa is a Japanese-Canadian poet who was born in a Japanese Internment camp. Many of her poems and her novel *Obasan* focus on themes of alienation, prejudice, and tolerance. See if you can identify references to these themes in the following poem.

WHERE THERE'S A WALL

where there's a wall
there's a way
around, over, or through
there's a gate
maybe a ladder
a door
a sentinel who
sometimes sleeps
there are secret passwords
you can overhear
there are methods of torture
for extracting clues
to maps of underground passageways
there are zeppelins
helicopters, rockets, bombs
bettering rams
armies with trumpets
whose all at once blast
shatters the foundations

where there's a wall
there are words
to whisper by a loose brick
wailing prayers to utter
special codes to tap
birds to carry messages
taped to their feet
there are letters to be written
novels even

on this side of the wall
I am standing staring at the top
lost in the clouds
I hear every sound you make
but cannot see you

I incline in the wrong direction

a voice cries faint as in a dream
from the belly
of the wall

—by Joy Kogawa

The poem focuses on the image of a wall—a metaphor for the alienation and separation foisted upon Japanese Canadians in World War II. Throughout the poem, there are allusions to war and conflict. Although the speaker tries hard to break down the barrier represented by the wall (gate, ladder, gateways, secret passwords, passageways—even prayers), the wall of prejudice is impenetrable. Nevertheless, it seems that the speaker recognizes that no one gives up—the very presence of the wall represents a challenge to be overcome. This concept is introduced and emphasized in the first lines of the poem, a play on the well-known saying "Where there's a will, there's a way."

The last stanza mourns the fact that the speaker can hear the sound of the person attempting to contact her on the opposite side of the wall, but despite their efforts, they cannot connect—contact remains as distant, as though the other person was in "the belly of the wall."

2.3.1c explain how the choices and motives of characters and people presented in texts may provide insight into the choices and motives of self and others

Choices and Motives of Character

A writer seldom has the space in a work to completely define every motivation of a particular character. Instead, writers often relate important experiences in the person's life—those things that influence their behaviour and decisions. A skillful writer will choose an event or situation that encourages the reader to attempt to understand the circumstances. Understanding the motives of a character in that situation helps provide insight that broadens the reader's own context for reading and the experience the reader gains from it.

Study the following poem by Susanna Moodie— a poet known for her first-hand experience of the difficulties faced by early Canadian settlers. It is the personal perspective of a resentful boy with respect to his young stepmother. At first, the boy is rude and unfriendly to a young woman who wishes no more than to gain his trust. The reader can follow the first person rendition of how the boy comes to love the new caregiver and how he grieves when she sacrifices her life for his. Readers are privy to the change in his perspective as he comes to trust his father's new wife as a result of her kind nature and loving spirit.

THE STEP MOTHER

Well I recall my Father's wife,
The day he brought her home.
The children looked for years of strife,
And troubles sure to come—
Ungraciously we welcomed her,
A thing to scorn and blame;
And swore we never would confer
On her, a Mother's name

I see her yet—a girl in years,
With eyes so blue and mild;
She greeted us with smiles and tears,
How sweetly too she smiled—
She bent to kiss my sullen brow,
With woman's gentle grace;
And laid her tiny hand of snow
On my averted face—

"Henry—is this your son? She said—
"Dear boy—he now is mine—
What not one kiss?—" I shook my head,
"I am no son of thine!—"
She sighed—and from her dimpled cheek
The rosy colour fled;
She turned away and did not speak,
My thoughts were with the dead—

"Henry—is this your son? She said—
"Dear boy—he now is mine—
What not one kiss?—" I shook my head,
"I am no son of thine!—"
She sighed—and from her dimpled cheek
The rosy colour fled;
She turned away and did not speak,
My thoughts were with the dead—

There leaped from out my Father's eyes
A jet of swarthy fire;
That flashed on me in fierce surprise—
I fled before his ire
I heard her gentle voice entreat—
"Forgiveness for her sake"—
Which added swiftness to my feet,
A sad and strange mistake—

A year had scarcely rolled away
When by that hated bride;
I loved to linger half the day,
In very joy and pride;
Her voice was music to mine ear,
So soft its accent fell;
"Dear Mother now"—and oh, how dear
No words of mine can tell—

She was so gentle, fair and kind,
So pure in soul and free from art;
That woman with her noble mind,
Subdued my rebel heart—
I just had learned to know her worth,
My Father's second choice to bless;
When God removed her from the earth,
And plunged us all in deep distress—

Hot fever smote with burning blight
Stretchd on a restless bed of pain;
I moaning lay from morn till night
With aching limbs and throbbing brain—
Four weary weeks beside my bed,
She sat within a darkened room;
Untiring held my aching head,
Nor heeded silence—cold and gloom—

And when my courage quite gave way,
And fainter grew my struggling breath;
She taught my stricken soul to pray
And calmly meet approaching death—
"Fear not God's angel, sent by Him,
The weary spirit to release;
Before the mortal eyes grow dim,

Floats down the white winged dove of peace"—
There came a change—but fingers small,
No longer smoothed my matted hair;
She sprang not to my feeble call,
Nor helped to lift me to my chair—
And I arose as from the dead,
A life for her dear life was given;
The angel who had watched my bed
Had vanished into Heaven!—

—by Susanna Moodie

A reader can relate to the antagonism he or she feels when a newcomer seems to usurp the position of a loved one. By appealing to an emotion most readers have experienced, Moodie creates an opportunity for them to understand the speaker. Readers observe how the kindness of the new mother-figure breaks through the barrier of a hurt child's resentment and mistrust.

In a cruel twist of fate, however, the young stepmother dies of the illness she nursed him through and he must grieve for two lost mothers. Suddenly, the perspective changes again, as readers understand how the young speaker in the poem has no choice but to develop into a young man who must accustom himself to the harsh realities of nineteenth century life in the Canadian bush.

Readers gather far more information from the manner in which a character reacts to a situation than from a mere description. Be careful to note reactions and motivations for characters, as they provide excellent insight into the aspects that are less obvious at first glance. This aids in better appreciation and can go a long way in expanding the personal context that readers bring to any text.

2.3.1.d identify and examine ways in which cultural and societal influences are reflected in a variety of Canadian and international texts

Cultural and Societal Influences

Among the many topics and themes that a writer might address in his or her work are those related to cultural and societal issues, or possibly to the clash that ensues when different cultures collide. Literature is an excellent platform for examining societal issues or voicing emotions and opinions regarding the human struggle to come to terms with cultural or personal history.

The following poem by Daniel David Moses takes its title from the stone landmarks made by Inuit people for the purposes of communication and direction. It relates the speaker's yearning for his lost bond with the world of nature and his (or his peoples') quest for direction in an increasingly modern world. Thus, its theme is alienation, or sadness at the realization that he is unable to reconnect with nature in the face of modernization. Sharp, cold images and metaphors are the basis for most of the poem, but the writer also makes skillful use of personification, allusion, and stylistic techniques to convey his emotions to the reader.

INUKSHUK

You were built from the stones,
they say, positioned
alone against the sky
here so they might take
you for something human

checking the migrations.
That's how you manage this,
standing upright despite
the blue wind that snow is
this close to Polaris.

Still, the wind worries
you some. It's your niches
that ought to be empty.
Nothing but lichen grows
there usually. Now

they're home to dreams. Most come
from the south, a few from
further north
out of their mouths comes from
no direction you know.

They keep singing about
the Great Blue Whale the world
is; how it swims through space
having nightmares about
hunters who only hunt
their brothers
the other's snow-white face.
How beautiful frozen
flesh is! Like ivory,
like carved bone, like the lights

of Polaris in hand.
So it goes on and one,
the hunting refrain. Dead
silence would be better,
the Pole Star overhead.

The wind agrees, at least
wants to stop up each niche.
How long can you stand it
--that song, the cold, the stones

that no longer hold you

up now that they hold you
down?

Soon the migrations
recommence. How steady
are you? Dreams, so they say,
also sing on the wing.

Stones are markers for direction, symbols of own culture and history.

2.3.2c analyze and assess settings and plots in terms of created reality and plausibility (for example, determine the authenticity of the setting of a work of historical fiction)

Importance of Setting

The setting is the where and when of a story, and as such, an important part of the work. Short stories only have one setting, but the action in a novel may occur in several places over an extended period of time, so a novel can have many different settings. The description of the setting helps to give the reader the atmosphere or mood of the story. For example, if the writer describes the setting as a dark wood with trees that have jagged branches and in which strange noises are heard, the atmosphere could be described as spooky or creepy.

The setting includes more than simply where a story occurs. It also includes aspects such as time in history, cultural customs, and how people dress.

In the case of historical fiction, setting is a very important literary element. Because the time and place are connected to a certain time in history, the information about the time period must be authentic and correct. To create such settings in their work, writers research the time period thoroughly. They must know how people lived, the social problems of the day, their living conditions, and what beliefs and vocations were an integral part of their lives.

Historical fiction allows the reader to identify with the characters of the time. Through them, the reader is invited to further explore a particular period of history. A writer may have a goal of examining the stereotypes or preconceived notions related to particular historical events. Or, a writer may wish to view a historical event from the particular perspective of a character, thus offering close, personal insight into an event.

Consider, for example, the novel *Oliver Twist*. If that story were told about an orphaned youngster today, Oliver would not be living in a poorhouse, or orphanage, being fed gruel for breakfast. He would have a social worker and a foster home, where foster parents would be paid by the government to see that he was well-fed, clothed, and sent to school. Modern times are very different from the Victorian times surrounding the Oliver story.

Historical context also influences how a story unfolds. Charles Dickens, who wrote during the time of the Industrial Revolution in England, deliberately intended to make the public, particularly those in the middle classes, more aware of the contemporary social problems such as child labour. *Oliver Twist* helped to change labour laws to protect factory workers and children. You could extend your knowledge and create a connection between your knowledge of the novel and your knowledge of life's realities today by writing a modern version of Oliver Twist, showing that children or unskilled workers continue to be exploited around the world today.

Another example of historical writing is the novel *Obasan* by Joy Kogawa. In this autobiographical story of the internment of Japanese Canadians, the writer recounts the treatment of her people by the Canadian government during World War II. Themes such as prejudice and racism are examined through the firsthand accounts in the book. Intense imagery and realistic portrayal of the time and places that are the setting for this novel succeed in bringing this period of history alive. By encouraging the reader to share the experience from the point of view of a character who is an integral part of a historical event, a writer allows the reader a much deeper insight than an entry in a history book.

As mentioned, one of the most important reasons for writing literature with plausible settings and plots is that it can generate interest for further research and learning. A skillfully written narrative can generate curiosity and awareness of a historical event.

2.3.2d analyze and assess character and characterization in terms of consistency of behaviour, motivation and plausibility, and in terms of contribution to theme (for example, determine the meanings suggested by a change in a character's behaviour or values)

CHARACTER

Throughout your lifetime, you will read and become familiar with different literary characters from a variety of settings. These characters will face conflicts and challenges in many different situations. However, human nature has remained consistent throughout history. Even in a science fiction story, there are greedy, curious, fearful, and courageous characters: any character types that exist in the real world. Think about these character types from literature, and compare and contrast their motivations as they confront similar situations and conflicts in different historical eras. For example, a character from the past, Oliver Twist, and one from contemporary literature, Harry Potter, can be compared and contrasted.

Similarities between Oliver Twist and Harry Potter:

- Both are orphans.
- Both are mistreated by abusive adults.

They both dream of eventually changing their circumstances—Oliver dreams of going to London, and Harry dreams of freeing himself from his stifling home life.

Differences between Oliver Twist and Harry Potter:

Oliver	Harry
faces physical survival challenges	faces emotional survival problems
is manipulated by people	learned to use his "gifts" to have power over his enemies

The connections demonstrated are between two characters from two very different historical periods. However, they share some characteristics. This is the case with many characters you will encounter as you continue to read. The more characters you meet and understand, the more insight you will collect, furthering your understanding of them and your ability to analyze them.

RECOGNIZABLE CHARACTERS

- **Stock characters** are those that have been used in literature over and over again. The audience knows what to expect from them, which makes it easier to immediately draw the audience into the story. It is then possible to move the character toward reality, or at least individuality.

- **Archetypal characters** have certain enduring character traits referred to as archetypal qualities. Characters with these qualities are called archetypes, and they are usually instantly recognizable. Examples of archetypes include the hero, the sidekick, and the foil (a character whose contrasts with the hero show off the hero's qualities). The reason that stock characters work well in literature is that they have the archetypal qualities that readers recognize and accept, and sometimes the distinction can be a matter of taste. Including these characters in a piece of literature ensures that the reader will almost certainly have a understanding of the character and is also likely to have certain expectations of the character.

How Character is Revealed

In this context, *character* refers to qualities such as courage, honesty, generosity, and intelligence—and their opposites. *Character* also refers to fundamental ideas and beliefs held by the character, which can be revealed through

- actions
- dialogue

thoughts revealed through internal dialogue or through other thought-revealing techniques, such as stream of consciousness narration

- the writer's narration

One limitation of film is the difficulty of revealing thoughts in any way other than action. Voice-over narration is one technique filmmakers use to get around this limitation.

Personality

Personality refers to things such as mannerisms, social skills, sense of humour, and all traits that contribute to the words and actions of a person.

Motivation

- Motivation is essential to character development and plot.
- Well-developed characters have believable motives—even multiple and conflicting motives.
- Motivation takes time to develop. That is one reason that characters in movies often have simple motivation.

Appearance

Except in a movie, appearance is usually an unimportant part of character, unless the story is actually about appearance.

- Some writers do not describe their characters' appearance at all. A reader is left to imagine what the character looks like.
- When appearance is described, first-person narration and third-person limited narration can present problems as a result of subjectivity.

Understanding Character

Understanding fictional characters requires the same analytical, inferential, and interpretive skills that are used to judge people in real life. Conclusions are made by the reader's observations and through what is revealed by the narrator. It is possible to make supported assumptions and to draw logical conclusions about fictional characters.

People share human thoughts, emotions, and motives. Through an active and sympathetic imagination, it is possible to understand people who are genuinely different. Understanding is possible through one's own experiences and by seeing something of oneself in a character's experiences. By coming to know or observing others, characters in fictional texts can be easier to understand. The better you know yourself and others, the better able you are to understand characters in fictional texts.

Skilful fiction and storytellers can make feelings and motives so clear that the world and the individual have new meaning. Empathy—the sense of personal identification with the experiences of a character—develops when a reader can identify with or relate to a character's experiences.

Characterization

Everything that a writer does to portray characters is referred to as characterization. Characters can be described directly or indirectly. The following chart contains examples of both types of characterization.

Direct characterization is received	Indirect characterization is inferred
from what one character says or thinks about another character	from what a character says—sometimes from what a character says about another character
from the writer's statements about a character. For example, "Jane was stubborn and persevering."	from what a character thinks about his or herself, others, and the world
from "indirect characterization" that is obvious or contrived	from what a character does, especially in small things or when under pressure
	from other characters' reactions to a character

One of the basic methods of characterization is to invent different kinds of characters that serve different purposes. Characters can be classified by type and function.

Types of Characters

flat	have only one quality or character trait; are one-sided; always act the same way
round	have different, even contradictory traits; are more like real people
stock	are like flat characters, except that stock characters have been used over and over and are instantly recognizable
archetypal	are like stock characters, except that archetypes are meant to present typical (even universal) examples of certain character traits
dynamic	change or grow in some way either for good or bad; are altered by events and by their own actions and choices
static	do not change; flat, round, stock, and archetypal characters can all be static
foil	used as a contrast to the main character or protagonist; the difference between the foil and the main character emphasizes the main character's qualities; the foil is used for indirect characterization

Good storytellers use all of these types of characters. The most important character in a story is usually rounded and dynamic. The taxi driver whose only function is to delay the protagonist by taking a wrong turn is usually flat. In fact, some characters must be flat because there is no time or space to portray every character as a real person.

The amount of characterization that a character is given by the writer is generally controlled by the character's function in the story.

Characters Classified by Function

protagonist	the main character; often the hero, but not always, as sometimes the main character is a villain; often a dynamic character
antagonist	the character the protagonist struggles against; often but not always the villain
major	help move the plot forward in some way; they are often round and dynamic; the protagonist and antagonist are major characters
minor	have minor roles; they affect an event in the plot, but they do not move the whole plot forward; are often flat or stock because they do not appear long enough to be fully developed

2.3.2f assess the significance of a text's theme or controlling idea, and the adequacy, relevance and effectiveness of its supporting details, examples or illustrations, and content in general

Theme

The theme of any work is its subject. The theme deals with the meaning the writer wants the work to be about. The theme can be divided into two parts: the subject itself and what is said about the subject.

In a skillfully constructed narrative, all of the parts of the story contribute to the theme. The chart below demonstrates how all the elements of the narrative contribute to the theme.

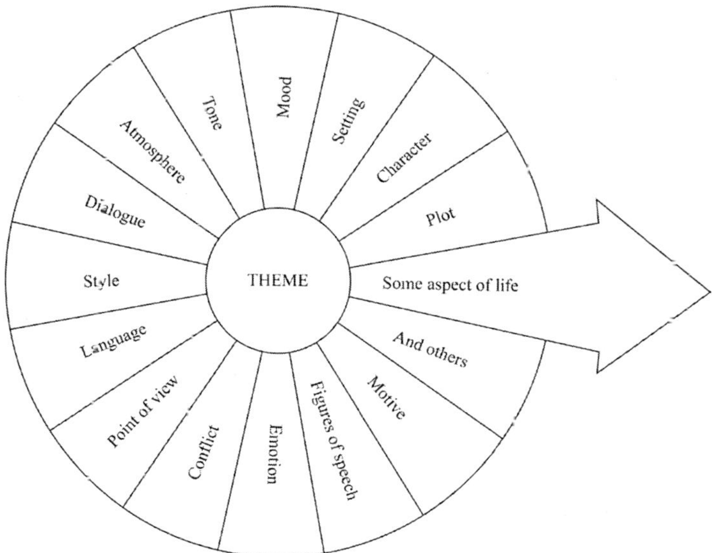

The moral of a story and its theme are connected, but they are not the same. A moral is a conclusion drawn from events in a story. It is a statement about the best way to behave. A story does not have to have a moral. If a story has a moral, then sometimes the writer states it. It is more common for the moral to be left for the reader to discover.

Recurring themes such as good versus evil appear across traditional and contemporary works of literature.

Example

The Struggle of Good Versus Evil

Traditional	**Contemporary**
Huckleberry Finn	*Star Wars*
Around the World in 80 Days	*Lord of the Rings*

Some common themes in literature, past and present, include:

- survival
- person versus nature
- triumph over adversity
- rags to riches
- courage and bravery
- heroes
- freedom
- friendship
- loyalty

Recognizing a common theme in a story, poem, play, or in several related literary works is a connection that will influence your attitude toward literature. Good literature is timeless and meaningful. Literature can become even more meaningful when you make connections between what you are reading and other knowledge you have.

Life Connections

Life connections are connections you find between your life and the literature you are reading. When something you read connects to your own life, it becomes a part of who you are as a developing young person. Often, people read books that contain situations or characters that remind them of aspects of their own lives. Think about your own favourite books to read: are there any similarities between your life and the lives of the characters in the book? Even fantasy or science fiction works can connect to a reader's life.

2.3.3b describe the effectiveness of various texts, including media texts, for presenting feelings, ideas and information, and for evoking response

Comprehension Strategies after Reading and Viewing

Reflecting on Predictions, Questions, Images, and Connections

After you have finished reading, it is important that you reflect on your pre-reading and reading strategies. Make a mental or physical note about your strategies:

- *Were your predictions correct?*
- *Have you answered the questions you created?*
- *Have the visualizations and images in your mind changed through the reading process, from your pre-reading images through your reading visualizations to your post-reading reflections?*
- *Were the connections you made before and during reading useful in helping you understand the text?*
- *What could you do differently to assist your comprehension of the text the next time you read?*

Reviewing Text and Purpose for Reading

Here are some questions to ask after reading a piece of text.

After Reading

- *Do I need to reread any parts that were difficult?*
- *What new information did I learn, and how does it fit into my background knowledge?*
- *What else do I still need to know about the topic?*
- *What are my thoughts about what I have read? Do I agree or disagree? Why?*
- *Do I like what I have read? Why or why not?*
- *Have I fulfilled the purpose I set for reading? If not, what do I need to do in order to meet that purpose?*

Making Inferences and Drawing Conclusions

As you read fiction, you make inferences and draw conclusions from the information in the text. Your responses to the text should always be supported by relevant aspects from the text itself or from your experiences in reading and in life.

The following examples show how to reach conclusions or inferences by using the clues in texts.

In Prose

In the following narrative, you could make several inferences about the boy and his grandfather, supported by stated or implied ideas in the text. Some questions about possible inferences follow this example.

IMPATIENCE

I get very impatient with my grandfather. He lives with us, and he does everything in slow motion. If we are walking somewhere, he walks so slow I feel like I could tip over trying to walk that speed. When I have to walk to the store for my mom, I just want to run down there, buy what she wants, and run home. That way I will miss less time with my friends or with my video games. But mom will call my name and ask me to run to the corner market, and I dread what follows. Grandpa will pipe up in his quavering old man's voice, "I'll go with the boy. I could use some fresh air." He says the same thing every time. I want to protest, but the look my mom gives me tells me I'd better keep my mouth shut. Once, I pitched a fit, complaining loudly about how slow he walks. Mom took away the video games for a week and lectured me about "respecting my elders," about how grandpa will not be here forever, and someday, I will look back and appreciate the time I had with him.

He does tell cool stories, though, while we move along the sidewalks at the speed of glaciers. He remembers when he saw the first automobile. It was a Ford Model T. Once, he took me to an antique auto show and showed me what they looked like. Part of this story always includes him telling me that his friend Frank, who is dead now, said they were a fad and wouldn't last. Grandpa told Frank he was wrong. He said he'd known the minute he set eyes on that first car that they would change the entire world. I try to imagine the world at that time the way grandpa has described it many times. Even though he makes me feel impatient, I will reach out sometimes and hold his hand as we walk. Just in case my mom is right.

Inference Questions

What kind of environment did the grandfather grow up in? How did his environment and his actions in life affect his beliefs?

What did the boy's mother teach him about life, about nature? What are some words you could use to describe his mother's character?

What kind of relationships has the boy had with values? What changes have taken place in his mind?

Being curious is the first step in making inferences. You probably know a lot more about a text than you may think, and asking questions is the first step to unlocking that information.

In Poetry

Inferences can also be made when you read poems. The mood, for instance, can be suggested in the rhythm, as you will see when you read the first few stanzas of "The Prospector."

PROSPECTOR

"Merchant ship to California" the sign did advertise.
The gold rush is on, don't miss it, be among the wise.
The "fourty-niner" set out with little, but the clothes upon his back,
This was his chance to be rich.
His chance to be Rich.
He prayed for safety from harm, and from any Indian attack.

Typhoid fever and cholera were his acquaintances along the bitter way
But he stuck it out, tough as nails, and wondered what his gold would weigh.
To Sutter's Mill he went, hoping to stake a claim
With riches his stature would rise, rise in everybody's eyes.
With riches he would be esteemed in everybody's eyes.
His piece of the American Dream became his only aim.

Laying track side by side, and mile after mile,
The Railroad grew, such a feat, by many feet, and utterly worthwhile.
But when the prospector did arrive, what did he behold?
Countless thousands.
Countless thousands.
All of them panning for gold.

What stood out to you in this poem? What parts of the language were striking, and which parts were descriptive? What literary devices are used? Here are some examples of inferences and conclusions about details of the poem.

- The regular rhythm throughout the entire poem suggests the action of the men panning for gold.

Here are some examples of highly descriptive figurative language in the second stanza:

- "tough as nails" (simile)
- "with riches his stature would rise, rise in everybody's eyes" (personification)

Consider, too, the other techniques that contribute to the effectiveness and the enduring appeal of this poem. Listeners respond well to repetition and parallel structures—they are pleasing to the ear and lend further emphasis and rhythm to a selection of poetry.

Writing

WRITING

3.1.1a select and monitor selected strategies as needed to refine the depth and breadth of inquiry or research and to identify the purpose, audience and form of presentation

3.1.1b describe the purpose of inquiry or research and the scope of the inquiry or research topic; identify the target audience' and identify the potential form for the presentation of inquiry or research finding, when applicable [such as a narrative, report, diary entry or bibliography]

PURPOSES (WRITING AND REPRESENTING)

DEVELOPING WRITING TASKS

By Grade 11, you should be confident using various forms of writing. The form of writing you choose will change according to your purpose for writing and your intended audience. These forms include analytic and argumentative essays, critical reviews, and expressive works, such as narrative or dramatic scenes, and independent research essays and reports. Because the general emphasis by the end of high school is on critical thinking essays (analytic and argumentative) and expressive works (narratives, dramatic scenes), examples of those forms are demonstrated for you in this ***KEY***.

DEFINING ESSAYS

Webster's Dictionary defines an essay as "a short literary composition on a particular theme or subject." That describes most of the published essays that you will be required to read in class. In a text, the essay definition would be a bit longer and might resemble this one:

> An essay is a multi-paragraph composition in which a writer develops a subject with supporting ideas and detail. A minimum of three paragraphs are required in order to develop an introduction with a controlling idea (thesis), a body, and a conclusion. Most essays produced by senior high students consist of at least five paragraphs. In many ways, an essay is an extension of a well-organized and developed paragraph.

TYPES OF ESSAY GENRES

In this context, the word *genres* refers to special types of essays that you will encounter in literary texts or that you may write yourself. The main genres or types of essays are descriptive, narrative, expository, reflective, and persuasive.

A **descriptive essay** describes something in detail, such as an object, place, person, procedure, emotional experience, etc.; for example, an essay describing a setting for a story, novel, or film, or a character sketch.

A **narrative essay** tells a story. These essays usually relate a personal experience or relate a person's involvement in an event; for example, first-person accounts from people who were on the Titanic or who were on board the Hindenburg when it crashed many years ago on its maiden flight from Europe to America.

An **expository essay** shows or explains a procedure, event, or topic; for example, an explanation of what causes a lunar eclipse or an article explaining anorexia.

A **reflective essay** considers a topic in a thoughtful (reflective) manner. A reflective essay usually does not present a single side of an issue, but rather, it asks the reader to consider various aspects of a topic. An essay on "Canadian Heroes" would be a reflective essay, as would one entitled "The Joys and Heartaches of Being Mother."

A **persuasive essay** is an opinion essay that seeks to win the reader over to a particular viewpoint on a topic or issue. Political essays tend to be examples of persuasive essays. Newspaper editorial essays are often persuasive in content and tone.

Organizing Essays

The graphic below contains an explanation of an easy-to-use formula for an essay. Think of how a hamburger is made when you think about how you want to structure your essay. Most of the literary essays you will read in class will be a variation of this basic pattern, since they will tend to be longer than five paragraphs. However, the five-paragraph essay is quite common, and with this diagram, you can see the essential components of the essay as a literary form.

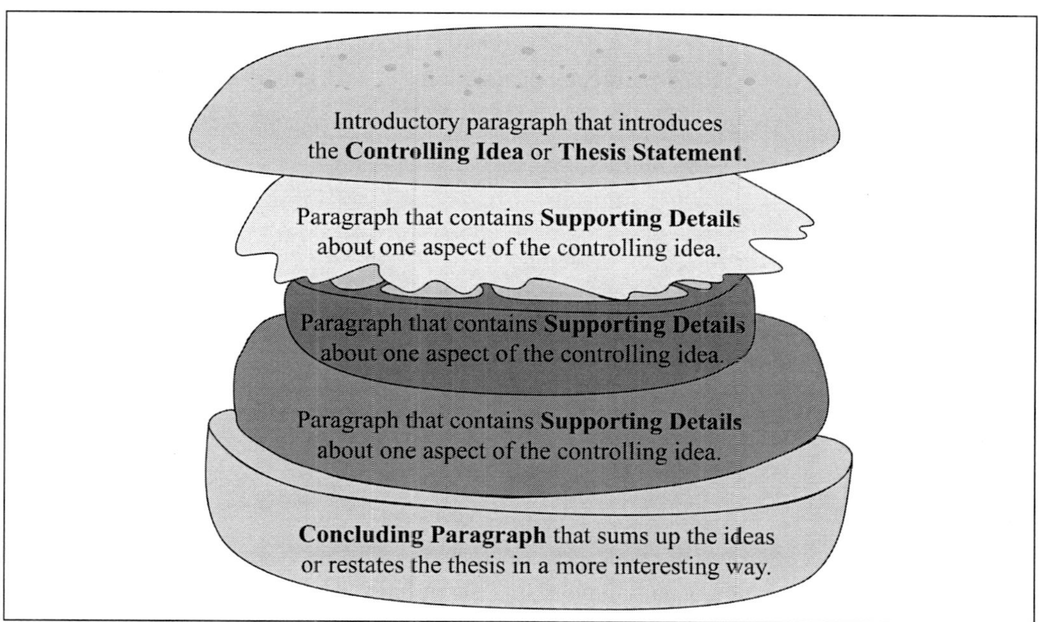

Not all essays follow this pattern; however, this is a basic essay structure that works in most situations. This is the pattern that is frequently required of students.

The graphic of the hamburger shows an essay structure that includes an introduction, a conclusion, and three items in between. Within this structure, you can have some freedom in terms of how long each paragraph is.

3.2.1a reflect on and describe strategies that may be used to select, record and organize information; select and monitor appropriate strategies' and modify selected strategies as needed

3.2.1b select information and other material appropriate to purpose from a variety of print and nonprint sources [for example, from museums, archives, government agencies, periodicals, microfiches, Internet, CD-ROMs, films, television and radio broadcasts, interviews, surveys, and print and online encyclopedias]

USING A VARIETY OF SOURCES TO COLLECT IDEAS AND INFORMATION

Information is all around you. Some examples of public documents in which you can locate information are shown in the table.

Consumer Documents	Workplace Documents	Public Documents
Consumer reports Guarantees Warranties Recall announcements Advertisements	Safety policies Dress codes Emergency evacuation procedures Internet use rules Email policies	Clean Air Act Safe Water Act Highways Act Littering laws Driver's handbook Library policies

Some examples of information books that are recognizable by their formats are

- encyclopedia
- dictionary
- thesaurus
- atlas
- almanac
- textbook
- manual

When you look for information, you usually have a specific purpose in mind. Each of the information sources listed below is appropriate for one or more specific purposes:

- lists
- phone books
- brochures
- recipe books
- newsletter
- biographies
- maps
- autobiographies
- schedules
- catalogues
- agendas
- booklets
- newspapers
- pamphlets
- magazines
- Internet
- TV guides
- travel guides
- handbooks
- yearbooks

The following table matches some purposes with information sources from the list.

Purpose	Information Source
Finding a new word	Dictionary, thesaurus
Planning a trip	Internet, travel brochure, travel guide, map
Finding annual weather patterns	Almanac
Finding current sports information	Newspaper, Internet
Finding out about replacing a DVD player that stopped working	Warranty, guarantee
Ordering some camping equipment	Catalogue, Internet
Checking the option courses at your school	School handbook

When you need to locate any type of information, there is usually an appropriate source close at hand. Just ask yourself the following questions:

- What do I need to find out?
- Where am I most likely to find this information?
- Who could help me if I do not know?

Online Library Catalogues

Online library catalogues can be accessed simply by typing the name of your local library into a search bar. You will find hyperlinks such as

- Library Catalogues
- Databases by Subject or Title
- FAQ or "Frequently Asked Questions" such as "How do I use the library catalogue?"

You can search your library to find materials that are related to your topic by typing in any piece of information from the list below:

- title
- keyword
- author
- subject
- call number
- series title
- ISBN / ISSN This last item is a cataloguing number found at the bottom of the credits page; it looks like this: 0-03-052664-75-048 04 03 02 [these particular numbers represent a text entitled *Elements of Language: a Second Course*].

Your catalogue search could produce titles and call numbers for several books on your topic, and you can take that information to your local library.

Dictionaries and General Encyclopaedias

Dictionaries are always a good place to start when you are looking for the meaning of a specialized term. Look for the meaning associated with the specific subject or content area. For instance, the word revolution, shown in the sample dictionary definition below, is used in both science and social studies, but with completely different meanings and associations.

> **rev•o•lu•tion** (rev′ə lōō'shən), n. **1.** the overthrow and replacement of an established government or political system by the people governed. **2.** a sudden, complete, or radical change. **3.** rotation on or as if on an axis. **4.** the orbiting of one celestial body around another. **5.** a single cycle in a rotation or orbit. –**rev′o•lu′•tion•ar′y,**
>
> adj., n., pl –ies. – **rev′o•lu′•tion•ist**, n.

In spite of increased use of the Internet as a means of finding information, encyclopedias continue to hold their own as solid sources of basic information on many topics, particularly historical events, famous people, inventions, and scientific topics. They do have to be used in the library, unless you have a good set at home. Remember that libraries also have electronic encyclopedias on CD-ROMS. The advantage of these is that the information is regularly updated as needed. Recording the bibliographic entry for a CD-ROM encyclopedia is somewhat different than recording one for a regular encyclopedia, as shown:

> CD-ROM – Author's name (if known). "Title of Article."
> Title of Database. Medium (CD-ROM)
> City: Electronic Publisher, publication date.
> Example: Merrill, Cyrus. "Sunspots – Solar Mystery."
> North American Science Encyclopedia. CD-ROM.

It is worth noting here that CD-ROM versions of many subjects and topics are available through your library. You record them the same way as the CD-ROM encyclopedia.

You can also access all major encyclopedias online from home; for example, the Encyclopaedia Britannica Online. However, except for a free trial period, your parents would have to pay a subscription fee of around $70 per year to allow you continued access.

Research Sources

In a research paper, you express your opinion on a subject. You must support your views by using other primary or secondary sources. Before you begin, it is a good idea to create a chart labeled "What I Know" and "What I Want to Know" about the subject. This will help you create clear, concise, and pertinent research questions. Now, you are ready to begin your research.

Primary Sources

A source is considered primary if it was created by a person who has direct, personal knowledge of the event. A primary source is a document such as a letter, speech, or picture created by a primary participant in the event being studied.

Examples of Primary Sources

- **Interviews** – you might decide to interview one of the astronauts from one of the Apollo Missions. How would you conduct the interview? Would you do it by phone? Email? In person? Remember to prepare open-ended questions (those that require a larger response than "yes" or "no") that are specific to the topic and to your interviewee's experiences. Take notes or use a recording device as you speak to the astronaut. Finally, remember to write a thank-you letter after the interview.
- **Photos** – you might be able to find firsthand photographic accounts that you could use to support your research.
- **Eyewitnesses** – you might be able to interview someone who witnessed one of the Apollo spaceships as it took off for its mission.
- **Original documents** – any original, authentic documents (such as newspaper and magazine articles, pamphlets, and blueprints) that were created by a person involved in the launch of one of the Apollo spaceships.

Secondary Sources

Secondary sources use primary sources or other secondary sources to report information. A secondary source usually contains reports, paraphrased material, or evaluations of events from the past. Quotations from primary sources are often found in secondary sources.

Examples of Secondary Sources

- **Libraries** – catalogues in libraries have print and electronic resources listed under three headings—author, title, and subject—to make it easier for you to find what you are looking for.
- **Internet sites** – the Internet has many sites from which you can gather more information about your subject. Be aware that anyone can post information on a website, so, even though an Internet site may be more up-to-date than encyclopedias and text books, the information may not always be accurate. Be sure to check all your facts against other sources.

  Knowing the following abbreviations at the end of a website address can help you eliminate unreliable websites:

  .com – is a business or company
  .edu – is an educational site
  .gov – is a government site (any country, not just the United States)
  .in – is an international organization site
  .org – is a not-for-profit organization site

- Books, encyclopedias, and reference books will have very accurate information, but will not necessarily be the most up-to-date.

Example

A student investigates what it would be like to be a doctor in a small town by studying both primary and secondary sources of information.

The comparison chart below illustrates some distinctions between the kinds of information available.

Secondary Sources: career pamphlet, career website, university handbook, career catalogue	**Primary Source:** interview with family physician
• educational requirements • specialties • salary range • personal aptitudes • range of career opportunities • professional skills • professional development	**Hardships:** long hours, being on-call disrupts life, tiring, demanding, limited family time, competition for hospital privileges, large patient load **Benefits:** satisfaction, small town friendliness, valued, respected, known in community, chances for community involvement, good salary
Generalized information	Personal, practical information

3.2.1e observe guidelines for Internet use [for example, keep passwords, telephone number and addresses confidential; visit appropriate sites; respect copyright; and observe rules for citing Internet sources, following correct procedures to avoid plagiarism

READING WEBSITES

The Internet allows anyone to make information public, so you must be very careful when performing research using Internet resources. Not everything you read will be true, and if it is, it might not be totally accurate. Although you should be critical of any text you read, it is especially important to use critical reading skills with Internet resources. Critical reading is especially necessary to check the quality and reliability of the information on the Internet.

Reading any text requires you to think critically and ask questions about the truth of the text. You should ask yourself some questions to help you to determine the validity and reliability of the information presented on a website.

Things to Consider Doing Research on the Internet

1. Take a look at who the writer or editor of the website is. Is it a professional academic journal or an amateur blog? How professional the writing sounds and polished the site looks are factors that can help you determine how reliable that site is. Does the site post information about the writer of the materials that are found there? Does the writer have training or recognized expertise in the field that the website represents? Can you find any other sites that mention that writer? Well-known writers will usually be referred to on many sites.

2. What is the content like? Is the information consistent with information from other sources, such as books or other websites? Usually, academic publishers are reliable sources of information about a subject. Is the information easy to understand? Does the site present more than one side of an issue?

3. Who is the intended audience? Does the writer seem to have a specific audience in mind? Does the site have advertisements? At whom do you think the ads are targeted? How has the site been funded—through corporate sponsorships or through non-profit organizations?

4. How is the site structured? Is it easy to navigate? Can you exit at any time? Can you go back to a previous page without hitting the "Back" button on the browser? Are there links to other sites that give you additional information?

After you have analyzed the different features of a site, it is time to evaluate the usefulness of the information on the site. Does it fit the topic of your research? Some sites may look great and have reliable information, but it may not necessarily relate to your assignment. Be careful that you do not fill up a research paper with lots of citations from sites that do not have much to do with what you are writing about. More is not always better. You may only find a few websites that help you, but if they are comprehensive and large sites,
you may only need a few Internet sources for your writing. Finally, remember that the Internet should not be the only resource you use. Books, newspapers, interviews, or academic journals are all excellent resources
as well.

Online Searches

- Use keywords and phrases related to your topic: e.g. "Pearl Harbor attack", "casualties of Pearl Harbor"
- Be as specific as possible; e.g., "terrorism in Afghanistan" would be more specific than "global terrorism" or "terrorism."
- Watch for hyperlinks to other related articles or websites.
- Remember that websites are listed in order of usage or "hits." Most often (but not always), the websites listed on the first page of your search results will be the most helpful with respect to information.
- Remember to record the website information for your bibliography if you use any of its content.

3.2.2c assess the accuracy, completeness, currency and relevance of information selected from sources; and assess the appropriateness of the information for purpose

Critiquing Logic and Quality of Evidence

Determining the Reliability of Sources

Generally, you would tend to think that information you find in encyclopedias is fact. However, not everything that is stated with authority is really fact. There are so many other resources, such as eyewitness accounts, newspaper accounts, supermarket tabloid accounts, and the Internet. These sources are often less reliable than reference materials you can find at the library. Information on the Internet often has errors or bias.

How do you determine what makes a resource reliable as a source of information? When is the information valid and authentic? What kinds of sources will mostly provide accurate information?

It is important to be critical of what you read, particularly when the information you are reading claims to be factual or truthful. Evaluate the facts stated carefully. Decide what evidence is convincing and what might need verification. Look for biases that suggest a particular viewpoint or opinion, even when the bias is not directly stated. If a newspaper, for example, reports mostly stories and articles that cast a particular politician or political party in a negative light, you could probably draw the conclusion that the paper does not support the policies of that politician or that party. It is a good idea to either not read a newspaper that has a bias or to balance your knowledge of issues by reading a variety of news sources.

Eyewitness Accounts

An eyewitness account is a first-hand description of events from the point of view of an eyewitness who was present as a participant or a bystander.

Example

> A commuter in the London Underground might have responded to a reporter's question about a blast that killed and injured many subway passengers a few years ago: "The deafening sound of the explosion made me sure we would all die. Then I saw the clouds of smoke and dust. I kept running, but I couldn't find the escalator or the lift."

Usually, an eyewitness tries to provide an accurate description of the event, but they may be hampered by faulty memory, location perspective, and unconsciously creative twists to the story. Some eyewitnesses deliberately misrepresent the situation or mislead the listener, particularly in cases of crimes or motor vehicle accidents. If possible, it is best to get an account of events from impartial witnesses. It is also a good idea to verify any facts reported by eyewitnesses.

Newspapers

Newspaper sources, both print and electronic, such as the *Ottawa Citizen*, *Montreal Gazette*, and the *Edmonton Journal*, are major city newspapers; they are usually reliable sources of local, national, and international news. If they make a mistake, the paper will typically print a correction the next day or as soon as the fact is verified. City newspapers tend to deal with "hard news": local, national, and international events that impact large numbers of people. News reporters are expected to be objective and impartial, leaving opinions for the editorial page. The owners of major newspapers have no desire to be sued for publishing lies or to lose their credibility. They must be credible or they risk losing sales and advertising revenues. However, newspapers often display a slant or perspective, known as a *media bias*.

Even a newspaper must be read critically. Letters to the editor sometimes convey strong disagreement with an article or photo that some readers feel to be in poor taste, misleading, or inappropriately placed on the front page.

Supermarket Tabloids

Tabloids sell papers with sensational front page headlines and photos. They spend thousands of dollars for hot tips, celebrity gossip, and photos of famous people. Stories that are embarrassing or scandalous sell well, and celebrities are sometimes forced to issue denials through their publicists or to demand apologies or retractions from the paper. Costly lawsuits are often the result of incorrect or unfair portrayals of well-known people in the entertainment business. Journalism like this is known in the industry as "soft news" and mostly should not be taken too seriously.

Internet

For many people, the Internet is a primary source of hard news and soft news. In some respects, the Internet is invaluable because it can be so quickly corrected or updated. However, the global spread of cellphone use for taking pictures has added a public dimension to the news that is uncontrolled. Access to such public views of the news is changing how news is reported and received. Pictures recorded by bystanders are nonetheless a positive development, especially when they act as evidence for or against allegations. They have even provided courts with documentation of an alleged incident, such as unnecessary police force used in an arrest.

You have to look at news that is on the Internet even more critically than you would read a newspaper. Research is probably the most common school-related student use of the Internet. When you are using the Internet for research, be sure that the information you are using is accurate before using it in your work. Ask the following questions about your Internet sources:

Is the writer or contributor mentioned on the site? Are the writer and publisher recognized as reliable authorities on the topic?

- Do you detect any bias? Does the reporting seem fair and objective?
- Can you check the accuracy of the information with other sources?
- What subtopics are covered? Are there links to more extensive coverage?
- How current is the coverage? Has it been revised or updated? How old is the information?

Supporting Your Opinions

Teachers are usually receptive to opinions that are different or that disagree with what is being taught as long as support for a different opinion is given with valid and convincing evidence. You can support your opinion by using

- significant quotations from a text, especially statements by respected experts on the topic or issue
- well-known or proven facts
- statistics
- examples from a text that support your point. You should always use specific examples from a story, for instance, to support your conclusions about a character. When you write about a poem, you should quote phrases or words that illustrate the poet's use of imagery to achieve a special mood or particular effect.

As you can see, one of the most important parts of succeeding at supporting your opinions is using ideas or facts that come from sources that are logical and of good quality. Generally, an argument or opinion is more convincing when evidence, whether from a text or statistics, is used as support.

3.2.2d identify and describe possible biases of sources and describe the possible effects of such biases on the credibility of information [for example, examine the credibility of the author or organization, the proportion of verifiable facts to generalizations, or the sponsor/author/purpose / date of a Web site]

Bias and Stereotyping

Bias and stereotyping are both rooted in prejudice. The following section explains how bias and stereotyping in text is important to recognize and analyze from a balanced point of view.

Biases

Bias is an unconscious or natural tendency to adopt a preferred view on something. It may be unspoken, but is often expressed in attitude or behaviour. It can certainly be positive, as in having an inner pride in being Canadian, which would be a pro-Canada bias, or having a bias to cheer for your home team no matter what. However, there are negative biases, such as

- **anti-youth bias**, which refers to assumptions made about young people, including misconceptions about their sense of responsibility or about their trustworthiness
- **anti-aging bias**, which refers to assumptions made about older people, which can include misconceptions about their abilities or attitudes because of their age
- **anti-authority bias**, which makes a person view teachers, parents, policemen, or other authority figures with hostility and suspicion
- **racial prejudice**, which makes a person dislike or hate anyone who looks different from their own ethnic group

Other biases include political biases, gender biases, economic biases, and religious biases. Negative biases prevent people from being tolerant of other people and different viewpoints.

Stereotypes

Stereotypes are over-generalized beliefs about individuals or groups. These generalizations are based on preconceived notions that may be the result of a personal bias or from being misinformed. Stereotypes assume that a whole group of individuals are all exactly the same; stereotypes do not acknowledge uniqueness and individuality. They create mistaken assumptions; for example, that tall people must be good basketball players, that people who wear glasses must be smart, or that unemployed people must be lazy.

Particularly in areas where there is a concentration of a visible minority ethnic group, adults may, unfortunately, pass racial stereotypes on to the younger generation. An example of where this occurred is the United States prior to the Civil Rights Movement. At that time, many white Americans were in solidarity with black Americans to change laws that were discriminating against them. The results of the protests were fully integrated schools of mixed races and basic freedoms for black Americans, such as the right to sit where they want on public transportation, use public restrooms and drinking fountains, and eat in restaurants of their choice.

It is important to be mindful of stereotypes when you read texts of any kind. Advertising and editorial writing often include stereotypes. Watch for bias or slants no matter what type of medium is being presented to you. Bias can occur through omission—when an advertiser or a reporter deliberately chooses to include some facts and omit others. The bottom line is that stereotyping and bias come from opinions based on fear, not fact.

The best action you can take is to read as much as you can about a topic in order to get a lot of information. Different sources about a topic will probably have different opinions and feature different facts. When you read as much as you can about a topic, you are giving yourself a balanced picture of that topic. Many writers will expose you to stereotypes and biases intentionally in order to educate you about respecting individuality, tolerating differences, and forming your own (hopefully unbiased) opinions.

4.1.1a reflect on the purposes for text creation [for example], to inform, explain, entertain or inspire] and on own motives for selecting strategies to engage an audience [for example, to communicate information, promote action or build relationships]; and consider potential consequences of choices regarding text creation [for example, follow-up information may be required to clarify information, a position may need to be defended and opposing viewpoints addressed, and topic and style must be appropriate for intended audience]

Setting a Purpose and Considering Audience

Writing with Purpose

By Grade 11, you are becoming a more experienced writer. You have already accomplished a wide variety of writing tasks. Every writing task, from a short paragraph to a research report, shares the same first steps:

- determining a reason or purpose for writing
- choosing a topic
- considering the prospective audience for your finished product

The process of successful writing is like preparing for and going on a journey. If you plan and follow the steps in the writing process, you will reach your destination. Before starting to write, then, it is wise to sit back and think about your topic, purpose, and audience.

Choosing a Topic

Choosing a topic can be difficult if you are not sure where to begin or if you are having trouble choosing between topics that interest you. Assigned topics and topics you choose yourself may offer different challenges when you start organizing your work.

Assigned Topics: Often, a topic or a list of acceptable topics will be provided by your teacher. You may be asked to write a research paper, a story, a poem, a movie or book review, a business letter, or other creative texts.

Self-Chosen Topics: If you decide to choose your own topic, some of the following guidelines may help you arrive at a decision.

- Think of issue-related topics. These are topics that generate a range of opinions, such as when teenagers should be eligible to drive, what world leaders should do about global warming, and so on.
- Think about topics of personal interest to you. If you are passionate about Canadian hockey, the harmful effects of cyber-bullying, or future trends in transportation, you are more motivated to research and explore the topic thoroughly.
- Brainstorm and eliminate. Quickly think of and list six topics. Do a quick Internet search to see how much information is available online—this usually means information about those topics will likely be available at the library as well. Some topics may immediately lead you to a brick wall because resources on the topic do not seem to be available. Cross these topics off your list. You probably do not have time to spend hours hunting for related information.

- Think of topics that would be of interest to your target audience. Since your audience often consists of your peers, you can probably think of topics that would interest your classmates. These topics are more likely to motivate you, too, because you probably share many of the same interests as your classmates.
- Break a broad topic into a manageable size. If your topic is too broad, you will need to sort through too much information. Narrowing your topic before you begin will make your writing task less frustrating and easier to handle.

Deciding on Your Purpose for Writing

Good writers usually have a specific purpose for writing a given text. Your purpose in writing an assignment can act as a way to focus and stay on topic. Generally, there are five purposes for writing:

To inform (to interpret in detail, to make clear): This form of writing is concerned with the "what" of a situation.

- Announcements, news broadcasts, catalogues, labels, and documentaries are all examples of communication meant to inform.

To explain (to interpret, to make clear): This form of writing is concerned with the "why" or "how" of a situation. It is also known as explanatory writing because readers are given explanations and not just informed about an event.

- Charts, recipes, brochures, invitations, and textbooks are examples of communication meant to explain.

To entertain: This form of writing is meant to be light and entertaining. It may be humorous, but it can encompass many different kinds of fiction.

- Action, science fiction, and romance novels are examples of communication meant to entertain.

To impress (to affect deeply): This form of writing aims to make readers feel strongly about a topic.

- Editorials, complaint letters, and self-help books are examples of communication meant to impress.

To convince (to persuade by argument): This form of writing aims to change the reader's beliefs; the writer will state a belief and then appeal to the reader's feelings or intellect.

- Advertisements, editorials, and debates are examples of communication meant to convince.

4.1.1b identify purpose and target audience for text creation and select strategies to accomplish purpose and engage audience

Choosing an Audience

Another factor that affects a writer's purpose is his or her audience. Before writing a composition, writers must decide who their audience is and how they want their audience to react. For example, if you are writing an assignment for your teacher, you should write the report in a formal manner, keeping in mind that your audience is your teacher and that correct grammar, spelling, punctuation, and formal style are usually required. If you are writing a friendly letter to a friend, the manner can be less formal, and conventional rules are less important.

The following list is not exhaustive, but it includes a range of potential audiences for your writing:

- peers/classmates
- teacher
- prospective employer
- general public
- children
- parents
- pen pal
- politician
- celebrity
- role model

Reviewing Content

Much of your writing at this stage of your life will be required writing for which you are given a set of topics that you must choose from. You then begin writing an essay that receives a grade and some feedback from your teacher. The first thing to keep in mind is that you should always choose a topic that seems interesting to you, for whatever reason. Even if most of the topics initially seem boring, you want to get through the assignment as successfully as possible, so it is a good idea to try to find one topic you think you could become interested in, even if you are not entirely interested at the beginning. Once you are underway, keeping a copy of the actual essay question somewhere nearby, if not actually printed out on top of the pages of your notes, will help keep your research and writing focused on the task at hand, and doing so will also help ensure that your final draft actually addresses the question initially presented by your teacher. Composing a brilliant essay that is off topic will not earn you the grade you deserve for your intelligence, effort, and otherwise excellent writing skills. So at each stage of the essay-writing process, you will want to double check your "answer" with the instructor's "question" and make sure that what you are writing actually lines up.

4.1.2a *select a text form appropriate to the purpose for text creation and consistent with the content to be presented in the text*

4.1.2b *explore a variety of structures consistent with form, content and purpose when creating texts [for example, explore definition, example and illustration, classification and other methods of development consistent with the essay form when creating an essay]*

Analyzing Writing Samples or Models

The Analytic Essay

"Miss Brill" is a short story in which character and theme are the dominant elements. This makes the story a natural choice for a character analysis. Because the theme is so closely related to Miss Brill's character and limited outlook on life, a joint analysis of theme and character is advisable.

In the context of a literary essay, supporting detail can refer to an actual detail, like a single incident, scene description, sensory image, or metaphor. As well, supporting detail can mean a discussion or explanation of plot, setting, the use of imagery, or the use of figurative language.

Using a Model

If you have difficulty in devising your own structure for essay writing, you may want to follow a straightforward structure, such as the one modelled here, that includes

- an introductory paragraph that introduces your thesis and the text(s) that will be examined to support it
- three body paragraphs, each establishing and developing support for the thesis
- a concluding paragraph that unifies the writing

Creating a Thesis Statement

Your thesis statement, which often comes at the end of your introductory paragraph, guides the rest of your response. Your thesis statement contains the controlling idea for your essay. This idea may be either implicit in your thesis statement or it may be stated explicitly. Analysis of character, goal, conflict/obstacle, and realization/resolution should lead naturally to your thesis statement/controlling idea.

Example

"Miss Brill," a short story by Katherine Mansfield

Character: Miss Brill, a woman who lives in a fantasy world; she imagines that she lives a glamorous life and that she plays an important part in the lives of others

Character's goal: Contentment, escape from isolation of her real life

Conflict/obstacle: She is mocked by a young couple

Realization/resolution: She eventually sees herself as others see her, realizes the loneliness and emptiness of her life, and is ultimately devastated

Themes: Reality versus illusion, desire for companionship versus the struggle to belong

Thesis statement (controlling idea is implicit):	
Miss Brill lives in an imaginary world where she experiences a sense of contentment as she sees herself as an important part of other people's lives.	Character/goal
She is eventually forced to face the gloomy reality of the life she lives,	Conflict
and her feelings of contentment and self-worth are destroyed.	Realization/resolution

Stated explicitly, the controlling idea is that allowing imagination to blur one's reality can lead to both positive and negative consequences.

INTRODUCTORY PARAGRAPHS

If you have difficulty writing introductions, use some of the following hints to help make the process easier

- Write a sentence that introduces the topic and text(s) you will be using.
- Write several sentences that explain the topic and present your thesis statement, including the order of the evidence you will be supporting.
- Explore alternative beginnings to find the one that works best for the idea that you are developing. The first sentence is an important sentence because it introduces the mood and tone of your writing.

Example

Introduces the topic of imagination and the text selected

Thesis statement—opinion with the three supports identified as:

1. She experiences a sense of contentment.
2. She imagines herself an important part of others' lives.
3. Her fragile world is shattered.

> In the short story "Miss Brill," Katherine Mansfield depicts an elderly woman who lives in a fantasy world created in her imagination. She resorts to this to escape from the isolation and loneliness of her real world and, in so doing, her life becomes more interesting and fulfilling. In her fantasy world, she experiences a sense of contentment as she images herself as an important part of other people's lives and as possessing a life better than those around her. Unfortunately, her fragile world is shattered, forcing her to face the gloomy reality of the life she truly lives. Her feelings of contentment and self-worth are destroyed once she realizes the emptiness and loneliness of her real world.

Developing Paragraphs

Developing paragraphs support your thesis. The first support for the main idea or the thesis is in the first body paragraph, the second support for the thesis is in the second body paragraph, and the third support for the thesis is in the third body paragraph. The second and third body paragraphs follow the same pattern as the first body paragraph. Each developing paragraph contains the following elements:

- An effective introductory and topic sentence that focuses on the support for the thesis that you will develop in the paragraph.
- A development of the supporting idea through explanatory sentences. To bring power to your position, you must include concrete evidence from the text(s). Direct quotations are only useful if they precisely support your idea. Direct references to events, character traits, and literary symbols are all considered useful evidence.
- An explanation of your interpretation of the evidence in detail. Readers need to see evidence of your thinking. You need to demonstrate your intellect, your thinking, and your ability to interpret literature.
- Elaboration that specifically and overtly connects the information in this paragraph to your thesis.
- A transitional sentence that keeps the flow from one paragraph to the next. Transitions are necessary between paragraphs. They can happen at the end of paragraphs or in the introduction to a new paragraph.

Example

Miss Brill is content and happy to live within her fantasy world; a world wonderful within her own mind. This world affords her delightful routines, which, on most occasions, bring her to the Jardins Publiques where she enjoys the surroundings of nature, music, and contented people. On one particular Sunday afternoon, she dresses up for her outing, completing her ensemble with her fox fur piece; a piece she has had for a long time and of which she is very proud. From her position on a park bench, she watches and internally comments on what she sees. Miss Brill is a keen observer of the people around her, and she weaves what she sees and hears into imaginative, glamorous events. She notices an elderly gentleman in a velvet coat, and a woman with knitting in her lap. She is disappointed that they are not speaking as she had become quite expert "at listening to people's conversations, as though she wasn't listening." She turns her attention to other people and their activities around her. As she sits, she does not ponder her own solitary life as she is happy to enjoy the splendour of the day.	*Topic sentence clearly identifies the first support: she experiences a sense of contentment* *Specific details from the story to demonstrate her contentment* *Concluding sentence*
Ironically, as Miss Brill observes the other people—especially those occupying benches and chair—she fails to see the parallel between herself and them. She notes that Sunday after Sunday the same people are drawn to the park and something is "funny" about all of them. They were odd, silent, nearly all old, and from the way they stared, they looked as though they'd come from dark little rooms or even cupboards. She perceives these people as being different; as being "less" than what she is. As well, she does not see herself as being rejected like the violets the young woman throws away or like the woman in the ermine toque who is being carelessly cast aside by the man in the suit. Miss Brill, wearing her own piece, cannot see her image mirrored in the woman who does not perceive herself to be as shabby as the ermine toque she wears. Rather, Miss Brill imagines herself as being superior to these people; an intricate part of the stage performance that is re-enacted in the park each week. She fantasizes that her absence would be noticed if she were not present, so integral is her role. She takes delight in this fantasy and envisions telling the old gentleman to whom she reads that she is not a mere English teacher, but an actress. She is enthralled by this fantasy and feels as though she is one with all the members of the company. Her imaginary world is, indeed, fulfilling.	*Transition and topic sentence that clearly identify the second support: imagining herself as superior to others and an important part of their lives* *Support, including symbols of her rejection that she ironically does not perceive* *Concluding sentence*

Transition and topic sentence clearly identify the third support: her fragile world is shattered	Despite her excitement with her imaginary world, Miss Brill overhears a conversation that completely shatters her illusions and alters her life. A boy and girl, in love, sit near her, and Miss Brill prepares to listen. The boy wishes to kiss the girl but she insists that she cannot let him because of that stupid old thing at the end there. The girl then begins to giggle at the poor soul wearing the fur that looks like a fried whiting (fish).
Support, including symbolism of her dark room and fur piece	Miss Brill is shattered when she realizes that the young couple is mocking her. She leaves the park, not bothering to stop for her ritualistic slice of honey cake, and hurries home. Once inside, she realizes how dark her room is, like a cupboard. Her world is no longer bright and splendid, but depressing and stark in reality. This reality is even bleaker when compared with the imaginary world of her fantasies. Her fur piece symbolizes the shabbiness of her life, and as she replaces it in the box, she imagines she hears something crying.
Concluding sentence	Although she seeks to deny that she is the one who is crying, she has come to an unhappy epiphany: the loneliness of her life is devastating.

Concluding Paragraph

In your concluding paragraph, you should always

- generalize your thesis beyond the text—make your idea explicit
- summarize your major points
- end with a strong sense of closure

Topic sentence explicitly states the controlling idea as a generalization beyond the text	In "Miss Brill," Mansfield emphasizes both the positive and negative effects of the imagination and what can result when imagination is allowed to blur one's view of reality.
Summary of support and significance of support	Initially, Miss Brill is content living within the parameters of her fantasy world. Feelings of fulfillment are deepened as she perceives herself as being integral to the performance and the people around her; she views her own life as being more than what it truly is.
Thoughtful observation connected to resolution/ effect on character	When her illusion is shattered, however, the harshness of the reality she is compelled to face is devastating.

Be sure to stay focused on your controlling idea or thesis right through to the concluding sentence of your essay.

4.1.3a take ownership of text creation, by selecting or crafting a topic, concept or idea that is personally meaningful and engaging

4.1.3b recognize and assess personal variables [such as personal experience and prior knowledge] and contextual variables [such as availability of time and resources] that influence the selection of a topic, concept or idea' and address these variable to increase the likelihood or successful text creation

Gathering and Summarizing Ideas from Personal Interest, Knowledge, and Inquiry

Generating and Developing Ideas

There are many different ideas that can be written about for a topic that you have chosen. Some can be taken from your personal experience, while others can come from your imagination or knowledge. Here are some examples of techniques that writers use to generate ideas once they have chosen a topic.

Brainstorming: Write down all ideas you have, no matter how trivial or silly they seem. Then, choose the ideas that are most compatible with your purpose and that you find the most interesting. Brainstorming is a technique that is often productive when you are in a group situation because many ideas are brought up.

Webbing: Also known as mapping or clustering, this technique involves using a diagram to sort out ideas. Place the general topic in a circle in the middle of a page. As you think of more specific details for the topic, place them on the page around the general topic. This technique allows you to create sub-details and expand on each specific detail.

Free writing: Many interesting ideas can come from simply spending some time writing on a topic without spending too much time planning out what you want to write about. With this technique, rules about spelling, capitalization, punctuation, and grammar are not very important. The focus of free writing is to stimulate thinking in order to generate ideas.

Lists: Choose the general topic of your writing and brainstorm ideas about that topic. For each idea, create further ideas. Once you have a lot of ideas, you can arrange the list in order from the least important to most important detail.

KWL chart: This chart allows you to list what you already know about the topic, what you want to find out about the topic, and what you have learned during your research. A KWL chart provides focus for your inquiry and research of a topic. You could also expand the chart to meet your requirements as shown here.

What I Already Know	What I Want to Find Out	Possible Resources for Research	What I Learned from My Research

Small group discussion: This type of group discussion can produce ideas for an opinion piece. Group discussions allow for a variety of opinions.

Questions to Guide Your Inquiry

Once you have chosen a topic, try to think of some questions that will help you to focus or direct your inquiry. For instance, if you chose the topic "The Element of Surprise at Pearl Harbor" you might ask the following questions:

- How exactly did the Japanese launch a surprise attack on Pearl Harbor?
- Where in Pearl Harbor did they attack?
- How did the Americans respond to the attack?
- What did the Americans learn from this event?
- Did the Japanese successfully complete any other surprise attacks during the Second World War? If so, where?
- How did the Americans later use the element of surprise to turn the tables on the Japanese?

To keep your research focused and effective, you need to evaluate your questions. You may choose to eliminate some questions that are not relevant enough to your topic, such as the last two questions on the list above.

You may wish to arrange the questions in a logical order to help you to organize the information for your paper. Often, key questions can be used as subtopics for your paper. For example, if the main topic for your paper is "Where in Pearl Harbor Did the Japanese Attack?" a subheading for your paper could be "Attack Targets."

Identifying Keywords and Phrases

The topic and inquiry questions you have generated can provide a great starting point for your research. As you begin to find books and Internet articles on your topic, watch for keywords and phrases that you can use to find more in-depth information. Some keywords and phrases that would help you with Pearl Harbor research, for example, might include

- Hickam Air Force Base
- Bellows Air Force Station
- Wheeler Army Airfield
- casualties at Pearl Harbor
- United States Intelligence, Pearl Harbor
- surprise attack on Pearl Harbor
- aftermath of Pearl Harbor
- warnings before the attack on Pearl Harbor

Staying organized with key terms and phrases will ensure that you do not forget any part of the assignment that you want to include. There are many different methods to get you started in developing the content of your work; try a variety of methods to see which work the best for you.

Organizing information helps you at several stages in the writing process. Staying organized while you are forming ideas at the developing stage of a writing assignment helps you understand what you want to write about. It also gives you ideas of the information you can use in your assignment. You can keep tabs on what information you want to use and what you might eventually like to leave out.

Once your ideas are developed, organizing your information helps your reader understand your ideas more precisely. Being organized in your writing helps you create clearly formed ideas and helps you get those ideas across to your reader. Use the methods that work the best for you. Time spent organizing before you sit down to write will save you a lot of time in the long run and will ensure that you create the best writing possible.

4.2.2a assess the beginning of a text in progress, and revise it as needed to establish purpose and engage audience [for example, the thesis statement of an essay, the initial monologue of a script, or the statement of purpose of a proposal]

Generating Text

Organizing Ideas

In Grade 11, you will use your writing and creative skills to produce assignments that meet criteria from your teacher. Since teachers usually give assignments to help you meet the expectations of the curriculum, it is important that you consistently try to follow teacher guidelines. If you are asked to write a business letter, for instance, follow the business letter guidelines provided in the classroom. If the teacher has assigned an essay, the criteria would probably involve some of the following requirements.

ESSAY STRUCTURE

Introduction

- This is the first paragraph or two of an essay.
- It is the point where the reader is made aware of the writer's intentions for the piece of writing.
- The introduction provides information on the topic and allows the reader to figure out what kind of essay it is.

Body

- This is the bulk of the essay, where most information is provided.

Conclusion

- This is the end of the essay, usually one or two paragraphs in length, where the writer wraps up his or her argument or otherwise ties together the content of the essay for the reader.

Thesis

- This is the main idea of the essay that ties the whole piece together. It is like the theme in a short story.

Transitions

- These are words that allow the reader to slide smoothly from one idea to the next or one from one paragraph to the next.

If the essay is persuasive, the teacher might also require an outline to show that your points of argument are organized effectively. Effective organization includes a clear introduction, well-supported arguments, and a conclusion that meaningfully restates your main idea.

Shaping Your Ideas

Once you have collected ideas and information about your topic, organized these ideas in groups, and written your thesis sentence, it is time to focus more specifically on the structure of your essay. A good method of structuring your essay is to shape your ideas into hierarchies. Establishing a hierarchy means deciding which ideas are more general and which more specific. The following example shows you how an outline for an essay can be structured.

Thesis Sentence

- **I. First argument**
  - **A.** First section of the first argument
    - **1.** First example or illustration
      - **a.** first fact or detail
      - **b.** second fact or detail
    - **2.** Second example or illustration
  - **B.** Second section of the first argument
- **II. Second argument**
  - **A.** First section of the first argument
    - **1.** First example or illustration
      - **a.** first fact or detail
      - **b.** second fact or detail
    - **2.** Second example or illustration
  - **B.** Second section of the first argument

You may have been asked to provide at least three arguments to support your thesis, so you would proceed to complete your outline following the pattern shown in the first argument.

Creating an outline before you begin to write the essay gives you the advantage of mapping out the ideas you plan to cover. With an outline, you are more likely to stay on topic. You should allow yourself some flexibility to change the outline as you begin to write. While writing, you may discover that one section of the argument proceeds more naturally to a different aspect than what is in your outline. Shifting parts of the essay around is a common practice, especially when revising the first draft. As you are writing, try to stay flexible enough to alter the course of your argument if necessary. Use your outline as a guide, not a fixed format.

4.2.2b assess the organizational components of a text in progress, and revise them as needed to strengthen their effectiveness as units of thought or experience or to strengthen their contribution to other intended effects

Adequately Developing Information and Ideas

Development refers to improving and shaping your ideas while you work on an assignment. Development includes such things as examples, illustrations, definitions, descriptions, facts, statistics, anecdotes, quotations, etc. The following elements of writing will help you develop ideas and help you to decide what kind of information you want to include in your writing.

Narration and Description

Narration involves telling the sequence of events, and description involves telling what a person, place, or thing looks like. Both narration and description should be used sparingly, since they do not advance arguments on their own. Instead these techniques can be used to briefly support the case you are making. You may be tempted to use narration and description in too great detail, especially if your assignment asks for a word count and you are not sure if you have enough to say. It is better to extend one of the arguments you are making instead. When used carefully, narration and description make an essay more engaging for a reader because they offer concrete examples to support abstract arguments.

Facts and Statistics

Facts are objective pieces of information, while statistics are collections of facts that are organized into numerical data. When quoting facts or statistics in an essay, remember the importance of the source from which you draw your quoted material. Usually, a conversation overheard on the street would not provide an authoritative source of information that you could use in an assignment. If you are quoting statistics, you need to use credible, unbiased sources. For example, statistics from a university researcher regarding the link between cigarette smoking and lung cancer would be more credible that those provided by a cigarette manufacturer.

Definitions

Defining a key term is an excellent way to begin an essay or to solidify an argument in the middle of one. Definitions do not have to come from a dictionary, although this is a very good source. Other reliable books, such as textbooks, manuals, and encyclopedias offer definitions that could be useful for supporting your argument. Often, definitions from other authoritative books are more specialized.

Unless your argument requires a definition, it should not take up too much room in the body of your paper. If you intend to use a definition, make sure that you are defining the word correctly. You will need to cite the source of your definition whether it is from a dictionary, a textbook, or a website. Providing a definition shows the way in which you plan to use the term for your argument, although there may be several other ways the term is used in everyday speech.

Be sure to develop your ideas and information, but always stay relevant to your topic or subtopic. Teachers can tell when a student is "padding" his or her paper. Padding your paper means adding non-essential or unrelated information to make your assignment appear longer. Longer is not necessarily better!

Organizing and Synthesizing Ideas and Information

Most forms of writing can be categorized according to how they are organized and developed. When you write about what you think, know, or feel about a subject, try to communicate in a unique and personal way. Even in unique and personalized writing, organizational patterns help your message have the most impact. The following organizational structures help to ensure that your ideas are presented in an interesting and original manner.

Inductive and Deductive Reasoning

Inductive reasoning consists of gathering facts and then using those facts to formulate a more general statement. It is important to have enough examples to justify your conclusion, but you also need to be prepared to review or alter your conclusions as new evidence comes to light.

Example

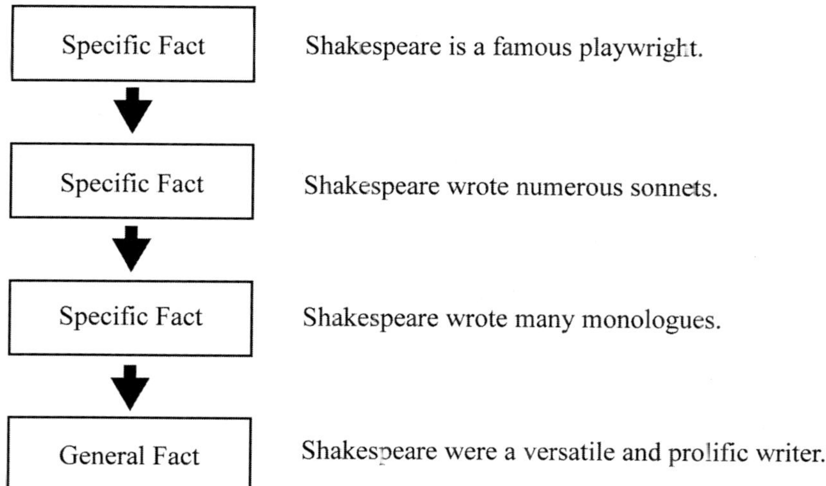

Deductive reasoning involves a different process. It begins with a generalization that you assume is true, and then specific facts are used to confirm that assumption.

Example

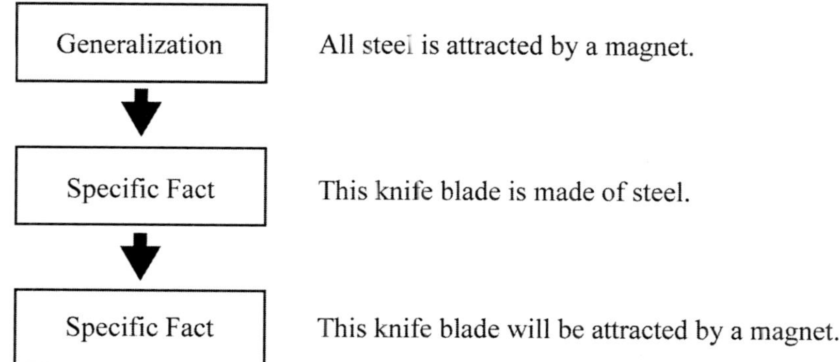

Analogy

Analogy is reasoning by using a brief comparison: if two things are similar in one respect, they will be similar in other respects. For example, imagine you were outside one day and got a sunburn. If you did not know why you got a sunburn, you might think of reasons for it. Perhaps, you would guess that it was because you were outside. If you thought this was the reason you got burned, through analogy, you would guess that any time you were outside at all, even if it were nighttime, you would get a sunburn. This is why analogy often does not make sense.

Process Analysis

Process analysis is used specifically in writing that informs or explains. Process analysis is used to explain how something works, how it is defined, or how it has been made. In a process analysis, chronological order is the most common structure to use because it outlines the steps in which something occurs.

Example

How to Program a VCR

1. Turn on VCR
2. Set channel on VCR to match channel on TV from which show to be recorded will be on
3. Set timer on VCR to indicate time that show starts and finishes
4. Press record

Climactic Order

Climatic order is achieved by developing a sequence of events or conflicts that build toward a climax. A climatic order chart could look like this.

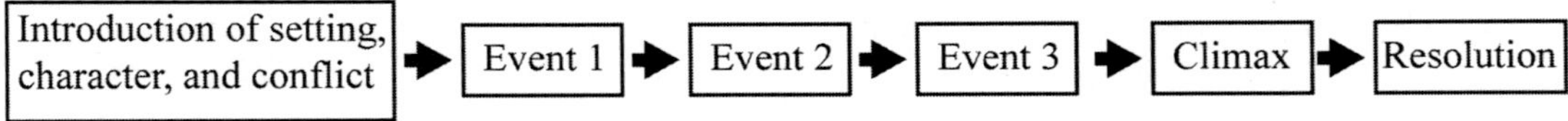

Chronological Order

Chronological order is often used to organize ideas in narrative and descriptive writing. It is a good idea to use transitions, such as first, second, then, finally, next, and later to connect your ideas.

Example

- One wintry day in 1926, as Lindbergh was flying his plane delivering mail, he was caught in a snowstorm. When his plane became unmanageable, he parachuted out. As he descended to Earth, he saw a barbed-wire fence below him, which he failed to miss—landing directly on top of it. Once he had untangled himself, he walked to the nearest farm to report the accident.

Cause and Effect

Cause and effect is frequently used in explanatory writing in order to present information clearly. It explains why something happened, what specific conditions exist, or what resulted from a certain action or condition. Cause and effect can be used in narrative writing to explain characters' actions, or it may be used in essays or reports to discuss how something progresses or the results of certain actions.

Cause-and-effect writing can be organized in the following three ways.

Effect to Cause

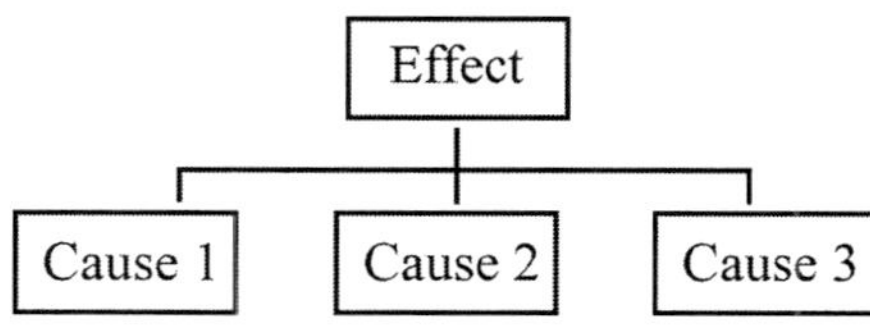

Cause to Effect

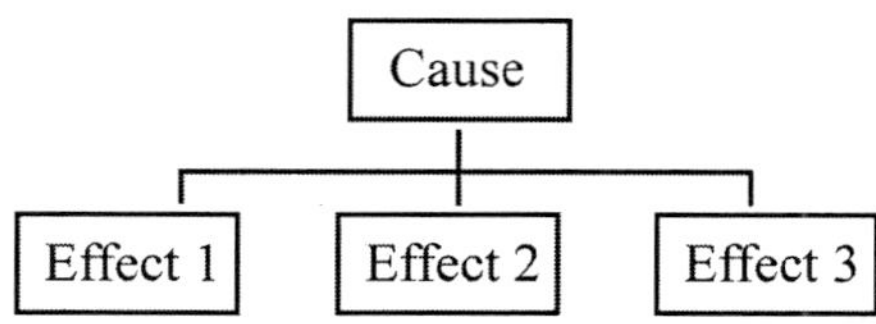

Cause and Effect Chain Reaction

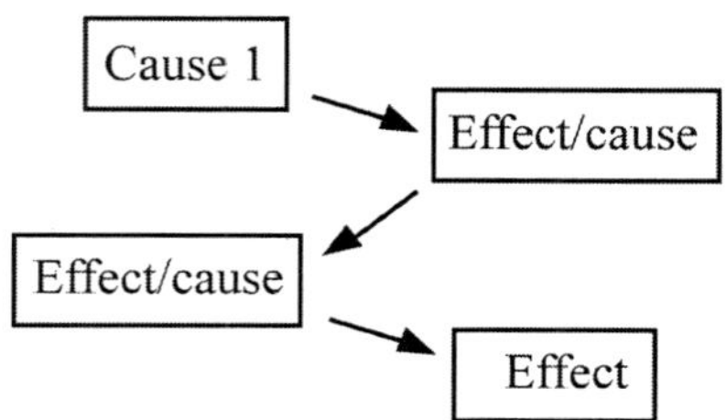

Regardless of the type of writing that you are doing (narrative, essay, critical reviews, or reports), make sure that you organize your writing well so that your ideas and information are logically presented. Logical organization gives your writing clarity. Experiment with different organizational methods to find the one that best suits the type of writing you are doing. An organizational structure gives you a skeleton upon which you can flesh out your ideas.

4.2.3a reflect on personal vocabulary and repertoire of stylistic choices and on their effectiveness; and expand vocabulary and repertoire of stylistic choices

VOCABULARY

Expanding your vocabulary has everything to do with using it. The more you use the words you learn, the better they will stick in your head and become part of your everyday speech and writing. Like your reading vocabulary, your writing vocabulary should be a constantly growing body of words that you are incorporating into your writing with increasing confidence.

You should only use words you understand in your writing. If you are looking for a more precise word, check a thesaurus.

The words in a thesaurus are arranged in alphabetical order. Here is an example of an entry for the word "bright."

Example

Bright: Adj (adjectives/synonyms) 1. sunny, fair, mild, balmy; brilliant, vivid, resplendent 2. smart, brainy, brilliant, clever, gifted, talented, sharp, keen

– (antonyms) 1. dull, flat, dingy, cloudy, faded, leaden, dim, pale, weak, faint 2. slow-witted, dim, slow, thick-headed, bland, desensitized

Do you need a synonym or an antonym? Do you want the literal/denotative meaning ("sunny") or a more connotative (associated) meaning like "brainy?" The thesaurus can help you to add variety to your writing, but avoid choosing words simply because they sound more elaborate. A simple word may be your best choice for the situation.

If you are using technical terms or "content" words in something like a research report, do not underestimate the dictionary as a useful reference.

Dictionaries are always a good place to start when you are looking for the meaning of a specialized term. Look for the meaning associated with the specific subject or content area.

Building Vocabulary

The following list describes different ways of building your vocabulary:

- engage in extensive and varied personal reading
- create personal lists of new words and phrases from texts you read
- make lists of subject-related words and their definitions
- use new words in conversation
- play word games
- create classroom word walls

Classroom word walls are interactive, and they usually involve a weekly or monthly addition to the wall. Each student posts up words he or she has learned and wants to share with the class. Even if word walls are not part of your classroom environment, you can create a "mini word wall" of your own in the back of your writing or English binder. Jotting down words from different sources in one easy-to-find location may encourage you to later use the words in your writing.

Using New Vocabulary

It is a good idea to keep personal vocabulary lists at the backs of binders or in separate vocabulary binders. If you learn a new word in any content area, try to remember to add the word and its definition to your list. If the word is an adjective, for instance, record its other forms, too.

Example

- *frugal* (adjective), meaning "reluctant to spend"
- *frugality* (noun), meaning "a reluctance to spend"

The best way to increase your vocabulary is to start using new words as often as you can after you learn them, in both speaking and writing. This will help you to internalize both the words and their meanings.

4.2.3b assess the appropriateness and effectiveness of diction, and revise word choice as needed to create intended effects

Diction

As you might have guessed from its similarity to the word dictionary, the word diction refers specifically to word choice. You can think of the words that hit the page as you write as the vehicles that carry along your thoughts and ideas to the minds of the readers who are going along with you for the ride. You do not want to use words that will make understanding your good ideas more challenging than is necessary. Instead, you should strive for accuracy and precision in word choice, using special terms only when more commonly used words are not available. Since diction is closely related to voice, the words you choose to express yourself also give readers an impression of where you are placing yourself in relation to them. If your writing contains many unnecessarily unusual or "big" words, some readers may feel put off by your diction and decide they would rather do something else with their time than read what you have written. If too many readers have that response, your time spent writing is being wasted. Instead of using such words, a good rule of thumb is to select common words, or the language of everyday speech, so that the reader's attention is not distracted from the interesting idea you are discussing.

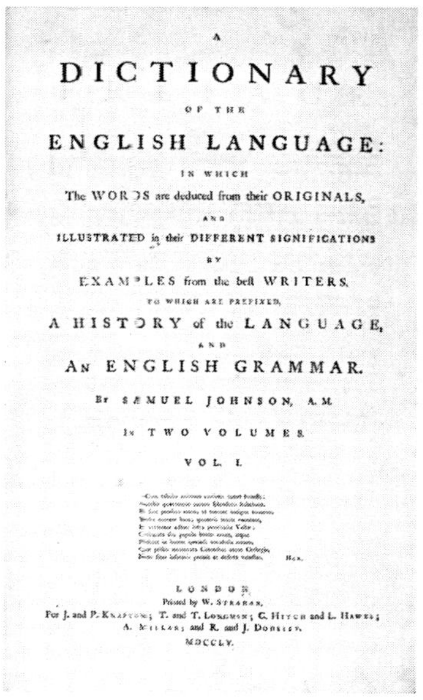

A
DICTIONARY
OF THE
ENGLISH LANGUAGE:
IN WHICH
The WORDS are deduced from their ORIGINALS,
AND
ILLUSTRATED in their DIFFERENT SIGNIFICATIONS
BY
EXAMPLES from the best WRITERS.
TO WHICH ARE PREFIXED,
A HISTORY of the LANGUAGE,
AND
AN ENGLISH GRAMMAR.
BY SAMUEL JOHNSON, A.M.
IN TWO VOLUMES.
VOL. I.

[illegible]

LONDON,
Printed by W. Strahan,
For J. and P. Knapton; T. and T. Longman; C. Hitch and L. Hawes;
A. Millar; and R. and J. Dodsley.
MDCCLV.

4.2.3d apply understanding of stylistic techniques and rhetorical devices when creating print and nonprint texts [for example, use imagery to create pathos, use parallel structure to create emphasis and use sound in multimedia texts to create humour]

Refining Specific Aspects and Features of Text

Once you have gathered, organized, and generated your text, you will need to enhance your writing with supporting details and examples. Below are some suggestions for this enhancement in different forms of text.

Writing Persuasive Compositions

If you are writing a persuasive composition, the opening paragraph requires close attention. The introductory paragraph is crucial to keeping your reader's attention. Persuasive writing appeals to a reader's emotions. The logic that you use must be stated clearly to ensure that your reader will understand. You must use examples that are drawn from an emotional source in order to fully convince your reader of the plausibility of your position.

Both logical arguments and emotional appeals are useful to persuade your reader, but try to create a good balance between the two.

Type of Appeal	Examples
Emotional	**1.** Gives personal anecdotes **2.** Asks questions **3.** Appeals to readers' emotions **4.** Uses emotional words
Logical	**1.** Provides facts **2.** Provides reasons **3.** Recognizes opposing arguments

Imagine that you are writing a persuasive argument on the topic of whether or not your school should adopt school uniforms. The first decision to make when writing a persuasive argument is to choose a position. Once you have chosen your position, you can start to research your position by finding existing arguments and information to help you. Suppose your position is that "wearing school uniforms is a way of protecting students and promoting learning." The following rhetorical devices can help you to support your argument in a persuasive way.

Rhetorical Devices

Provide your audience with statistics and researched information.

Example

- Research has shown that schools that require student uniforms have better attendance rates, higher academic achievement, and less fighting.

Appeal to your reader's emotions or ethical beliefs.

Example

- Teachers have been frustrated in the past because their classes are regularly disrupted by students looking at themselves in a mirror, painting their fingernails, combing their hair, or comparing designer labels. Parents who have a tight budget often watch in dismay and helplessness as their children are bullied for wearing "uncool" clothes.

Relate a personal anecdote to bring your audience closer to your position. Rather than sharing statistics or numbers, a personal story can make an audience feel the emotional impact that your issue can have.

Example

- When I went to school, we had to wear uniforms. I remember a time when a student misbehaved on the bus going home: a passenger (who recognized the uniform as belonging to our school) reported the incident to our principal. The principal was very quick to reprimand the culprit, who was identified by his bright red hair and freckled face!

Give examples of cases that support your argument.

Example

- An individual does not lose his personality when wearing a uniform. People in many walks of life, such as flight attendants, bus or train drivers, postal workers, restaurant employees, military personnel, members of school sports teams, and choirs or bands, wear uniforms. These people are able to wear uniforms without any loss of personality or personal freedoms.

Clarifying and Defending Your Position

Being clear in defending your position means making sure that your reader knows what you are trying to say. Get a classmate or friend to read over a text you have written that is opinion-based. Does he or she understand what you are trying to say after reading it through only one time? That is a good sign that your ideas and opinions are clear. To clarify and defend your position, use precise and relevant evidence including facts, expert opinions, quotations, expressions of commonly accepted beliefs, and logical reasoning.

As you prepare your arguments, ask people their views and record them. Additionally, you could research the findings of someone like Dr. David Brunsma from the University of Alabama who has written numerous books and articles on the subject of school uniforms; you might use the Internet to look up court cases and appeals involving school boards that have a school uniform policy; or, you could read the statements on the WHEN (World Home Education Network) website regarding school uniforms.
The more facts you can find to support your argument, the more persuasive your writing will be.

Addressing Your Audience

As you prepare your composition, you must be prepared to address concerns from both sides of your argument. Since your position is that the "wearing school uniforms is a way of protecting students and promoting learning," you must be able to respond to various other points such as the following points.

- The safety of Canadian students is fundamentally more important than any loss of freedom of expression that might occur by introducing school uniforms.
- It is an infringement on citizens' clearly established constitutional rights to tell students what to wear to school.
- School uniforms are not nearly as important as a good school atmosphere, clear rules and expectations, and parental involvement in student learning.

4.2.3e recognize personal voice in text created; and continue to develop personal craft through practice, using various methods

Voice

The term "voice" can have several meanings in the context of writing. This includes the passive and active voices of verbs. The term "voice" also refers to your own distinctive writing style: your way of expressing yourself that is uniquely your own and that sets you apart from your fellow writers. Your personality shines through your writing to some extent, and this quality is called the "voice" of your writing. Some students might cleverly decide to call the spelling and grammatical errors they happen to make or the colloquialisms and slang they use their "voice." A good writer, however, keeps in mind the requirements of each writing occasion and tailors the tone of his or her voice accordingly. If you are writing a literary essay for school, your voice should be formal. If you are writing an anecdotal piece for a magazine, your voice could be more conversational, or informal. Either way, the basic rules of clear expression still apply, including those of spelling, grammar, and organization that are discussed in an English class. Over time, your own voice will emerge and become clearer as you continue to work at expressing your ideas effectively.

Voice refers to how the narrator or speaker of a text sounds to the reader. Using a voice and style appropriate to academic and personal writing and format is an important choice that should be evident in your writing. Depending on the formality of the occasion, for example, it would be more appropriate to write "Good Evening, Ladies and Gentlemen" than "It's great to see everyone here tonight" at the beginning of your banquet speech.

Expressive Writing

Your own expressive writing through which you respond to texts you have read in class can help you understand those texts in greater detail. For example, an expressive poem or dramatic scene based on a novel can help you pinpoint the main themes or symbols within the novel. That is one reason your teacher may require students to adapt an episode in a novel to a different time period or setting, or to create a dramatic scene from a short story. For example, many students have recreated scenes from Shakespearean plays and put them into the language of modern English. Expressive writing is enjoyable, and it can teach you how to change the voice of your writing.

Personal Responses to Texts

When you write responses to literature—that is, when you write an analysis of a literary work—you must avoid giving only a summary of the plot. Rather, you should

- use correct literary terms
- make sure your facts are accurate
- discuss the use of figurative language
- interact with the literature by giving examples from the text that support your ideas

This can be accomplished by:

1. demonstrating a comprehensive grasp of the significant ideas of the literary work.
2. making sure that you read the literature carefully and take notes on the passages that affect you
3. supporting important ideas and viewpoints through accurate and detailed references to the text or to other works
4. demonstrating awareness of the writer's use of stylistic devices and an appreciation for the effects created
5. identifying and assessing the impact of perceived ambiguities, nuances, and complexities within the text

A Writer's Voice

What is a writer's voice? Generally, a writer's voice can be described as how the writing sounds or its overall effect on the writer's audience. A writer's voice is a unique blend of careful word choices that express what the writer means, as well as the writer's attitude toward his or her topic. Voice becomes an important part of the writer's writing style, combining word choices, phrasing, and word arrangement in distinctive sentence patterns. Even punctuation plays a part. As you discover your own writer's voice in different writing assignments, remember that using "big" words are not nearly as important as the way those words are put together. Voice should be deliberate, appropriate, and consistently adapted to your form, audience, and purpose for writing.

Voice and Form

In a book report, for example, your form should include some sort of evaluation of the book's merits, supported by evidence. However, your voice would vary according to the form. For example, an interview would probably use a voice that imitates speaking style of at least one character. A letter to an adult would likely have a polite and formal voice.

Voice and Audience

You should adjust the level of formality in your writing to match your intended audience. Your readers could be adults, peers, or children. Another part of voice that could change would be the technical language you use. You should try to use technical language that suits the level of expertise of the audience. For example, a research report might require a voice that explains difficult words or technical terms. You would probably have to assume that your audience is uninformed and lacks background information. A sports article for the school newspaper, on the other hand, might be in a more familiar voice, with contractions, exaggerations, and possibly some slang or jokes that you know your readers will understand.

Voice and Purpose

To an extent, your purpose for writing will determine the voice of your writing.

If you are sharing or relating a personal experience, your text would probably be written in first person voice and would include specific details along with personal thoughts, feelings, and reactions.

If your purpose is to inform, your text would most likely be written in third person objective voice. You would want a more detached, unemotional voice. Adding humour might sound out of place or might detract from the information you are presenting.

If your purpose is to entertain or inform, the voice in which you write might vary. If you were writing an article for a school newspaper section, for example, your voice might change according to the type of article you are writing. On the front page, your voice should be precise, clear, and objective, while in the sports section, your voice might include lively, age-appropriate description, exaggeration, humour, and even slang.

Voice Consistency

As a writer, try to keep a consistent voice throughout your writing piece. Consistency makes your writing clear. Different people use different language. Depending on what kind of assignment you are writing for, you may want to experiment with using a different voice. Trying to write using someone else's voice can be challenging but rewarding. For example, if you decide to write from the point of view of a young child, listen to how younger children interact with you. What words do they use? How do they express emotions?
When you go to write, try to imitate their voice.

As you read the following examples, notice how voice changes depending on the person who is writing.

In the following example, a 16-year-old boy has just received word that he has won an achievement award in the "20 Under 20" contest sponsored nationwide by the CBC for a homeless awareness program that he initiated in his Toronto high school. As a result of this young man's leadership, hundreds of blankets, jackets, toques, gloves, and scarves have been provided to inner-city shelters over the winter. Additionally, the boy has arranged for non-perishable foods and coffee from the community's independent grocery store to be distributed to the needy. Among many congratulatory messages, he has received the following two emails and a letter from his local MP.

Example

Email from Dad in Vancouver on Business

When my Blackberry started to flash in the middle of my meeting, I knew it was Mom with the news. I am so proud to be your Dad. I wanted to interrupt the meeting and shout to the chandeliers, but the company president, who was presenting our quarterly sales figures at the time, might not have appreciated my enthusiasm. Mom and I have always tried to remind you that not everyone is as fortunate as you and your sister. Son, I can't give you any advice for the future, except to keep growing in all the right directions. I am so glad that our country recognizes youthful role models. The people of Canada can definitely learn much from the young. I will be home for the presentation ceremony on Friday. Save me a good spot!

Love,
Dad

Email from Best Friend

So, dude! You made the Big Leagues! Whazzup for the next run—youngest Prime Minister? I knew when you were nominated you would make the top 50, but top 20? You cool with all that attention? Don't forget your friends when you move into the fast lane of fame and fortune. I'm always here for ya, bud.

See you soon,
Randy

Letter from Local MP

Dear Mr. Smith:

I am writing to congratulate you on behalf of your town, constituency, and country for being recognized as a top 20 Under 20. Your accomplishments with the homeless awareness program are truly commendable. Your contributions to society at such a young age are truly remarkable.

From your community and your country, I am pleased to acknowledge your endeavors and anticipate more great contributions from such a generous and industrious young man.

Sincerely,
John Smith, MP

A different voice and tone are observable in each of the three messages. The father's voice is informal and loving, but adult in vocabulary and tone. As you would expect, the friend is even more informal, admiring but reluctant to be overly complimentary. He uses some slang expressions as well. The letter from the MP is concise, containing very formal language and tone.

4.2.4a use handbooks and other tools, including electronic tools, as resources to assist with text creation [for example, dictionaries, thesauri, spell checkers and handbooks]

Producing Finished Works

A finished work should be neat, well-organized, and polished. The final stages of writing involve double-checking your work for spelling, grammar, and punctuation. During the revision and editing stages of the writing process, grammar, style, and format should be checked with a recognized print or electronic style guide. The following list of recognized style guides may be helpful. Your teacher may also recommend a style guide.

Recognized Style Guides

Publication Manual of the American Psychological Association. Fifth Edition. Washington, DC: American Psychological Association, 2001.

Rozakis, Laurie. *The Complete Idiot's Guide to Grammar and Style.* New York: Alpha Books, 2003.

Sabin, William, et al. *The Gregg Reference Manual.* Seventh Canadian Edition. Toronto: McGraw-Hill Ryerson, 2006.

Tasko, Patti, Editor. *The Canadian Press Stylebook.* 14th Edition. Toronto: The Canadian Press, 2006.

Troyka, Lynn. *Simon and Schuster Handbook for Writers.* New Jersey: Prentice Hall, 1990.

Style Information Online

If you do an online search for English language conventions, your results will provide links to websites where you can purchase guides. Others provide information electronically. You could vary your search according to the specific style information you are seeking.

4.2.4b know and be able to apply capitalization and punctuation conventions correctly, including end punctuation, commas, colons, apostrophes, quotation marks, hyphen, dashes, ellipse, parentheses, underlining and italics

Punctuation

Imagine if people never paused when they were speaking. It would be difficult to understand when thoughts started and ended, or when someone was asking a question. Punctuation translates many conventions of speech, such as pausing, into writing. It has its own set of rules that are necessary for clear writing. Punctuation gives clarity and definition to your writing and can be used for a wide variety of rhetorical and stylistic effects.

Periods

The period is used at the end of most sentences and after fragments used as sentences:

- I walked to the end of the world. And stopped.

Do not use a period after a complete sentence that is contained by brackets or quotation marks within another sentence:

- The company then sent him a registered letter (he was not answering e-mails or telephone messages) to explain the situation.
- That's my friend Sonja (the Matchmaker).
- When she said, "Class dismissed," chaos erupted.

Notice that the bracketed sentences in the first and second examples do not begin with a capital letter, but the quotation in the third example does. The quotation is also set off with both quotation marks and commas.

Punctuating Possessives

Most possessives are formed by adding an apostrophe and an s:

- a girl's smile
- one country's history
- a coat's buttons

The possessive of a noun that ends in s is generally formed with an apostrophe and an s:

- the boss's car
- the countess's speech
- James's, Charles's, Alex's

The possessive of plural nouns is formed by adding an apostrophe after the s of the plural:

- five girls' smiles
- three countries' histories
- the actresses' Oscars
- the girls' car

Commas with Conjunctions

Coordinating conjunctions (*for*, *and*, *nor*, *but*, *or*, *yet*, *so*—think FANBOYS) are used with a comma if they join two independent clauses:

- He will be late, *for* he must complete the game.
- Go to the edge of the cliff, *and* tell me what you see there.
- She will not learn from her failures, *nor* will she learn from her successes.

When a coordinating conjunction joins two short independent clauses, a comma may not be necessary:

- She's late *and* she's tired.

When subordinating conjunctions (which include after, because, although, before, since, though, and unless) are used in an introductory clause, a comma follows the clause:

- *Because* you have been elected, you must serve.
- *Before* she leaves, she plans to write a note of farewell.

Do not use a semicolon to follow an introductory clause:

- Because you have been elected; you must serve. (incorrect)

When the subordinate clause follows the independent clause, a comma is usually not used:

- She plans to write a note of farewell *before* she leaves.
- You must serve *because* you have been elected.

However, a comma should be used when it is necessary to avoid confusion:

- He has done all his work since his failure last term threatened his final grade. (unclear)
- He has done all his work, since his failure last term threatened his final grade. (clear)

The original sentence seems to mean that he has done all his work from the time that his failure threatened his final grade. It is only once you reach the end of the sentence that the meaning is clear. A comma after "work" makes it clear that "since" is a subordinating conjunction and not a preposition.

Colons

When used in sentences, a colon can only follow an independent clause to introduce a list, explanation, or appositive:

- You should bring the following items: a sleeping bag, a change of clothes, and matches.
- There is only one honest thing to do: admit you made a mistake and apologize.
- Everything about him was summed up in his nickname: Old Ornery.

When a list is set up in point form, the same rule applies:

- The introductory course will cover three topics:
  1. algebra
  2. geometry
  3. trigonometry

If a list does not follow an independent clause, no colon is used:

- You must bring a sleeping bag, a change of clothes, and matches.

Similarly, the following list does not require a colon:

- The introductory course will cover
  1. algebra
  2. geometry
  3. trigonometry

A simple way of checking colon use is to cover up all the words after the colon. Can the first part of the sentence now stand alone as a sentence? If it can, use a colon. If it cannot, do not use a colon.

Quotation Marks

Use quotation marks at the beginning and end of all words in a direct quotation. Watch for the use of quotation marks before and after speech tags:

- Alfred said, “We are ready.”
- “I’m finished the job,” said Alfred. “We can go now.”
- “When we are ready,” said Alfred, “we will go.”

Notice that the closing quotation mark is placed after a comma or a period and that a comma is used after a speech tag (“Alfred said,”).
Closing quotation marks are also used with exclamation marks and question marks. When these punctuation marks belong to the sentence, they are placed outside the closing quotation marks:

- Didn’t you hear him say, “I’m in trouble”?

If the quotation marks belong to the quotation, they are placed inside the quotation marks:

- He asked sadly, “Why is it always me?”

The same rules apply to closing quotation marks used for other purposes.

Periods and commas are always placed inside the quotation marks:

- You could say that her acting was “over the top.”

Exclamation marks and question marks belong either outside or inside the quotation marks, depending on whether they belong to the sentence as a whole or to the words inside the quotation marks:

- She asked, “Are these seats taken?”
- I can’t believe you call that dilapidated wreck a “car”!

Indirect quotations never require quotation marks:

- Alfred asked if we were ready.
- Alfred said that he had finished the job and we could go.
- Alfred said that when we were ready, we could go.

Quotation marks are also used for the titles of short stories and poems and to indicate that a word is being used in an unusual sense:

- “Housekeeping” on the space station is challenging.

Quotation marks can also indicate sarcasm or irony:

- The “suicide” of Jan Masaryk marked the end of democracy in Czechoslovakia.

It seems that their “help” has put this project three weeks behind.

Punctuation for Effect

Consider the following examples, remembering that punctuation is your tool, not your taskmaster.

- John closes the door and asks Alice what is wrong.
- John closes the door and asks Alice, "What is wrong?"
- John closes the door and asks, "Alice, what is wrong?"

- We mustn't believe everything we hear is the truth.
- We mustn't! Believe! Everything we hear is the truth!

- Consider yourself one of the family.
- Consider yourself one of the family!
- Consider yourself one of the family? Never!

- Why? Because we can. Because we must. Because we care.

Sentence fragments can be used deliberately with sentence punctuation to create a rhetorical effect.

Italics and Underlining

Certain titles are printed in italic script. Italicize or underline the titles of all major works, such as books, long poems, newspapers, magazines, movies, and television series.

Example

A Tale of Two Cities
Time Magazine
The Times
The Wizard of Oz
Star Trek

Italics are also used to indicate words and sometimes letters that are considered as objects rather than as structural parts of a sentence:

- *The* can be a subordinate conjunction or a preposition.
- Add *s* or *es* to form the plural of a noun.

Italics should only be used sparingly for emphasis. It is more acceptable to use italics for emphasis in creative writing than it is for formal writing. Formal writing should use words and arguments so compelling that no extra emphasis is needed. In creative writing, for example, it can be useful to use italics for showing emphasis in the dialogue of characters.

Use quotation marks to set off shorter works or parts of works, such as chapters, short stories, short poems, songs, articles, and episodes in a television series.

PROOFREADING

When proofreading for spelling, not every mistake will jump out at you. Look for mistakes like kernel (for colonel), *reciept* (for receipt), or *dessert* (for desert). Mistakes like these can be hard to catch. A good method for finding easy-to-miss mistakes is to read sentences backward. This allows each word to be seen as an individual item and not as part of a sentence. With the pattern of meaning removed, it is easier to find errors. The same method may help you to proofread your own work in the written-response questions on examinations.

When you have finished writing the content of a piece of written work (including revising and rewriting), you should proofread and edit it for correct grammar, punctuation, capitalization, and spelling. Though you may have spent a great deal of time organizing and writing your ideas down, your reader's ability to understand and enjoy them will suffer if the final document contains basic errors and inconsistencies.

4.2.4c know and be able to use spelling conventions consistently and independently

Spelling Rules

One of the reasons that most people do not become accomplished writers overnight is that writing requires so many levels of expression, from argument to organization, style, diction, grammar, and spelling. Spelling might seem like just a minor detail, but if you consider your own reaction to an email, letter, or document that has spelling mistakes, you will begin to realize that providing clean copy, without spelling errors of any kind, is an important way to create a good impression with your writing. When your writing contains spelling errors, not only will your readers assume a weakness in your writing that they may link to your thinking, they may also assume that you do not care enough about your writing to tidy up the mistakes. Fixing spelling errors involves more than simply running the text through a spell checker, since homonyms will not be flagged by this software. Instead, you must carefully and alertly reread your document, keeping an eye out for any spelling mistakes that may have slipped in.

You may have heard the complaint that there are always exceptions to spelling and grammar rules; however, spelling rules are still a good place to start. The rules take care of most cases and leave you free to pay attention to exceptions. The "I before E" rhyme is a good example:

I before E except after C or when sounding like A, as in neighbour and weigh.

The rule this rhyme explains covers the majority of cases. It is possible to sort the common exceptions into groups.

- Words of foreign origin: German (*Geiger*, *stein*, *poltergeist*) or Greek (*protein*, *kaleidoscope*, *seismograph*)
- Words that have some connection. A group of words loosely connected with government, law, or property can be matched with *reign*, which does follow the rule. Then think of *reign*, *sovereign*, *foreign*, *heir*, *heiress*, *seize*, *counterfeit*, and *forfeit* as being a group.
- Words whose pattern matches a subset of words that follow the rule: *height* and *sleight* match *neighbour*, *weigh*, *weight*, and *freight*.
- A few more or less common words are left over. Simply pay attention to their spelling: *either*, *neither*, *leisure*, *weird*, *heifer*, *feisty*
- Words like *reinforce* can be ignored, since the pronunciation of the prefix makes it just about impossible to spell the *ei* incorrectly.

Use a writing guide or the Internet to look up a list of spelling rules for review.

Homonyms and Other Easily Confused Words

Words can be confused because they sound exactly the same (*its*, *it's*) or almost the same (*insure*, *ensure*).

Certain contractions (when two words are combined with an apostrophe) and pronouns are also easily confused:

- Your list is complete.
  You're almost ready.
- Their supper is ready.
  They're about to sit down.
  There is the book.
- Its collar came off.
  It's a great pity.

Remember that no possessive pronoun is ever written with an apostrophe.

Because possessives written with apostrophes sound the same as plural forms when spoken, they are often confused when written.

- The quarter's shape is distinctive.
- I have four quarters in my pocket.

The complete list of homonyms, near-homonyms, and easily confused words is long. The following list provides some examples of commonly confused homonyms:

• allowed, aloud • bow, bough • not, knot • pore, pour, poor • principal, principle • prophet, profit • red, read • waste, waist	• seen, scene • sight, site, cite • sign, sine • slight, sleight • sweet, suite • there, their, they're • to, too, two

The following chart displays more examples of easily confused words that a computer spell check might not find.

all right, alright	In standard written English, only *all right* is recognized; *alright* is strictly informal.
practice, practise	*Practice* is a noun (two hours of practice). *Practise* is a verb (He has been practising for two hours).
licence, license	*Licence* is a noun (driver's licence), and *license* is a verb (The state licenses us to drive).
stationary, stationery	*Stationary* means staying in one place; *stationery* is the writing materials sold by a *stationer*, originally a merchant who set up a station, or booth, to sell pens and paper.
a lot, allot	There is only one way to spell these two words when they are used together: *a lot.* The word *allot* means to allocate or give out.
it's, its	All the possessive pronouns are formed the same way: *yours*, *his*, *hers*, *its*, *theirs*, *whose*. Pronouns spelled with apostrophes are contractions: *you're* (you are), *he's* (he is), *she's* (she is), *it's* (it is), *they're*, (they are), *who's* (who is).

Frequently Misspelled Words

Certain words in the English language are frequently misspelled, even by people who consider themselves to be good spellers. Some of these words are listed below. Try to master them now. The tricky parts of these words have been underlined for you.

across
argument
calendar
column
committed
conscience
definitely
discipline
embarrass
equipment
experience
foreign
government
height
lightning

neighbour
occasionally
possession
really
relevant
restaurant
rhyme
rhythm
schedule
separate
until
weird
grateful
immediate
mischievous

Frequently Confused Words

Here are some examples of frequently confused words:

- **accept/except:** Everyone was pleased to accept their reward, except Melody.
- **a lot:** Two words, as in "a lot of homework." This word gets confused with allot, which means to distribute a portion: Each child was allotted some personal space in the new classroom.
- **believe/receive:** These two words follow the i before e rule: "i before e, except after c."
- **its/it's:** Its without the apostrophe is a possessive pronoun, as in "The cat injured its tail." The word shows possession, just like the pronoun "yours." With the apostrophe, it's is a contraction of the phrase it is. The apostrophe is used to replace the missing letter.
- **principal/principle:** A *principal* is the headmaster of a school, as in "the principal's office." *Principal* also means main, as in "The principal reason I am moving is…" The word principle, however, refers to a belief or idea, as in "The school's anti-bullying policy is based on the principle that all children deserve to feel safe at school."
- **their/there/they're**: "*Their* new house," "*They* live over there," and "He said *they're* coming."
- **to/too/two:** To is a preposition, as in "to the track meet." Too means also or in excess, as in "She wants to go, too" and "He ate too much." Two represents a number, as in "He has two sisters."
- **weather/whether:** "*Whether* or not we attend the game depends on the *weather*."

4.2.4d understand the importance of grammatical agreement and assess and revise texts in progress to ensure correctness of grammatical agreement, including correct pronoun reference and pronoun-antecedent agreement, and correct use of modifiers and other parts of speech

Grammar

Grammar gives structure to language so that communication can be as clear as possible. Understanding grammar—the names of the parts of speech, kinds of sentences, rules for the agreement of sentence parts—gives you a common vocabulary so that you can speak about language. If your teacher writes a comment on a paper such as "use the objective case of that pronoun," it is helpful for you to understand the objective case.

Pronouns take the place of nouns: *I, she, it, we, that, all, whatever, some*. In your writing, ensure that there are no misunderstandings regarding the nouns to which your pronouns refer.

Example

Both girls agreed that their projects had been prepared thoroughly. They were ready for the science fair. (What or who was ready? The girls? The projects?)

When I got to the tax office, they told me they were closing for the day. (This sentence is fine for informal speech, but in written English, they can only refer to the tax office, and a tax office cannot be *they*.)

Ensure that your pronouns and their antecedents are clear.

Personal pronouns replace persons or things and are used to identify point of view, particularly in narrative texts such as short stories, novels, and plays.

First Person:	I/Me	We/Us
Second Person:	You	
Third Person:	He/Him They/Them She/Her	 It

Using the Correct Case

For the most part, English is not inflected. This means that most words do not change their endings to show how they are used in sentences. Pronouns are one exception: they are inflected.

Pronouns have three cases, as shown in the following chart.

henever you use these pronouns, check the pronoun case and check for the correct spelling.

Subjective case is used for the subject of a sentence or clause and for the complement of a linking verb	**Objective case is used for the object of a verb or preposition, gerund, participle, or infinitive**	**Possessive case is used to show ownership**	
		Used as an adjective	**Used as a subject or as the complement of a linking verb**
I	Me	My	Mine
You	You	Your	Yours
He/she/it	Him/her/it	His/her/its	His/hers/its
We	Us	Our	Ours
You	You	Your	Yours
They	Them	Their	Theirs
Who	Whom	Whose	Whose

The possessive pronoun *its* follows the same pattern as *his*, *hers*, *yours*, and *theirs*. Remember that the possessive of pronouns is never formed with an apostrophe.

When the pronoun is the subject, use the subjective case:

- *You* have been elected.
- Despite the weather, *we* are certainly going.
- *He* and *she* ran the marathon.
- Even after a late start, *they* still won the marathon.

If the pronoun is the subject and a possessive, use the second form of the possessive case:

- *Mine* is nearly ready.
- *Yours* is already finished, but *theirs* is not *ready*.

When the pronoun is the object (either direct or indirect), use the objective case:

- Give it to *her*.
- The government mailed *me* a letter.
- The fall smashed *it* to pieces.
- When the paper is ready, give *it* to *her* and *me*.

A pronoun following a linking verb is a noun complement (or predicate nominative or subject completion), and it is in the subjective case:

- It is *he*.
- Yes, I've seen Miss Jones. It was *she* who walked past just now.
- I am *he*.
- It is *I*.

When writing comparisons using *than* or *as*, use the objective case:

- He likes me more than him.
- Evan can type as accurately as her.

These examples illustrate the problem of different levels of language in different situations. Consider the sentence "It is I." The sentence is grammatically correct, but it may appear to be stuffy, even pretentious. However, in a formal or solemn context, such sentences are not only correct, they are suitable. On the other hand, in everyday life, few would complain about, "It's me." Sometimes, pronoun agreements cause trouble. The following is a useful rule of thumb:

- Most of those who might say Him and me did it would never say *Me did it* or *Him did it.* Whenever you have more than one pronoun, try the sentence with one of the pronouns at a time. *He* did it + I did it = *He* and I did it.

When the pronoun that follows a linking verb is a possessive, use the form of the possessive case that would be used for the subject of a sentence:

- The red one is *mine*. Did you hear me? *Mine* is the red one.
- This car is *hers*—or is it *theirs*? No, *theirs* is the car on the right.

Note the difference when a pronoun is used as an adjective and when it is used as a predicate complement:

- *Their* win was amazing.
- The win was *theirs*.

You would not want to memorize all the pronouns, but it is a good idea to be aware of them and of their uses.

Kinds of Pronouns	Examples
Demonstrative I want to enter *this* in the exhibition.	This, that, these, those
Interrogative *Who* said that?	Who, whom, which, what, whoever, whomever, whichever, whatever
Relative Choose *whichever* you like.	Who, whom, that, which, whoever, whomever, whichever
Indefinite *Many* have asked that question.	All, another, any, anybody, anyone, anything, each, everybody, everyone, everything, few, many, nobody, none, one, several, some, somebody, someone
Reflexive She did the job *herself.*	Myself, yourself, herself, himself, itself, ourselves, yourselves, themselves
Intensive The professor *himself* was not sure of the answer.	Myself, yourself, herself, himself, itself, ourselves, yourselves, themselves

Notice the reflexive and intensive pronouns, which are often used incorrectly: "Give it to myself." The examples given in the chart show the only correct uses of the reflexive pronoun. Notice that when the reflexive is used immediately after the noun, it is an intensifier.

What about the pronouns *who* and *whom*? Although the distinction between these two pronouns may be disappearing in spoken English, you should be able to use both of them in formal writing. Who is an interrogative subjective pronoun. Use it whenever the pronoun is the subject of a sentence or a clause:

- *Who* are you?
- *Who* is going?

The candidate *who* should be elected is Julia.

Whom is an interrogative objective pronoun. Use it whenever the pronoun is the object of a predicate or a preposition:

- The prize will be given to *whom*?
- *Whom* did you tell?
- To *whom* did they refer?

A simple mnemonic for remembering the difference is "he/who" and "him/whom."

If the sentence could use he, then use who; if the sentence could use him, then use whom:

- *He* will win. Who will win?
- Give it to him. Give it to *whom*?
- The crowd followed after *him*. The crowd followed after *whom*?
- The robbers left *him* for dead. The robbers left *whom* for dead?
- For *him*, we would do anything. For *whom* would we do anything?
- Yes, it is *he* that won. *Who* was it that won?

Of course, there is an extra mental step if the pronoun is not masculine:

- Give it to *her*. Give it to *whom*?
- For *her*, we would do anything. For *whom* would we do anything?
- Yes, it is *she* that won. *Who* was it that won?

Verbs: Voice and Mood

The mood and voice you choose for the verbs you use in your writing makes a difference. The following section describes different voices and the subjunctive mood in writing.

Active and Passive Voice

The active voice is transitive, which means that the verb requires an object. The active voice is stronger and more direct than the passive voice, and it usually makes your writing more effective. A sentence is written in the active voice when the subject clearly does the action; a sentence is written in the passive voice when the subject of the sentence receives the action. The following examples will help you to understand how much stronger and more direct the active voice is than the passive voice

- John completed his exam.

The active voice emphasizes the "doer" of the action. This makes a stronger statement and helps the writer avoid dangling or misplaced modifiers:

- Her dog was walked wearing a bright orange skirt. *(incorrect)*
- Wearing a bright orange skirt, she walked her dog. *(correct)*

The placement of the modifier in the first sentence makes it seem that the dog is wearing the skirt.

The passive voice is intransitive, which means the verb does not take an object. The action is implied:

- "The exam was completed early."

The passive voice emphasizes the receiver of the action and minimizes the importance of the doer.

Example

- *Active Voice* My dad packed the car for the trip.
- *Passive Voice* The car was packed for the trip by my dad.
- *Active Voice* Sue ate her birthday cake.
- *Passive Voice* The birthday cake was eaten by Sue.

Passive Voice in Writing

The passive voice can come across as unnecessarily wordy. The passive voice is a form of the verb where who or what is doing the action is implied but never actually stated. The active voice is preferred over the passive voice for clear, engaging writing. The active voice indicates the agent who performs the action.

Politicians often use the passive voice because they do not want to identify a specific individual responsible for some problem in government. They may say, "There has recently been a decline in economic activity." The passive voice does not state who or what is responsible for this economic decline. Critics of government, on the other hand, use the active voice because they do want to identify who is responsible for some government problem. They may say, "The finance minister's recent budget has caused a decline in economic activity." The active voice, "The new budget has caused…," offers an agent that the critics feel is to blame for the economic decline.

In the active voice, the subject of each sentence is placed before the object. Active language conveys the same ideas in fewer words.

Subjunctive Mood

The subjunctive mood expresses a wish or condition that is not actually true. Verbs such as *could, would,* and *should* are commonly used in the subjunctive mood.

Example

- If I were prime minister, I would *allow* everyone to work a four-day week.
- If Colin *could* take his dream vacation, he *would* spend it in Antarctica.

4.2.4i assess strengths and areas of need [for example develop a checklist of skills mastered and skills to be developed and set goals for language growth]

Evaluating Your Process

Metacognition consists of two processes occurring at the same time: monitoring your progress as you learn, and changing and adapting your strategies if necessary. In writing, this involves identifying what strategies you found most helpful before, during, and after writing and what steps you can take to improve as a writer. After you have finished a writing project, think back to how you developed your ideas for writing, the research you did, and how you sorted and organized it. This will help you to identify the strategies you used. The next time you do similar writing, use the strategies that worked best for you and reconsider the others.

For example, a Grade 11 student came up with the following examples of strategies that he had used during the first half of the year.

My Writing Strategies

Before Writing

- Went online to find information about topics when I could, like the topic natural disasters after we read the short story "The Worst Day Ever."
- Jotted down books, TV shows, music titles related to topic
- Talked with mom about topic choice
- Wrote down purpose, audience
- Made a web plan or outline

During Writing

- Spread out notes and outlines by computer
- Tried to follow outlines
- Checked with assignment criteria
- Tried to write correctly
- Tried to use good transitions
- Tried to include things teacher was emphasizing, like different sentence openers, "said is dead" replacements, etc.

After Writing

- Labelled my revisions to make sure I was intentionally including teacher suggestions
- Read drafts aloud from computer screen while revising and editing.
- Worked with my peer partner so we could help each other improve.

Next, the student explained the strategy he found the most helpful. The strategy he chose was the idea of labelling revisions to require thinking specifically about what he was changing and why. Since the students were sharing their metacognition activities with the teacher, he submitted the following paragraph:

Example

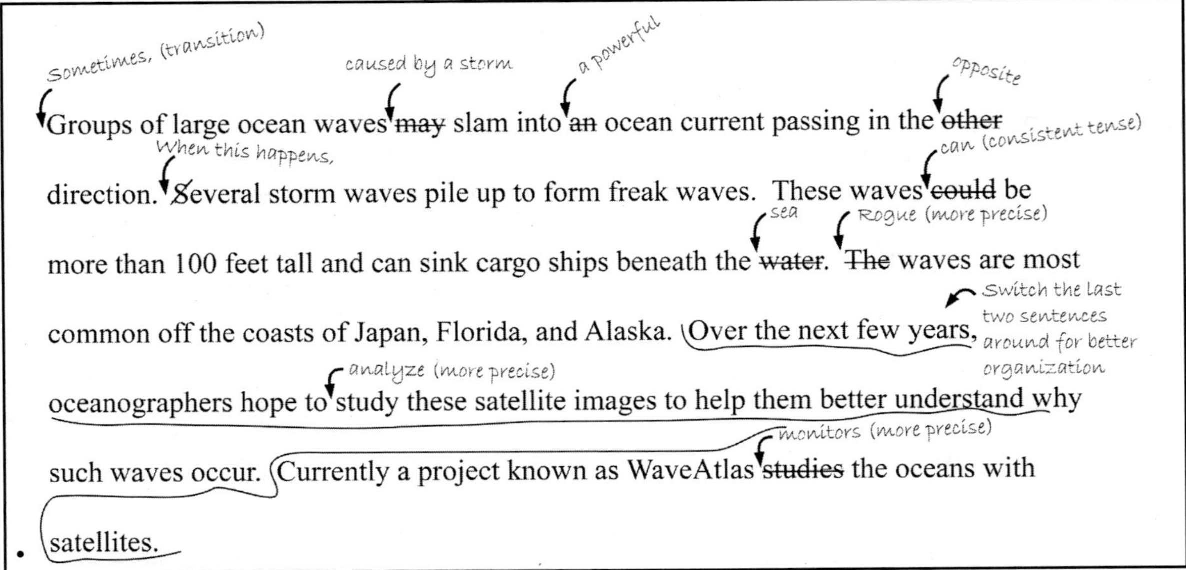

Groups of large ocean waves may slam into an ocean current passing in the other direction. Several storm waves pile up to form freak waves. These waves could be more than 100 feet tall and can sink cargo ships beneath the water. The waves are most common off the coasts of Japan, Florida, and Alaska. Over the next few years, oceanographers hope to study these satellite images to help them better understand why such waves occur. Currently a project known as WaveAtlas studies the oceans with satellites.

In a note to the teacher under the paragraph, the student added the following note.

Example

Ms. Harmon: Thanks for making us stop to think about our growth as writers. It is helping me improve. I just wanted to add that there should not be many errors in the paragraph because I really tried to be careful and to write correctly. That did make the revision easier.
Your student, Lyall
P.S. I tried to use the points you listed on the board when I was revising, like improving organization/using transitions; making ideas consistent and clear, and making details precise

Finally, the student identified several steps he could take to improve as a writer. His list included the following ideas:

1. Keep a writing log with sections: Spelling Errors, Writing Errors, Story Ideas
2. Start a list of words I want to use in my writing
3. Look online for sites where I can share some of my writing

After collecting the class's reflections, Ms. Harmon gave the students two 4 × 6 cards to tape inside their writing logs. The cards contained reminders to help the students think about each piece of writing.

This Piece

- What is best?
- What could I improve?
- What stage was smoothest?
- What ideas could I use for new writing?

Learning from this Piece

- Have I learned any new techniques?
- Did I try something new?
- Have I eliminated personal errors that I have commonly made in the past, like sentence fragments?

Writer's Reflection

Reflecting on your writing is something you probably have to do in class. The following example shows you an example of answers a fictional student has written in response to metacognition questions from his or her class. You may have to answer questions similar to these in class about your own writing and language skills. See if you can answer the following questions yourself.

Example

Before Grade 11, what did you know or understand to be your strengths as a writer? Has this changed?

I always thought that my greatest strength was writing humour. It was because I found it easy to remember the punch line of a good joke, and I could always seem to make my friends laugh. Sometimes at the wrong time, like in the middle of your class on sentence fragments. When you asked us to think hard about our strengths in September and to think of ways to branch out from those strengths, I realized that one reason I can describe things in a humorous way is that I am a people watcher. I am always watching what people do, how they react, and what they say in certain situations. I used that strength to branch out when I wrote my one-act play on peer pressure.
With realistic sounding dialogue and characters based on what I had really seen around me, I think I was able to get some serious points across using humour. During your comments after my group presented my play, you said our dialogue was convincing and real.

What did you learn about yourself as a writer as a result of the group writing experience?

You mean the short story project. The truth is, I wasn't too happy at first. I actually like writing independent stories from my own head, so it was annoying to have to stop and pay attention to the other two guys in my group. One hated writing, period, and the other didn't want to write anything but fantasy, which I have never read. We wasted a bit of time in the beginning, but when you started posting deadlines on the board, we had to think of something. We had just learned about parodies, so we decided to write a modernized parody of a well-known fairy tale. The partner who hated writing didn't mind working from a basic plot we all knew—"Little Red Riding Hood." He even started to contribute a few ideas. My other partner added some twists,
I added some ideas for humour, and we all liked the result because it turned out like a bit of a fantasy. What I learned about myself as a writer was that:

- I am more creative than I realized.
- Sometimes, other points of view can improve writing.
- I can motivate a peer who thinks writing is an unpleasant chore.

How do you determine whether the peer feedback you receive is valid or not?

I pay the closest attention to revision ideas. I figure if my ideas are boring or confusing to any reader, especially a peer, I need to fix that. Sometimes, it's just the organization that is confusing, so I make it more chronological or use better transitions. When a peer suggests different spelling or punctuation, I look at it, but not as hard, unless the peer is a classmate I know to be a strong speller or one who makes very few errors in their own writing. Even when I don't agree with the peer feedback, it does force me to take another look at my writing before publishing the final draft.

How you learn matters. Keeping track of what has affected your language skills is important. How easy was it to answer the three questions in the example? Could you think of any other questions that might be good to ask about your learning? Metacognition means thinking about your learning while you are learning. The more you ask yourself questions like the ones in the given example, the more aware you will become of your learning.

NOTES

KEY Strategies for Success on Tests

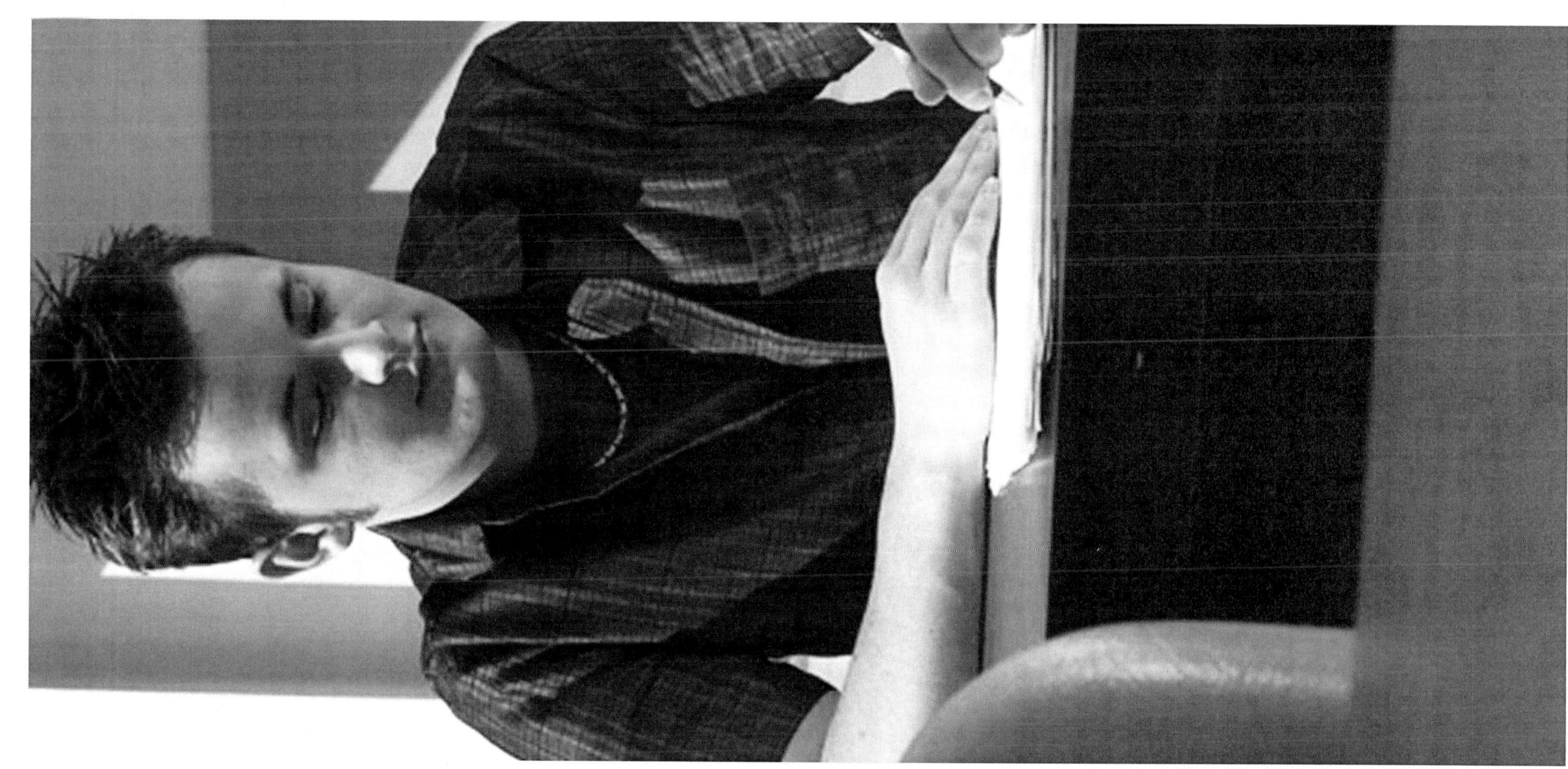

KEY STRATEGIES FOR SUCCESS ON TESTS

THINGS TO CONSIDER WHEN TAKING A TEST

It is normal to feel anxious before you write a test. You can manage this anxiety by

- Thinking positive thoughts. Imagine yourself doing well on the test.
- Making a conscious effort to relax by taking several slow, deep, controlled breaths. Concentrate on the air going in and out of your body.
- Before you begin the test, ask questions if you are unsure of anything.
- Jot down key words or phrases from any instructions your teacher gives you.
- Look over the entire test to find out the number and kinds of questions on the test.
- Read each question closely and reread if necessary.
- Pay close attention to key vocabulary words. Sometimes these are **bolded** or *italicized*, and they are usually important words in the question.
- If you are putting your answers on an answer sheet, mark your answers carefully. Always print clearly. If you wish to change an answer, erase the mark completely and then ensure your final answer is darker than the one you have erased.
- Use highlighting to note directions, key words, and vocabulary that you find confusing or that are important to answering the question.
- Double-check to make sure you have answered everything before handing in your test.

When taking tests, students often overlook the easy words. Failure to pay close attention to these words can result in an incorrect answer. One way to avoid this is to be aware of these words and to underline, circle, or highlight them while you are taking the test.

Even though some words are easy to understand, they can change the meaning of the entire question, so it is important that you pay attention to them. Here are some examples.

all	always	most likely	probably	best	not
difference	usually	except	most	unlikely	likely

Example

1. During the race, Susan is **most likely** feeling

A. sad

B. weak

C. scared

D. determined

HELPFUL STRATEGIES FOR ANSWERING MULTIPLE-CHOICE QUESTIONS

A multiple-choice question gives you some information, and then asks you to select an answer from four choices. Each question has one correct answer. The other answers are distractors, which are incorrect. Below are some strategies to help you when answering multiple-choice questions.

- Quickly skim through the entire test. Find out how many questions there are and plan your time accordingly.
- Read and reread questions carefully. Underline key words and try to think of an answer before looking at the choices.
- If there is a graphic, look at the graphic, read the question, and go back to the graphic. Then, you may want to underline the important information from the question.
- Carefully read the choices. Read the question first and then each answer that goes with it.
- When choosing an answer, try to eliminate those choices that are clearly wrong or do not make sense.
- Some questions may ask you to select the best answer. These questions will always include words like *best, most appropriate*, or *most likely*. All of the answers will be correct to some degree, but one of the choices will be better than the others in some way. Carefully read all four choices before choosing the answer you think is the best.
- If you do not know the answer, or if the question does not make sense to you, it is better to guess than to leave it blank.
- Do not spend too much time on any one question. Make a mark (*) beside a difficult question and come back to it later. If you are leaving a question to come back to later, make sure you also leave the space on the answer sheet, if you are using one.
- Remember to go back to the difficult questions at the end of the test; sometimes clues are given throughout the test that will provide you with answers.
- Note any negative words like *no* or *not* and be sure your choice fits the question.
- Before changing an answer, be sure you have a very good reason to do so.
- Do not look for patterns on your answer sheet, if you are using one.

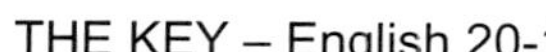

HELPFUL STRATEGIES FOR ANSWERING OPEN-RESPONSE QUESTIONS

A written response requires you to respond to a question or directive such as *explain*, *predict*, *list*, *describe*, *show your work*, *solve*, or *calculate*. In preparing for open-response tasks you may wish to:

- Read and reread the question carefully.
- Recognize and pay close attention to directing words such as *explain*, *show your work*, and *describe*.
- Underline key words and phrases that indicate what is required in your answer, such as *explain*, *estimate*, *answer*, *calculate*, or *show your work*.
- Write down rough, point-form notes regarding the information you want to include in your answer.
- Think about what you want to say and organize information and ideas in a coherent and concise manner within the time limit you have for the question.
- Be sure to answer every part of the question that is asked.
- Include as much information as you can when you are asked to explain your thinking.
- Include a picture or diagram if it will help to explain your thinking.
- Try to put your final answer to a problem in a complete sentence to be sure it is reasonable.
- Reread your response to ensure you have answered the question.
- Think: does your answer make sense
- Listen: does it sound right?
- Use appropriate subject vocabulary and terms in your response.

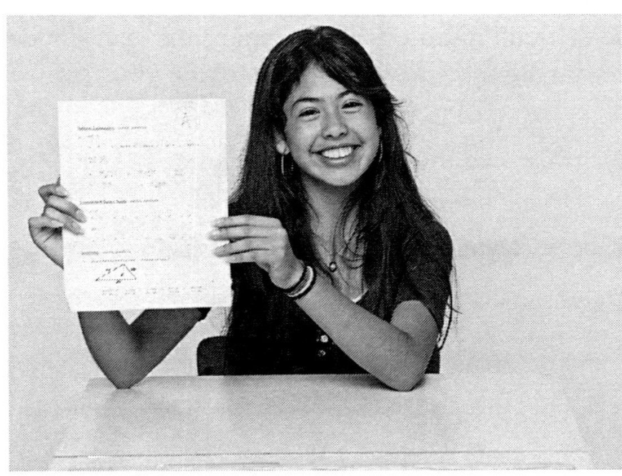

TEST PREPARATION COUNTDOWN

If you develop a plan for studying and test preparation, you will perform well on tests.

Here is a general plan to follow seven days before you write a test.

Countdown: 7 Days before the Test

1. Use "Finding Out About the Test" to help you make your own personal test preparation plan.
2. Review the following information:
   - areas to be included on the test
   - types of test items
   - general and specific test tips
3. Start preparing for the test at least 7 days before the test. Develop your test preparation plan and set time aside to prepare and study.

Countdown: 6, 5, 4, 3, 2 Days before the Test

4. Review old homework assignments, quizzes, and tests.
5. Rework problems on quizzes and tests to make sure you still know how to solve them.
6. Correct any errors made on quizzes and tests.
7. Review key concepts, processes, formulas, and vocabulary.
8. Create practice test questions for yourself and then answer them. Work out many sample problems.

Countdown: The Night before the Test

1. The night before the test is for final preparation, which includes reviewing and gathering material needed for the test before going to bed.
2. Most important is getting a good night's rest and knowing you have done everything possible to do well on the test.

Test Day

1. Eat a healthy and nutritious breakfast.
2. Ensure you have all the necessary materials.
3. Think positive thoughts: "I can do this." "I am ready." "I know I can do well."
4. Arrive at your school early so you are not rushing, which can cause you anxiety and stress.

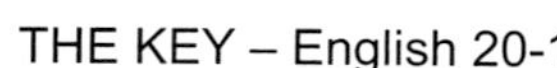

SUMMARY OF HOW TO BE SUCCESSFUL DURING A TEST

You may find some of the following strategies useful for writing a test.

- Take two or three deep breaths to help you relax.
- Read the directions carefully and underline, circle, or highlight any important words.
- Look over the entire test to understand what you will need to do.
- Budget your time.
- Begin with an easy question, or a question you know you can answer correctly, rather than following the numerical question order of the test.
- If you cannot remember how to answer a question, try repeating the deep breathing and physical relaxation activities first. Then, move on to visualization and positive self-talk to get yourself going.
- When answering a question with graphics (pictures, diagrams, tables, or graphs), look at the question carefully.
    1. Read the title of the graphic and any key words.
    2. Read the test question carefully to figure out what information you need to find in the graphic.
    3. Go back to the graphic to find the information you need.
- Write down anything you remember about the subject on the reverse side of your test paper. This activity sometimes helps to remind you that you do know something and you are capable of writing the test.
- Look over your test when you have finished and double-check your answers to be sure you did not forget anything.

Practice Tests

PRACTICE TESTS

Table of Correlations

Specific Outcome		Reading Practice Test	Writing Practice Test
Students will			
2.1	*Construct meaning from text and context*		
2.1.1c.	*explain the relationship between text and context in terms of how elements in an environment can affect the way in which text is created [for example, the historical context in which the text is written; gender-biased language can provide information about the context in which a text was created in terms of prominant culture]*	14, 61	
2.1.2a.	*use a variety of strategies to comprehend literature and other texts [for example, reading passages out loud, forming questions, making predictions, using context to determine the connotative meanings of words, using graphic organizers and making annotations], and develop strategies for close reading of literature in order to understand contextual elements [for example, understanding subtext]*	2, 6, 8, 13, 15, 19, 31, 37, 41, 63	
2.1.2 b.	*describe how supporting ideas and supporting details strengthen a text's controlling idea*	5, 12, 54, 55	
2.1.2 c.	*describe the relationships among plot, setting, character, atmosphere and theme when studying a narrative*	30, 33, 42, 43	
2.1.2 f.	*interpret figurative language, symbol and allusions; recognize imagery; and explain how imagery contributes to atmosphere, characterization and theme in a text*	20, 23, 24, 32, 34	
2.1.2 g.	*analyze visual and aural elements, and explain how they contribute to the meaning of texts*	29	
2.1.3a.	*reflect on and describe strategies used to engage prior knowledge as a means of assisting comprehension of new texts; and select, monitor and modify strategies as needed*	44	
2.2	*Understand and appreciate textual forms, elements, and techniques*		
2.2.1	*Relate form, structure and medium to purpose, audience and content*		
2.2.1a.	*identify a variety of text forms, including communications forms and literary forms [for example, letters, memoranda, poems, narratives and dramatizations]; and describe the relationships of form to purpose and content*	9, 10, 38	
2.2.1b.	*describe audience factors that may have influenced a text creator's choice of form and medium [for example, age, gender and culture of the audience]*	62	
2.2.1c.	*explain how a variety of organizational patterns and structural features contribute to purpose and content*	48, 53	
2.2.2	*Relate elements, devices and techniques to created effects*		
2.2.2a.	*explain how rhetorical devices and stylistic techniques used in print and nonprint texts create clarity, coherence and emphasis*	16, 26, 60	
2.2.2b.	*explain how various textual elements and stylistic techniques contribute to the creation of atmosphere, tone and voice [for example, qualification and interrupted movement]*	7, 25, 28, 40, 47, 58, 65	

2.2.2 c.	*analyze the use of irony and satire to create effects in print and nonprint texts [for example, dramatic irony to create suspense, verbal irony to create humour, and satire to evoke response]*	4, 39, 45	
2.2.2 d.	*describe the effects of musical devices, figures of speech and sensory details in print and nonprint texts [for example, alliteration used to create emphasis, metaphor used to evoke images, and sensory details used to evoke pathos]*	49, 64	
2.2.2 e.	*explain the contribution of motif and symbol to controlling idea and theme*	22	
2.3	*Respond to a variety of print and nonprint texts*		
2.3.1	*Connect self, text, culture and milieu*		
2.3.1a.	*identify and consider personal, moral, ethical and cultural perspectives when studying literature and other texts; and reflect on and monitor how perspectives change as a result of interpretation and discussion*	17, 56, 59	
2.3.2	*Evaluate the verisimilitude, appropriateness and significance of print and nonprint texts*		
2.3.2 c.	*analyze and assess settings and plots in terms of created reality and plausibility [for example, determine the authenticity of the setting of a work of historical fiction]*	18	
2.3.2d.	*analyze and assess character and characterization in terms of consistency of behaviour, motivation and plausibility, and in terms of contribution to theme [for example, determine the eanings suggested by a change in a character's behaviour or values]*	1, 3, 35, 36, 45	
2.3.2 f.	*assess the significance of a text's theme or controlling idea, and the adequacy, relevance and effectiveness of its supporting details, examples or illustrations, and content in general*	11, 21, 50, 52	
2.3.3	*Appreciate the effectiveness and artistry of print and nonprint texts*		
2.3.3 b.	*describe the effectiveness of various texts, including media texts, for presenting feelings, ideas and information, and for evoking response*	57	
4.1	*Develop and present a variety of print and nonprint texts*		
4.1.1b.	*identify purpose and target audience for text creation, and select strategies to accomplish purpose and engage audience [for example, plan a campaign—public relations, advertising or lobbying— identifying the text forms to be used to influence the attitudes of the audience with respect to the chosen issue]*		Writing Prompt
4.1.2	*Consider and address form, structure and medium*		
4.1.2 a.	*select a text form appropriate to the purpose for text creation and consistent with the content to be presented in the text [for example, select a photo essay to demonstrate a personal or critical/analytical response to poetry or other literature when the content to be presented is well suited to the creation of a visual text]*		Writing Prompt
4.1.2b	*explore a variety of structures consistent with form, content and purpose when creating texts [for example, explore definition, example and illustration, classification and other methods of development consistent with the essay form when creating anessay]*		Writing Prompt
4.1.3	*Develop content*		

4.1.3a.	*take ownership of text creation, by selecting or crafting a topic, concept or idea that is personally meaningful and engaging*		Writing Prompt
4.1.3 b.	*recognize and assess personal variables [such as personal experience and prior knowledge] and contextual variables [such as availability of time and resources] that influence the selection of a topic, concept or idea; and address these variables to increase the likelihood of successful text creation*		Writing Prompt
4.2	*Improve thoughtfulness, effectiveness and correctness of communication*		
4.2.2a.	*assess the beginning of a text in progress, and revise it as needed to establish purpose and engage audience [for example, the thesis statement of an essay, the initial monologue of a script, or the statement of purpose of a proposal]*		Writing Prompt
4.2.2b.	*assess the organizational components of a text in progress, and revise them as needed to strengthen their effectiveness as units of thought or experience or to strengthen their contribution to other intended effects [such as emphasis or transition]*		Writing Prompt
4.2.3a.	*reflect on personal vocabulary and repertoire of stylistic choices and on their effectiveness; and expand vocabulary and repertoire of stylistic choices*		Writing Prompt
4.2.3 b.	*assess the appropriateness and effectiveness of diction, and revise word choice as needed to create intended effects*		Writing Prompt
4.2.3 d.	*apply understanding of stylistic techniques and rhetorical devices when creating print and nonprint texts [for example, use imagery to create pathos, use parallel structure to create emphasis, and use sound in multimedia texts to create humour]*		Writing Prompt
4.2.3 e.	*recognize personal voice in texts created; and continue to develop personal craft through practice, using various methods*		Writing Prompt
4.2.4 b.	*know and be able to apply capitalization and punctuation conventions correctly, including end punctuation, commas, semicolons, colons, apostrophes, quotation marks, hyphens, dashes, ellipses, parentheses, underlining and italics*		Writing Prompt
4.2.4 c.	*know and be able to apply spelling conventions consistently and independently*		Writing Prompt
4.2.4 d.	*understand the importance of grammatical agreement; and assess and revise texts in progress to ensure correctness of grammatical agreement, including correct pronoun reference and pronoun–antecedent agreement, and correct use of modifiers and other parts of speech*	27, 51	Writing Prompt

PRACTICE TEST—READING

Reading One

Catherine Morland, the protagonist of Jane Austen's Northanger Abbey, is unfit for her role as a heroine. The reason for her unsuitability is found in the nature of the Gothic romances that were popular at the time. The Gothic genre required a heroine to possess remarkable beauty and unusual abilities. She would also be expected to endure grotesque and horrible events, supernatural horrors, and isolation in a ruinous castle or an abbey (a monastery). She would be caught up in dark secrets or the results of ancient crimes, and she might find an evil monk or nun adding to the darkness and gloom. The Gothic genre also required brooding, tyrannical male characters that might include a harsh and unreasonable father or an eligible bachelor with a tortured past. All of these Gothic elements, and Catherine's lack thereof, make her an unlikely heroine.

from NORTHANGER ABBEY

No one who had ever seen Catherine Morland in her infancy would have supposed her born to be a heroine. Her situation in life, the character of her father and mother, her own person and disposition, were all equally against her. Her father was a clergyman, without being neglected, or poor, and a very respectable man, though his name was Richard – and he had never been handsome. He had a considerable independence besides two good livings – and he was not in the least addicted to locking up his daughters. Her mother was a woman of useful plain sense, with a good temper, and, what is more remarkable, with a good constitution. She had three sons before Catherine was born; and instead of dying in bringing the latter into the world, as anybody might expect, she still lived on – lived to have six children more – to see them growing up and around her, and to enjoy excellent health herself.

A family of ten children will be always called a fine family, where there are heads and arms and legs enough for the number; but the Morlands had little other right to the word, for they were in general very plain, and Catherine, for many years of her life, as plain as any. She had a thin awkward figure, a sallow skin without colour, dark lank hair, and strong features – so much for her person; and not less unpropitious for heroism seemed her mind. She was fond of all boys' plays, and greatly preferred cricket not merely to dolls, but to the more heroic enjoyments of infancy, nursing a dormouse, feeding a canary-bird, or watering a rose-bush. Indeed she had no taste for a garden; and if she gathered flowers at all, it was chiefly for the pleasure of mischief – at least so it was conjectured from her always preferring those which she was forbidden to take. Such were her propensities – her abilities were quite as extraordinary. She never could learn or understand anything before she was taught; and sometimes not even then, for she was often inattentive, and occasionally stupid. Her mother was three months in teaching her only to repeat the "Beggar's Petition"; and after all, her next sister, Sally, could say it better than she did. Not that Catherine was always stupid – by no means; she learnt the fable of "the Hare and Many Friends" as quickly as any girl in England.

Her mother wished her to learn music; and Catherine was sure she should like it, for she was very fond of tinkling the keys of the old forlorn spinnet; so, at eight years old she began. She learnt a year, and could not bear it; and Mrs. Morland, who did not insist on her daughters being accomplished in spite of incapacity or distaste, allowed her to leave off. The day which dismissed the music-master was one of the happiest of Catherine's life.

Her taste for drawing was not superior; though whenever she could obtain the outside of a letter from her mother or seize upon any other odd piece of paper, she did what she could in that way, by drawing houses and trees, hens and chickens, all very much like one another. Writing and accounts she was taught by her father; French by her mother. Her proficiency in either was not remarkable, and she shirked her lessons in both whenever she could.

What a strange, unaccountable character! – for with all these symptoms of profligacy at ten years old, she had neither a bad heart nor a bad temper, was seldom stubborn, scarcely ever quarrelsome, and very kind to the little ones, with few interruptions of tyranny. She was, moreover, noisy and wild, hated confinement and cleanliness, and loved nothing so well in the world as rolling down the green slope at the back of the house.

Such was Catherine Morland at ten. At fifteen, appearances were mending; she began to curl her hair and long for balls; her complexion improved, her features were softened by plumpness and colour, her eyes gained more animation, and her figure more consequence. Her love of dirt gave way to an inclination for finery, and she grew clean as she grew smart; she had now the pleasure of sometimes hearing her father and mother remark on her personal improvement. "Catherine grows quite a good-looking girl – she is almost pretty today," were words which caught her ears now and then; and how welcome were the sounds! To look almost pretty is an acquisition of higher delight to a girl who has been looking plain the first fifteen years of her life than a beauty from her cradle can ever receive.

Mrs. Morland was a very good woman, and wished to see her children everything they ought to be; but her time was so much occupied in lying-in and teaching the little ones, that her elder daughters were inevitably left to shift for themselves; and it was not very wonderful that Catherine, who had by nature nothing heroic about her, should prefer cricket, baseball, riding on horseback, and running about the country at the age of fourteen, to books – or at least books of information – for, provided that nothing like useful knowledge could be gained from them, provided they were all story an no reflection, she had never any objection to books at all. But from fifteen to seventeen she was in training for a heroine; she read all such works as heroines must read to supply their memories with those quotations which are so serviceable and so soothing in the vicissitudes of their eventful lives.

From Pope, she learnt to censure those who

"bear about the mockery of woe."

From Gray, that

"Many a flower is born to blush unseen,
And waste its sweetness on the desert air."

From Thompson, that –

"It is a delightful task
To teach the young idea how to shoot."

And from Shakespeare she gained a great store of information – amongst the rest, that –

"Trifles light as air,
Are, to the jealous, confirmation strong,
As proofs of Holy Writ."

That

> "The poor beetle, which we tread upon,
> In corporal sufferance feels a pang as great
> As when a giant dies."

And that a young woman in love always looks –

> "like Patience on a monument,
> Smiling at Grief."

So far her improvement was sufficient – and in many other points she came on exceedingly well; for though she could not write sonnets, she brought herself to read them; and though there seemed no chance of her throwing a whole party into raptures by a prelude on the pianoforte of her own composition, she could listen to other people's performance with very little fatigue. Her greatest deficiency was in the pencil – she had no notion of drawing – not enough even to attempt a sketch of her lover's profile, that she might be detected in the design. There she fell miserably short of the true heroic height. At present she did not know her own poverty, for she had no lover to portray. She had reached the age of seventeen, without having seen one amiable youth who could call forth her sensibility, without having inspired one real passion, and without having excited even any admiration but what was very moderate and very transient. This was strange indeed! But strange things may be generally accounted for if their cause be fairly searched out. There was not one lord in the neighbourhood; no – not even a baronet. There was not one family among their acquaintance who had reared and supported a boy accidentally found at their door – not one young man whose origin was unknown. Her father had no ward, and the squire of the parish no children. But when a young lady is to be a heroine, the perverseness of forty surrounding families cannot prevent her. Something must and will happen to throw a hero in her way.

Mr. Allen, who owned the chief of the property about Fullerton, the village in Wiltshire where the Morlands lived, was ordered to Bath for the benefit of a gouty constitution – and his lady, a good-humoured woman, fond of Miss Morland, and probably aware that if adventures will not befall a young lady in her own village, she must seek them abroad, invited her to go with them. Mr. and Mrs. Morland were all compliance, and Catherine all happiness.

—*by* Jane Austen (1775–1817)

An English novelist, Austen wrote her elegant and realistic novels of manners at a time when sensational and improbable Gothic romances were popular.

1. Which of the following quotations most directly explains the narrator's surprise that Catherine Morland is the heroine of this story?
   A. "Her father was a clergyman, without being neglected, or poor, and a very respectable man, though his name was Richard – and he had never been handsome" (lines 3–5)
   B. "Her mother wished her to learn music…She learnt a year, and could not bear it; and Mrs. Morland, who did not insist on her daughters being accomplished in spite of incapacity or distaste, allowed her to leave off" (lines 26–29)
   C. "Writing and accounts she was taught be her father, French by her mother; her proficiency in either was not remarkable, and she shirked her lessons in both whenever she could" (lines 33–35)
   D. "She was, moreover, noisy and wild, hated confinement and cleanliness, and loved nothing so well in the world as rolling down the green slope at the back of the house". (lines 38–40)

2. The word "propensities" (line 20) most likely means
   A. ideas
   B. skills
   C. abilities
   D. inclinations

3. At ten years of age, Catherine still does not seem to be much of a heroine because, according to the narrator,
   A. her mother "had three sons before Catherine was born" (line 7–8)
   B. "The day which dismissed her music-master was one of the happiest of Catherine's life" (lines 29–30)
   C. "she shirked her lessons…whenever she could" (line 35)
   D. "she had neither a bad heart nor a bad temper" (lines 37)

4. The description of Catherine as "a strange, unaccountable character!" (line 36) is most clearly explained as
   A. irony that shows she was perfectly normal
   B. metaphor that shows she was an awkward ten-year-old
   C. parody that shows the narrator is easily surprised by her
   D. metonymy that shows she did really have a bad character after all

5. The most complete description of Catherine's "propensities" and "abilities" is that they are
   A. described in terms of what she cannot do
   B. quite remarkable for someone so young
   C. focused on heroic deeds in the future
   D. more mischievous than anything else

6. From this introduction to Catherine, it is most likely that the rest of the story will

A. show how she deserves to be called a heroine

B. continue to tell how ordinary she is

C. describe the rest of her family

D. give her complete biography

7. The best description of the narrator's tone in this passage is

A. ironic

B. Gothic

C. derisive

D. insincere

8. In the context of lines 85 to 88, "sensibility" most clearly means

A. feelings

B. admiration

C. social rank

D. common sense

9. This excerpt is really about the

A. importance of education

B. qualities necessary for heroism

C. foolishness of certain kinds of stories

D. unequal education given to girls in the 1800s

10. The genre of this extract may be most accurately described as

A. burlesque

B. romance

C. parody

D. Gothic

Reading Two

from PLATO'S REPUBLIC

In this excerpt from one of the dialogues recorded by the Greek philosopher Plato, Socrates (the "I") tells of speaking with Glaucon (the "he") about the human situation. The brief replies made by Glaucon are typical of a Socratic dialogue. The dialectic teaching method of question and answer is called the Socratic method.

THE MYTH OF THE CAVE

And now, I said, let me show in a figure how far our nature is enlightened or unenlightened: – Behold! Human beings living in an underground den, which has a mouth open toward the light and reaching all along the den; here they have been from their childhood, and have their legs and necks chained so that they cannot move, and can only see before them, being prevented by the chains from turning round their heads. Above and behind them a fire is blazing at a distance, and between the fire and the prisoners there is a raised way; and you will see, if you look, a low wall built along the way, like the screen which marionette players have in front of them, over which they show the puppets.

I see.

And do you see, I said, men passing along the wall carrying all sorts of vessels, and statues and figures of animals made of wood and stone and various materials, which appear over the wall? Some of them are talking, others silent.

You have shown me a strange image, and they are strange prisoners.

Like ourselves, I replied; and they see only their own shadows, or the shadows of one another, which the fire throws on the opposite wall of the cave?

True, he said; how could they see anything but the shadows if they were never allowed to move their heads?

And of the objects which are being carried in like manner they would only see the shadows?

Yes, he said.

And if they were able to converse with one another, would they not suppose that they were naming what was actually before them?

Very true.

And suppose further that the prison had an echo which came from the other side, would they not be sure to fancy when one of the passers-by spoke that the voice which they heard came from the passing shadow?

No question, he replied.

To them, I said, the truth would be literally nothing but the shadows of the images.

That is certain.

And now look again, and see what will naturally follow if the prisoners are released and disabused of their error. At first, when any of them is liberated and compelled suddenly to stand up and turn his neck round and walk and look toward the light, he will suffer sharp pains; the glare will distress him, and he will be unable to see the realities of which in his former state he had seen the shadows; and then conceive someone saying to him, that what he saw before was an illusion, but that now, when he is approaching nearer to being and his eye is turned toward more real existence, he has a clearer vision – what will be his reply? And you may further imagine that his instructor is pointing to the objects as they pass and requiring him to name them – will he not be perplexed? Will he not fancy that the shadows which he formerly saw are truer than the objects which are now shown to him?

Far truer.

And if he is compelled to look straight at the light, will he not have a pain in his eyes which will make him turn away to take refuge in the objects of vision which he can see, and which he will conceive to be in reality clearer than the things which are now being shown to him?

True, he said.

And suppose once more, that he is reluctantly dragged up a steep and rugged ascent, and held fast until he is forced into the presence of the sun himself, is he not likely to be pained and irritated? When he approaches the light his eyes will be dazzled, and he will not be able to see anything at all of what are now called realities.

Not all in a moment, he said.

He will require to grow accustomed to the sight of the upper world. And first he will see the shadows best, next the reflections of men and other objects in the water, and then the objects themselves; then he will gaze upon the light of the moon and the stars and the spangled heaven; and he will see the sky and the stars by night better than the sun or the light of the sun by day?

Certainly.

Last of all he will be able to see the sun, and not mere reflections of him in the water, but he will see him in his own proper place, and not in another; and he will contemplate him as he is.

Certainly.

He will then proceed to argue that this is he who gives the season and the years, and is the guardian of all that is in the visible world, and in a certain way the cause of all things which he and his fellows have been accustomed to behold?

Clearly, he said, he would first see the sun and then reason about him.

And when he remembered his old habitation, and the wisdom of the den and his fellow-prisoners, do you not suppose that he would felicitate himself on the change, and pity them?

Certainly, he would.

And if they were in the habit of conferring honours among themselves on those who were quickest to observe the passing shadows and to remark which of them went before, and which followed after, and which were together; and who were therefore best able to draw conclusions as to the future, do you think that he would care for such honours and glories, or envy the possessors of them? Would he not say with Homer,

Better to be the poor servant of a poor master, and to endure anything, rather than think as they do and live after their manner?

Yes, he said, I think that he would rather suffer anything than entertain these false notions and live in this miserable manner.

Imagine once more, I said, such a one coming suddenly out of the sun to be replaced in his old situation; would he not be certain to have his eyes full of darkness?

To be sure, he said.

And if there were a contest, and he had to compete in measuring the shadows with the prisoners who had never moved out of the den, while his sight was still weak, and before his eyes had become steady (and the time which would be needed to acquire this new habit of sight might be very considerable) would he not be ridiculous? Men would say of him that up he went and down he came without his eyes; and that it was better not even to think of ascending; and if anyone tried to loose another and lead him up to the light, let them only catch the offender, and they would put him to death.

No question, he said.

This entire allegory, I said, you may now append, dear Glaucon, to the previous argument; the prison-house is the world of sight, the light of the fire is the sun, and you will not misapprehend me if you interpret the journey upwards to be the ascent of the soul into the intellectual world according to my poor belief, which, at your desire, I have expressed whether rightly or wrongly, God knows. But, whether true or false, my opinion is that in the world of knowledge the idea of good appears last of all, and is seen only with an effort; and, when seen, is also inferred to be the universal author of all things beautiful and right, parent of light and of the lord of light in this visible world, and the immediate source of reason and truth in the intellectual; and that this is the power upon which he who would act rationally either in public or private life must have his eye fixed.

—by Plato (427–347 BC)

Most of what we know about the ideas of Socrates (469–399 BC) is found in the writings of Plato

11. Which of the following quotations most strongly presents the theme of limited perception?

A. "Behold! Human beings living in an underground den, which has a mouth open toward the light and reaching all along the den" (lines 2–3)

B. "here they have been from their childhood, and have their legs and necks chained to that they cannot move, and can only see before them, being prevented by the chains from turning round their heads" (lines 3–5)

C. "and you will see, if you look, a low all built along the way like the screen which marionette players have in front of them, over which they show the puppets" (lines 6–8)

D. "And do you see, I said, men passing along the wall carrying all sorts of vessels, and statues and figures of animals made of wood and stone and various materials, which appear over the wall?" (lines 10–11)

12. According to Socrates, the liberated prisoner will paradoxically

A. regret his liberation

B. throw caution to the wind

C. have to be forced to leave the prison

D. experience more intense levels of pain

13. A liberated prisoner who returned to the cave would be least likely to be

A. put to death

B. seen to be ridiculous

C. unable to see as well as the others

D. at a disadvantage compared to those who had never left

14. In this context, the main function of a "myth" such as the one told by Socrates is to

A. express a truth about the human condition

B. make a vivid image which the reader can "see"

C. state in images a thought that is too difficult for ordinary words

D. briefly summarize a moral principle that is sometimes stated at the end of a story

15. The first paragraph explains that through this myth, the writer will show "how far our nature is enlightened or unenlightened," and then goes on to posit that man is

A. unenlightened because of the immobilizing chains

B. enlightened because of the "fire blazing at a distance"

C. unenlightened because of external causes beyond our control

D. both enlightened and unenlightened because of the shadows cast by the fire

16. The function of the dialogue in the telling of this myth is best summarized as a way

A. to simplify a complicated story

B. for the reader to infer the meaning of the argument

C. of teaching by proceeding one step at a time through question and answer

D. to provide a "yes-man" that will cause unconscious agreement with the argument

17. The narrator's overall attitude toward human nature is best stated as

A. cynical

B. realistic

C. optimistic

D. pessimistic

18. In the analogy of the myth, the location that is most real is

A. "an underground den" (line 2)

B. the fire which is blazing "above and behind" them (line 5)

C. the other side of "a low wall built along the way" (lines 6 to 7)

D. "the shadows of the images" (line 27)

19. The meaning of the phrase "show in a figure" (line 1) is most clearly explained as

A. a shadow play

B. a figure of speech

C. the result of calculation

D. an illustration that demonstrates truth

20. In lines 84 to 88, Socrates is saying that anyone who wants to behave rationally should

A. be guided by the light of the sun

B. remember that the world is a prison

C. understand that nothing that we see is really true

D. remember that good is the source of truth in everything

21. According to Socrates, truth is understood through

A. inference

B. figures of speech

C. studying shadows

D. the light of the sun

Reading Three

CROSSING THE BAR

Sunset and evening star,
And one clear call for me!
And may there be no moaning of the bar,
When I put out to sea,
But such a tide as moving seems asleep,
Too full for sound and foam,
When that which drew from out the boundless deep
Turns again home.
Twilight and evening bell,
And after that the dark!
And may there be no sadness of farewell,
When I embark;
For though from out our bourne of Time and Place
The flood may bear me far,
I hope to see my Pilot face to face
When I have crossed the bar.

—*by Alfred, Lord Tennyson* (1809–92)

Tennyson was one of the best-known Victorian poets. He requested that "Crossing the Bar" always be the last poem printed in any collection of his works.

22. The theme of this poem is **best** described as the

A. inevitable

B. silence of eternity

C. approach of death

D. acceptance of death

23. The phrase "moaning of the bar" is **best** explained as

A. weeping

B. suffering

C. ship-board noises

D. the rush of the tide over gravel

24. In line 15, "my Pilot" **most likely** refers to

A. God

B. eternity

C. the ship's guide

D. someone who can show the way

25. Which of the following quotations **most clearly** expresses the poet's attitude?

A. "Twilight and evening bell, / And after that the dark!" (lines 9–10)

B. "When that which drew from out the boundless deep / Turns again home" (lines 7–8)

C. "But such a tide as moving seems asleep" (line 5)

D. "And may there be no moaning of the bar, / When I put out to sea" (lines 3–4)

26. In lines 13 and 15, three words other than the first words of each line are capitalized because

A. of poetic licence

B. proper nouns are always capitalized

C. of their importance in the poet's thought

D. in Tennyson's day, English had different rules for capitalization

27. In the quotation "When that which drew from out the boundless deep" (line 7), the pronoun "that" does not have a clear antecedent—it might not even refer to anything mentioned before. The antecedent of the pronoun "that" is the

A. "I" (line 12) who is embarking on a journey

B. tide that moves to and from "the boundless deep"

C. soul leaving the boundary of time and space (line 13)

D. Pilot (line 15) who guides the ship once it has left harbour

28. The tone of this poem is **best described** as

A. calm

B. anxious

C. grieving

D. hopeless

Reading Four

from THE TEMPEST, Act III, scene iii

CHARACTERS

ALONSO, King of Naples

SEBASTIAN, his brother

PROSPERO, the right Duke of Milan

ANTONIO, his brother, the usurping Duke of Milan

FERDINAND, son to the King of Naples

MIRANDA, daughter to Prospero

GONZALO, an honest old Counsellor

ADRIAN, FRANCISCO, Lords

ARIEL, an airy spirit

On an almost uninhabited island somewhere in the Mediterranean Sea, Prospero lives with his daughter Miranda. Prospero, who has become a powerful magician, is also the rightful Duke of Milan. Twelve years ago, Prospero's brother Antonio, with the help of Alonso, the King of Naples, seized Milan. Antonio and Alonso conspired to have Prospero and the infant Miranda, whom they dared not murder outright, put out to sea in a leaky boat to drown. However, the two castaways did not drown, partly because Gonzalo, one of Alonso's lords, secretly provided them with supplies as well as books—including the all-important book of magic—from Prospero's library.

Over the next twelve years, Prospero's power has grown and he now has powerful spirits of the air for his servants. When Antonio, Alonso, and others of their courts pass near the island on ship, Prospero arranges a great storm and an apparent shipwreck. He now has them all in his power.

As this scene begins, the characters, confused by magic, have been wandering in circles for some time.

Enter ALONSO, SEBASTIAN, ANTONIO, GONZALO, ADRIAN, FRANCISCO, and others.

GONZALO**:** By'r lakin, I can go no further, sir;
My old bones ache: here's a maze trod indeed
Through forth-rights and meanders! By your patience,
I needs must rest me.

ALONSO: Old lord, I cannot blame thee,
Who am myself attach'd with weariness,
To the dulling of my spirits: sit down, and rest.
Even here I will put off my hope and keep it

No longer for my flatterer: he is drown'd

Whom thus we stray to find, and the sea mocks

Our frustrate search on land. Well, let him go.

ANTONIO: [Aside to SEBASTIAN] I am right glad that he's so out of hope.

Do not, for one repulse, forego the purpose

That you resolved to effect.

SEBASTIAN: [Aside to ANTONIO] The next advantage

Will we take throughly.

ANTONIO: [Aside to SEBASTIAN] Let it be to-night;

For, now they are oppress'd with travel, they

Will not, nor cannot, use such vigilance

As when they are fresh.

SEBASTIAN: [Aside to ANTONIO] I say, to-night: no more.

[Solemn and strange music]

ALONSO: What harmony is this? My good friends, hark!

GONZALO: Marvellous sweet music!

Enter PROSPERO above, invisible. Enter several strange Shapes, bringing in a banquet; they dance about it with gentle actions of salutation; and, inviting the King, etc. to eat, they depart

ALONSO: Give us kind keepers, heavens! What were these?

SEBASTIAN: A living drollery. Now I will believe

That there are unicorns, that in Arabia

There is one tree, the phoenix' throne, one phoenix

At this hour reigning there.

ANTONIO: I'll believe both;

And what does else want credit, come to me,

And I'll be sworn 'tis true: travelers ne'er did lie,

Though fools at home condemn 'em.

GONZALO: If in Naples

I should report this now, would they believe me?

If I should say, I saw such islanders –
For, certes, these are people of the island –
Who, though they are of monstrous shape, yet, note,
Their manners are more gentle-kind than of
Our human generation you shall find
Many, nay, almost any.
PROSPERO: [Aside] Honest lord,
Thou hast said well; for some of you there present
Are worse than devils.
ALONSO: I cannot too much muse
Such shapes, such gesture and such sound, expressing,
Although they want the use of tongue, a kind
Of excellent dumb discourse.
PROSPERO: [Aside] Praise in departing.
FRANCISCO: They vanish'd strangely.
SEBASTIAN: No matter, since
they have left their viands behind; for we have stomachs.
Will't please you taste of what is here?
ALONSO: Not I.
GONZALO: Faith, sir, you need not fear. When we were boys,
Who would believe that there were mountaineers
Dew-lapp'd like bulls, whose throats had hanging at 'em
Wallets of flesh? or that there were such men
Whose heads stood in their breasts? which we now find
Each putter-out of five for one will bring us
Good warrant of.
ALONSO: I will stand to and feed,
Although my last: no matter, since I feel
The best is past. Brother, my lord the duke,
Stand to and do as we.

Thunder and lightning. Enter ARIEL, like a harpy; claps his wings upon the table; and, with a quaint device, the banquet vanishes.

ARIEL: You are three men of sin, whom Destiny –
That hath to instrument this lower world
And what is in't – the never-surfeited sea
Hath caused to belch up you; and on this island
Where man doth not inhabit; you 'mongst men
Being most unfit to live. I have made you mad;
And even with such-like valour men hang and drown
Their proper selves.
[ALONSO, SEBASTIAN, etc. draw their swords]
You fools! I and my fellows
Are ministers of Fate: the elements,
Of whom your swords are temper'd, may as well
Wound the loud winds, or with bemock'd-at stabs
Kill the still-closing waters, as diminish
One dowle that's in my plume: my fellow-ministers
Are like invulnerable. If you could hurt,
Your swords are not too massy for your strengths
And will not be uplifted. But remember –
For that's my business to you – that you three
From Milan did supplant good Prospero;
Exposed unto the sea, which hath requit it,
Him and his innocent child: for which foul deed
The powers, delaying, not forgetting, have
Incensed the seas and shores, yea, all the creatures,
Against your peace. Thee of thy son, Alonso,
They have bereft; and do pronounce by me
Lingering perdition, worse than any death

Can be at once, shall step by step attend
You and your ways; whose wraths to guard you from –
Which here, in this most desolate isle, else falls
Upon your heads – is nothing but heart-sorrow
And a clear life ensuing.

He vanishes in thunder; then, to soft music enter the Shapes again, and dance, with mocks and mows, and carrying out the table.

PROSPERO: Bravely the figure of this harpy hast thou
Perform'd, my Ariel; a grace it had, devouring:
Of my instruction hast though nothing bated
In what thou hadst to say: so, with good life
And observation strange, my meaner ministers
Their several kinds have done. My high charms work
And these mine enemies are all knit up
In their distractions; they now are in my power;
And in these fits I leave them, while I visit
Young Ferdinand, whom they suppose is drown'd,
And his and mind loved darling.

[Exit above]

GONZALO: I' the name of something holy, sir, why stand you
In this strange stare?

ALONSO: O, it is monstrous, monstrous:
Methought the billows spoke and told me of it;
The winds did sing it to me, and the thunder,
That deep and dreadful organ-pipe, pronounced
The name of Prosper: it did bass my trespass.
Therefore my son i' the ooze is bedded, and
I'll seek him deeper than e'er plummet sounded
And with him there lie mudded.

[Exit]

SEBASTIAN: But one fiend at a time,
I'll fight their legions o'er.
ANTONIO: I'll be thy second.
[Exeunt SEBASTIAN, and ANTONIO]
GONZALO: All three of them are desperate: their great guilt,
Like poison given to work a great time after,
Now 'gins to bite the spirits. I do beseech you
that are of suppler joints, follow them swiftly
And hinder them from what this ecstasy
May now provoke them to.
ADRIAN: Follow, I pray you.
[Exeunt]

29. Line 33 begins with only a few words printed at the end of the line that contains the character's name. The most likely reason for this is that

A. the space contained directions that are not needed in this short excerpt

B. the short line completes the iambic pentameter begun by the previous speaker

C. many of the lines vary in length and the short lines actually have no significance

D. the short first line is a poetic device intended to give relief from the monotonous rhythm

30. Gonzalo's words "here's a maze trod indeed / Through forth-rights and meanders!" (lines 3 to 4) are an example of

A. a figure of speech

B. dramatic poetry

C. scene-setting

D. metaphor

31. At the beginning of the scene, Antonio says, "I am right glad that he's so out of hope" (line 13). By "out of hope," Antonio means that Alonso

A. is weakened by exhaustion

B. feels trapped on the island

C. is troubled by remorse

D. thinks his son is dead

32. Sebastian's quotation, "A living drollery. Now I will believe / That there are unicorns, that in Arabia / There is one tree, the phoenix' throne, one phoenix / At this hour reigning there" (lines 29 to 32), contains examples of

A. allusion

B. metaphor

C. metonymy

D. synecdoche

33. After his speech in lines 119–126, Alonso exits in order to

A. look for his missing son

B. flee from his guilt

C. fight the fiends

D. seek death

34. Ariel appearing like a harpy and making the food vanish suggests

A. the hunger of the shipwrecked men

B. an allusion to classical mythology

C. a punishment for crime

D. increasing horror

35. In lines 117 to 118, Gonzalo says to Alonzo, "I' the name of something holy, sir, why stand you / In this strange stare?" because

A. he is trying to stir Alonzo out of his strange mood

B. Alonzo is on the point of confessing his crime

C. only the three guilty ones heard and saw Ariel

D. he is concerned for Alonso's sanity

36. Which of the following quotations best show Alonso's guilty feelings?

A. "Even here I will put off my hope and keep it / No longer for my flatterer" (lines 9–10)

B. "the sea mocks / Our frustrate search on land. Well, let him go" (lines 11–12)

C. "no matter, since I feel / The best is past" (lines 66–67)

D. "That deep and dreadful organ-pipe, pronounced / The name of Prosper; it did bass my trespass" (lines 122 – 123)

37. When Gonzalo uses the word "ecstasy" in line 136, he means

A. intense feeling or activity

B. loss of self-control

C. spiritual uplifting

D. intense delight

Reading Five

from DEACON BRODIE, or THE DOUBLE LIFE: A MELODRAMA IN FIVE ACTS AND EIGHT TABLEAUX

CHARACTERS

WILLIAM BRODIE, Deacon of the Wrights, housebreaker and master carpenter

OLD BRODIE, the Deacon's father

WILLIAM LAWSON, Procurator-Fiscal, the Deacon's uncle

WALTER LESLIE

MARY BRODIE, the Deacon's sister

SYNOPSIS OF ACTS AND TABLEAUX

ACT I:

TABLEAU I The Double Life

TABLEAU II Hunt the Runner

TABLEAU III Mother Clarke's

ACT II:

TABLEAU IV Evil and Good

ACT III:

TABLEAU V King's Evidence

TABLEAU VI Unmasked

ACT IV:

TABLEAU VII The Robbery

ACT V:

TABLEAU VIII The Open Door

William Brodie (1741–88) actually lived in Edinburgh, Scotland, and was Deacon of Wrights (Head of the Guild of Master Carpenters). He was a very respectable and prosperous citizen, but he led a secret double life: he gambled and lost heavily, kept two mistresses and had five children by them, and he used his craftsman's skills to burgle the houses of his fellow tradesmen. According to legend, he was the first criminal to be hanged on the new kind of gallows that he himself had designed and built.

The Stage represents a room in the Deacon's house, furnished partly as a sittingroom, partly as a bedroom, in the style of an easy burgess of about 1780. C., a door; L. C., a second and smaller door; R. C., practicable window; L., alcove, supposed to contain a bed; at the back, a clothes-press and a corner cupboard containing bottles, etc. MARY BRODIE at needlework; OLD BRODIE, a paralytic, in a wheeled chair, at the fireside, L.

SCENE I

To these LESLIE, C.

LESLIE: May I come in, Mary?

MARY: Why not?

LESLIE: I scarce knew where to find you.

MARY: The dad and I must have a corner, must we not? So when my brother's friends are in the parlour he allows us to sit in his room: 'Tis a great favour, I can tell you; the place is sacred.

LESLIE: Are you sure that 'sacred' is strong enough?

MARY: You are satirical!

LESLIE: I? And with regard to the Deacon? Believe me, I am not so ill-advised: You have trained me well, and I feel by him as solemnly as a true-born Brodie.

MARY: And now you are impertinent! Do you mean to go any further? We are a fighting race, we Brodies: Oh, you may laugh, sir! But 'tis no child's play to jest us on our Deacon, or, for that matter, on our Deacon's chamber either: It was his father's before him: he works in it by day and sleeps in it by night; and scarce anything it contains but is that labour of his hands: Do you see this table, Walter? He made it while he was yet a 'prentice: I remember how I used to sit and watch him at his work: It would be grand, I thought, to be able to do as he did, and handle edge-tools without cutting my fingers, and getting my ears pulled for a meddlesome minx! He used to give me his mallet to keep and his nails to hold; and didn't I fly when he called for them! And wasn't I proud to be ordered about with them! And then, you know, there is the tall cabinet yonder; that it was that proved him the first of Edinburgh joiners, and worthy to be their Deacon and their head: And the father's chair, and the sister's workbox, and the dear dead mother's footstool – what are they all but proofs of the Deacon's skill, and tokens of the Deacon's care for those about him?

LESLIE: I am all penitence: Forgive me this last time, and I promise you I never will again.

MARY: Candidly, now, do you think you deserve forgiveness?

LESLIE: Candidly, I do not.

MARY: Then I suppose you must have it: What have you done with Willie and my uncle?

LESLIE: I left them talking deeply: The dear old Procurator has not much thought just now for anything but those mysterious burglaries –

MARY: I know! –

LESLIE: Still, all of him that is not magistrate and official is politician and citizen; and he has been striving his hardest to undermine the Deacon's principles, and win the Deacon's vote and interest.

MARY: They are worth having, are they not?

LESLIE: The Procurator seems to think that having them makes the difference between winning and losing.

MARY: Did he say so? You may rely upon it that he knows: there are not many in Edinburgh who can match with our Will.

LESLIE: There shall be as many as you please, and not one more.

MARY: How should I like to have heard you! What did uncle say? Did he speak of the Town Council again? Did he tell Will what a wonderful Bailie he would make? O why did you come away?

LESLIE: I could not pretend to listen any longer: The election is months off yet; and if it were not – if it were tramping upstairs this moment – drums, flags, cockades, guineas, candidates, and all! – how should I care for it? What are Whig and Tory to me?

MARY: O fie on you! It is for every man to concern himself in the common weal: Mr. Leslie – Leslie of the Craig! – should know that much at least.

LESLIE: And be a politician like the Deacon? All in good time, but not now: I hearkened while I could, and when I could not more I slipped out and followed my heart: I hoped I should be welcome.

MARY: I suppose you mean to be unkind.

LESLIE: Tit for tat: Did you not ask me why I came away? And is it unusual for a young lady to say 'Mr.' to the man she means to marry?

MARY: That is for the young lady to decide, sir.

LESLIE: And against that judgment there shall be no appeal?

MARY: O, if you mean to argue! –

LESLIE: I do not mean to argue: I am content to love and be loved: I think I am the happiest man in the world.

MARY: That is as it should be; for I am the happiest girl.

LESLIE: Why not say the happiest wife? I have your word, and you have mine: Is not that enough?

MARY: Have you so soon forgotten? Did I not tell you how it must be as my brother wills? I can do only as he bids me.

LESLIE: Then you have not spoken as you promised?

MARY: I have been too happy to speak.

LESLIE: I am his friend: Precious as you are, he will trust you to me: He has but to know how I love you, Mary, and how your life is all in your love of me, to give us his blessing with a full heart.

MARY: I am sure of him: It is that which makes my happiness complete: Even to our marriage I should find it hard to say 'Yes' when he said 'No.'

LESLIE: Your father is trying to speak: I'll wager he echoes you.

MARY (to OLD BRODIE): My poor dearie! Do you want to say anything to me? No? Is it to Mr. Leslie, then?

LESLIE: I am listening, Mr. Brodie.

MARY: What is it, daddie?

OLD BRODIE: My son – the Deacon – Deacon Brodie – the first at school.

LESLIE: I know it, Mr. Brodie: Was I not the last in the same class? (to MARY.) But he seems to have forgotten us.

MARY: O yes! His mind is well-nigh gone: He will sit for hours as you see him, and never speak nor stir but at the touch of Will's hand or the sound of Will's name.

LESLIE: It is so good to sit beside you: By and by it will be always like this: You will not let me speak to the Deacon? You are fast set upon speaking yourself? I could be so eloquent, Mary – I would touch him: I cannot tell you how I fear to trust my happiness to anyone else – even to you!

MARY: He must hear of my good fortune from none but me: And besides, you do not understand: We are not like families, we Brodies: We are so clannish, we hold so close together.

LESLIE: You Brodies, and your Deacon!

OLD BRODIE: Deacon of his craft, sir – Deacon of the Wrights – my son! If his mother – his mother – had but lived to see!

MARY: You hear how he runs on: A word about my brother and he catches it: 'Tis as if he were awake in his poor blind way to all the Deacon's care for him and all the Deacon's kindness to me: I believe he only lives in the thought of the Deacon. There, it is not so long since I was one with him: But indeed I think we are all Deacon-mad, we Brodies: Are we not, daddie dear?

BRODIE (without, and entering): You are a mighty magistrate, Procurator, but you seem to have met your match.

SCENE II

To these, BRODIE and LAWSON.

MARY (curtseying): So, uncle! you have honoured us at last.

LAWSON: Quam primum, my dear, quam primum.

BRODIE: Well, father, do you know me? (he sits beside his father and takes his hand.)

OLD BRODIE: William – ay – Deacon: Greater man – than – his father.

BRODIE: You see, Procurator, the news is as fresh to him as it was five years ago: He was struck down before he got the Deaconship, and lives his lost life in mine.

LAWSON: Ay, I mind: He was aye ettling after a bit handle to his name: He was kind of hurt when first they made me Procurator.

MARY: And what have you been talking of?

LAWSON: Just o' thae robberies, Mary: Baith as a burgher and a Crown offeecial, I tak' the maist absorbing interest in thae robberies.

LESLIE: Egad, Procurator, and so do I.

BRODIE (with a quick look at Leslie): A dilettante interest, doubtless! See what it is to be idle.

LESLIE: Faith, Brodie, I hardly know how to style it.

BRODIE: At any rate, 'tis not the interest of a victim, or we should certainly have known of it before; nor a practical tool-mongering interest, like my own; nor an interest professional and official, like the Procurator's: You can answer for that, I suppose?

LESLIE: I think I can; if for no more: It's an interest of my own, you see, and is best described as indescribable, and of no manner of moment to anybody: It will take no hurt if we put off its discussion till a month of Sundays.

BRODIE: You are more fortunate than you deserve: What do you say, Procurator?

LAWSON: Ay is he! There is no a house in Edinburgh safe: The law is clean helpless, clean helpless! A week syne it was auld Andra Simpson's in the Lawnmarket: Then naething would set the catamarans but to forgather privily wi' the Provost's ain butler, and tak' unto themselves the Provost's ain plate: And the day, information was laid before me offeecially that the limmers had made infraction, vi et clam, into Leddy Mar'get Dalziel's, and left her leddyship wi' no sae muckle's a spune to sup her parritch wi': It's unbelievable, it's awful, it's anti-christian!

MARY: If you only knew them, uncle, what an example you would make! But tell me, is it not strange that men should dare such things, in the midst of a city, and nothing, nothing be known of them—nothing at all?

LESLIE: Little, indeed! But we do know that there are several in the gang, and that one at least is an unrivalled workman.

LAWSON: Ye're right, sir; ye're vera right, Mr. Leslie: It had been deponed to me offeecially that no a tradesman – no the Deacon here himsel' – could have made a cleaner job wi' Andra Simpson's shutters: And as for the lock o' the bank – but that's an auld sang.

BRODIE: I think you believe too much, Procurator: Rumour's an ignorant jade, I tell you: I've had occasion to see some little of their handiwork – broken cabinets, broken shutters, broken doors – and I find them bunglers: Why, I could do it better myself!

LESLIE: Gad, Brodie, you and I might go into partnership: I back myself to watch outside, and I suppose you could do the work of skill within?

BRODIE: An opposition company? Leslie, your mind is full of good things: Suppose we begin to-night, and give the Procurator's house the honours of our innocence?

MARY: You could do anything, you two!

LAWSON: Onyway, Deacon, ye'd put your ill-gotten gains to a right use; they might come by the wind but they wouldna gang wi' the water; and that's aye a solatium, as we say: If I am to be robbit, I would like to be robbit wi' decent folk; and no think o' my bonnie clean siller dirling among jads and dicers: Faith, William, the mair I think on't, the mair I'm o' Mr. Leslie's mind: Come the night, or come the morn, and I'se gie ye my free permission, and lend ye a hand in at the window forbye!

BRODIE: Come, come, Procurator, lead not our poor clay into temptation: (LESLIE and MARY talk apart.)

LAWSON: I'm no muckle afraid for your puir clay, as ye ca't. But hark i' your ear: ye're likely, joking apart, to be gey and sune in partnership wi' Mr. Leslie: He and Mary are gey and pack, a body can see that. Man, because my wig's pouthered do ye think I havena a green heart? I was aince a lad mysel', and I ken fine by the glint o' the e'e when a lad's fain and a lassie's willing: And, man, it's the town's talk; communis error facit jus, ye ken.

OLD BRODIE: Oh!

LAWSON: See, ye're hurting your faither's hand.

BRODIE: Dear dad, it is not good to have an ill-tempered son.

LAWSON: What the deevil ails ye at the match? 'Od, man, he has a nice bit divot o' Fife corn-land, I can tell ye, and some Bordeaux wine in his cellar! But I needna speak o' the Bordeaux; ye'll ken the smack o't as weel's I do mysel'; onyway it's grand wine: tantum et tale: I tell ye the pro's, find you the con's, if ye're able.

BRODIE: You are talking in the air, as lawyers will: I prefer to drop the subject.

LESLIE: At four o'clock to-morrow? At my house? (to MARY).

MARY: As soon as church is done. (exit MARY.)

LAWSON: Ye needna be sae high and mighty, onyway.

BRODIE: I ask your pardon, Procurator: But we Brodies—you know our failings! A bad temper and a humour of privacy.

LAWSON: Weel, I maun be about my business: But I could tak' a doch-an-dorach, William; superflua non nocent, as we say; an extra dram hurts naebody, Mr. Leslie.

BRODIE (with bottle and glasses): Here's your old friend, Procurator: Help yourself, Leslie: Oh no, thank you, not any for me: You strong people have the advantage of me there: With my attacks, you know, I must always live a bit of a hermit's life.

LAWSON: 'Od, man, that's fine; that's health o' mind and body: Mr. Leslie, here's to you, sir: 'Od, it's harder to end than to begin wi' stuff like that.

— *by* W. E. Henley and R. L. Stevenson
Henley (1849–1903) is best remembered for the lines, I am master of my fate: / I am captain of my soul. Robert Louis Stevenson (1850–94) is best remembered for his novel Treasure Island

38. The most likely reason for the inclusion of the tableaux is that they

A. add variety to the play

B. show off the costumes and the detailed set

C. are a dramatic way of presenting the situation

D. are an ironical commentary on the audience's expectations

39. When Mary says "You are satirical!" (line 14), the word "satirical" is

A. correct

B. incorrect; she should use the word ironical

C. correct, but the word sarcastic would be better

D. partly correct, but the word ridiculing would be better

40. Leslie's tone as he speaks to Mary in the dialogue beginning in line 8 is best described as

A. jeering

B. teasing

C. satirical

D. mocking

41. When Brodie says in lines 176 to 177 "With my attacks, you know," he is referring to his

A. injuries

B. poor health

C. criminal behaviour

D. disapproval of liquor

42. The detail that best shows Deacon Brodie's hold over his family is

A. "'Tis a great favour, I can tell you; the place is sacred" (line 12)

B. "and wasn't I proud to be ordered about with them!" (line 25)

C. "Did I not tell you how it must be as my brother wills? I can only do as he bids me" (lines 68–69)

D. "But indeed I think we are all Deacon-mad, we Brodies" (line 99)

43. The detail that best displays the Deacon's dislike of Mary's plan to marry Leslie is

A. "A dilettante interest, doubtless! See what it is to be idle" (line 116)

B. "You are more fortunate than you deserve" (line 124)

C. "See, ye're hurting your faither's hand" (line 161)

D. "You are talking in the air, as lawyers will: I prefer to drop the subject" (line 167)

44. The procurator most likely uses Latin phrases because he is

A. a pompous old fool

B. hoping to impress the Deacon

C. often under the influence of alcohol

D. a magistrate and used to using Latin in court

45. Which of the following quotations contains the best example of dramatic irony?

A. "You have trained me well, and I feel by him as solemnly as a true-born Brodie." (lines 15–16)

B. "…he has been striving his hardest to undermine the Deacon's principles, and win the Deacon's vote and interest." (lines 37–39)

C. "At any rate, 'tis not the interest of a victim, or we should certainly have known of it before; nor a practical tool-mongering interest, like my own" (lines 118–119)

D. "Why, I could do it better myself!" (line 141)

46. Which of the following details best shows that the Procurator is very talkative?

A. "Baith as a burgher and a Crown offeecial, I tak' the maist absorbing interest in thae robberies" (lines 113–114)

B. "Come the night, or come the morn, and I'se gie ye my free permission, and lend ye a hand in at the window forbye" (lines 151–152)

C. "I was aince a lad mysel', and I ken fine by the glint o' the e'e when a lad's fain and a lassie's willin" (lines 157–158)

D. "But I needna speak o' the Bordeaux; ye'll ken the smack o't as weel's I do mysel'; onyway it's grand wine" (lines 164–165)

47. The tone of this extract is best described as

A. grim

B. comic

C. ironic

D. light-hearted

Reading Six

NOT MARBLE, NOR THE GILDED MONUMENTS

Not marble, nor the gilded monuments
Of princes, shall outlive this powerful rhyme;
But you shall shine more bright in these contents
Than unswept stone, besmeared with sluttish time.
When wasteful war shall statues overturn,
And broils root out the work of masonry,
Nor Mars his sword nor war's quick fire shall burn
The living record of your memory.
'Gainst death and all-oblivious enmity
Shall you pace forth; your praise shall still find room
Even in the eyes of all posterity
That wear this world out to the ending doom.
So, till the judgement that yourself arise,
You live in this, and dwell in lovers' eyes.

—*by* William Shakespeare (1564–1616)

48. The main purpose of the rhyming couplet (lines 13–14) is to

A. provide closure to the sonnet

B. immortalize the speaker's love

C. summarize the ideas in the rest of the sonnet

D. express despair resulting from "doom" (line 12) and "judgement" (line 13)

49. The best interpretation of the phrase "and dwell in lovers' eyes" (line 14) is that the

A. subject of this poem will dwell wherever love is expressed between lovers

B. most significant quality about the speaker's love is her expressive eyes

C. subject of this poem will be immortalized by this poem's stating she will live in her lover's eyes

D. eyes of lovers will serve as a "judgement" or "standard" for other lovers

50. The theme of the immortality of art is most strongly represented in the quotation

A. "Not marble, nor the gilded monuments / Of princes, shall outlive this powerful rhyme" (lines 1–2)

B. "you shall shine more bright in these contents / Than unswept stone, besmeared with sluttish time" (lines 3–4)

C. "When wasteful war shall statues overturn, / And broils root out the work of masonry" (lines 5–6)

D. "'Gainst death and all-oblivious enmity / Shall you pace forth" (lines 9–10)

51. The "you" that the speaker addresses in this poem is

A. the poem itself

B. the reader of the poem

C. "all posterity" (line 11)

D. the speaker's love (line 14)

52. The most complete statement of this poem's controlling idea is that

A. love is stronger than death

B. deathless poetry can make someone immortal

C. this poem will keep the lover alive in memory until she lives again

D. poetry is stronger than war and death and lasts longer than brick or marble

53. This sonnet most clearly follows the pattern of

A. two quatrains containing premises (or statements) followed by a third quatrain containing a conclusion derived from the first two

B. one quatrain containing a statement (or thesis) followed by a second quatrain containing a contradictory statement (or antithesis) and a third quatrain containing a conclusion (or synthesis)

C. two groups of lines containing contradictory statements: an octave containing a statement (or argument) followed by a sextet containing an opposing statement (or contradiction)

D. three quatrains containing statements that express the same premise in different ways followed by a couplet sums up the rest of the poem

Reading Seven

from WALDEN, or, LIFE IN THE WOODS

The mass of men lead lives of quiet desperation. What is called resignation is confirmed desperation. From the desperate city you go into the desperate country, and have to console yourself with the bravery of minks and muskrats. A stereotyped but unconscious despair is concealed even under what are called the games and amusements of mankind. There is no play in them, for this comes after work. But it is a characteristic of wisdom not to do desperate things.

When we consider what, to use the words of the catechism, is the chief end of man, and what are the true necessaries and means of life, it appears as if men had deliberately chosen the common mode of living because they preferred it to any other. Yet they honestly think there is no choice left. But alert and healthy natures remember that the sun rose clear. It is never too late to give up our prejudices. No way of thinking or doing, however ancient, can be trusted without proof. What everybody echoes or in silence passes by as true to-day may turn out to be falsehood to-morrow, mere smoke of opinion, which some had trusted for a cloud that would sprinkle fertilizing rain on their fields. What old people say you cannot do you try and find that you can. Old deeds for old people, and new deeds for new. Old people did not know enough once, perchance, to fetch fresh fuel to keep the fire a-going; new people put a little dry wood under a pot, and are whirled round the globe with the speed of birds, in a way to kill old people, as the phrase is. Age is no better, hardly so well, qualified for an instructor as youth for it has not profited so much as it has lost. One may almost doubt if the wisest man has learned anything of absolute value by living. Practically, the old have no very important advice to give the young, their own experience has been so partial, and their lives have been such miserable failures, for private reasons, as they must believe; and it may be that they have some faith left which belies that experience, and they are only less young than they were. I have lived some thirty years on this planet, and I have yet to hear the first syllable of valuable or even earnest advice form my seniors. They have told me nothing, and probably cannot tell me anything to the purpose. Here is life, an experiment to a great extent untried by me; but it does not avail me that they have tried it. If I have any experience which I think valuable, I am sure to reflect that this my Mentors said nothing about.

One farmer says to me, "You cannot live on vegetable food solely, for it furnishes nothing to make bones with"; and so he religiously devotes a part of his day to supplying his system with the raw material of bones; walking all the while he talks behind his oxen, which, with vegetable-made bones, jerk him and his lumbering plow along in spite of every obstacle. Some things are really necessaries of life in some circles, the most helpless and diseased, which in others are luxuries merely, and in others still are entirely unknown. The whole ground of human life seems to some to have been gone over by their predecessors, both the heights and the valleys, and all things to have been cared for. According to Evelyn, "the wise Solomon prescribed ordinances for the very distances of trees; and the Roman praetors have decided how often you may go into your neighbor's land to gather the acorns which fall on it without trespass, and what share belongs to that neighbour." Hippocrates has even left directions how we should cut our nails; that is, even with the ends of the fingers, neither shorter nor longer. Undoubtedly the very tedium and ennui which presume to have exhausted the variety and joys of life are as old as Adam.

—*by* Henry David Thoreau (1817–62)
American author and philosopher; he was an advocate of independence and simple living; he was also strongly opposed to slavery

54. According to the context of this passage, the "chief end of man" (line 7) is best defined as

A. following the advice of one's community

B. listening to the wisdom of the elderly

C. being guided by ancient traditions

D. making free choices

55. Instead of listening to advice from elders, the speaker recommends that people mainly

A. listen to advice from juniors

B. get as much experience as possible

C. leave civilization to live closer to nature

D. live as an example to those around themselves

56. The most notable aspect of Thoreau's comments about the elderly is

A. his limited contact with the elderly

B. his bias against his own grandparents

C. the totality of his rejection of their advice

D. his fear of what they might have to say to him

57. The most likely reason for Thoreau to allude to Evelyn, Solomon, Hippocrates, and the magistrates of ancient Rome is

A. to quote them to support his thesis

B. because they were distinguished for their wisdom

C. as examples of the emptiness of common experience

D. to mention their ideas to point out the weakness of current opinion

58. The best description of the speaker's tone in this passage is

A. genial

B. spiteful

C. humorous

D. argumentative

Reading Eight

from **THIS LIME-TREE BOWER MY PRISON**

This poem was written during the long-awaited visit of some friends. On the morning the friends arrived, the writer's foot was badly burned in a kitchen accident and he was unable to walk for the entire time of the visit. One day while his friends were out walking, he wrote these lines while sitting in the garden.

Well, they are gone, and here must I remain,
This lime-tree bower my prison! I have lost
Beauties and feelings, such as would have been
Most sweet to my remembrance even when age
Had dimm'd mine eyes to blindness! They, meanwhile,
Friends, whom I never more may meet again,
On springy heath, along the hill-top edge,
Wander in gladness, and wind down, perchance,
To that still roaring dell, of which I told;
The roaring dell, o'erwooded, narrow, deep,
And only speckled by the mid-day sun;
Where its slim trunk the ash from rock to rock
Flings arching like a bridge; – that branchless ash,
Unsunn'd and damp, whose few poor yellow leaves
Ne'er tremble in the gale, yet tremble still,
Fann'd by the water-fall! And there my friends
Behold the dark green file of long lank weeds,
That all at once (a most fantastic sight!)
Still nod and drip beneath the dripping edge
Of the blue clay-stone.

— *by* Samuel Taylor Coleridge (1772–1834)
English poet; with William Wordsworth, he helped change the character of lyric poetry

59. The mood of the speaker is most fully represented in the lines

A. "Well, they are gone" (line 1)

B. "I have lost / Beauties and feelings" (lines 2–3)

C. "Friends, whom I never more may meet again" (line 6)

D. "wander in gladness" (line 8)

60. The exclamation mark in line 2 emphasizes the

A. importance of the lime-tree

B. speaker's feeling of self-pity

C. fact that his friends have left him

D. discomfort of any place that feels like a prison

61. The poem "This Lime-Tree Bower My Prison" is a good example of writing from the Romantic period in that it

A. is very sober and rational

B. is about memory and blindness

C. derives its power from nature imagery

D. describes a disagreement with the speaker's friends

62. The speaker of this poem is apparently speaking to

A. no one

B. himself

C. the reader

D. his absent friends

63. In lines 5 to 19, the speaker's friends

A. see the "still roaring dell" (line 9)

B. cross over the bridge (line 13)

C. see "the dark green file of long lank weeds" (line 17)

D. might have gone to the dell, but the reader cannot know for certain

64. The images found in lines 10 to 17 are best described as reinforcing the

A. description of nature

B. romantic mood of the poem

C. author's melancholy feelings

D. mention of old age and blindness in line 5

65. The tone of this poem is best described as

A. romantic

B. melancholy

C. reminiscent

D. self-pitying

ANSWERS AND SOLUTIONS—PRACTICE TEST—READING

1. D	14. A	27. C	40. B	53. D
2. D	15. C	28. A	41. B	54. D
3. C	16. C	29. B	42. C	55. B
4. A	17. B	30. C	43. C	56. C
5. D	18. C	31. D	44. D	57. C
6. A	19. D	32. A	45. D	58. D
7. A	20. D	33. D	46. D	59. B
8. A	21. A	34. C	47. D	60 A
9. C	22. D	35. C	48. C	61. C
10. C	23. B	36. D	49. A	62. C
11. B	24. A	37. B	50. A	63. D
12. C	25. C	38. C	51. D	64. C
13. A	26. C	39. B	52. C	65 B

1. D

To some degree, all of the responses explain the narrator's "surprise" at Catherine being a heroine.

A. Her father was plain, boring, respectable, and he had never suffered any interesting difficulties. Such a father is a handicap for a heroine, but not more than a really determined young woman couldn't overcome.

B. Heroines are supposed to be good at music—it is one of the Romantic conventions of the Gothic—but this response is really only an extension of B.

C. Catherine herself could be lazy, and she was not good at arithmetic, languages, or music. These are more promising handicaps. But look at lines 52 to 73, which show the kind of learning that is really important to a heroine.

D. It is the image of a noisy, wild, grubby child rolling down a slope that really does not fit the ideal of a romantic heroine.

2. D

This is a context question. The best definition for propensities can be found by looking at how it is used. Lines 12 to 18 describe Catherine and they include the words *fond of*, *preferred*, *no taste for*, and *always preferring*.

These words all refer to matters of disposition, taste, or **inclination**. *Ideas*, *skills*, and *abilities* are all things learned or achieved—perhaps in spite of one's *propensities* or *inclinations*.

3. C

This question is about the supposed qualities of a heroine and requires the use of inference and interpretation.

A. Being a middle child in a large family is not heroic, but this handicap is not part of the heroine herself.

B. The narrator implies that a heroine ought to be talented at music, but there is no statement that Catherine shirked music as well as her other lessons, so this handicap does not show her at her worst.

C. This is the response that shows Catherine at her worst: shirking her lessons (that is, avoiding work).

D. A heroine can be proud and willful, but she can't have a bad heart or be bad-tempered. As far as this goes, this response is in Catherine's favour.

4. A

The narrator, of course, does not really mean that Catherine was strange and unaccountable.

A. Saying the opposite of what is meant is irony. This statement is really saying that Catherine was quite ordinary.

B. Strange and unaccountable (even when used ironically) have nothing to do with awkwardness—either physical or social. Also metaphor is a comparison in the form of a direct statement—there is no comparison in the statement.

C. Parody is a comic imitation of a work of art (or of a genre). A parody is a work of art: the whole of Northanger Abbey is a parody,* but the term cannot be applied to this brief statement.

**Northanger Abbey* is also a satire and a love story

5. D

The quote does show that Catherine did not have a bad character after all, but metonymy is a figure of speech that uses an attribute of something to stand for the whole. If Catherine were to be described as Miss Ordinary, then that would be metonymy.

Two of the responses fit the question; which of them is most complete?

A. It is true that much of what is said about Catherine is said in terms of what she cannot do—but none of what is said really matters.

B. Catherine has no abilities that are quite remarkable for someone so young. Her "disabilities" are to be expected in a child.

C. The story-telling is "focussed on heroic deeds in the future," but the question itself is about Catherine, not about her future.

D. None of her supposed faults is more than childish mischief, which is more or less the narrator's point.

6. A

This question requires a prediction. What will the rest of the story be about?

A. The opening of the extract makes it clear that Catherine does become a heroine. The rest of the story must be about how that happens.

B. You have heard quite enough about how ordinary she is. Jane Austen did not become a great writer by not knowing when to stop.

C. Unless there is a plot twist that you cannot foresee, the story is about Catherine, not about her family.

D. Complete biographies belong in biographies, not in novels. A novel rarely includes details that are not part of a story.

7. A

Tone is the way something is said or written; tone is an indication of what a speaker or author is thinking; tone indicates attitude toward the subject and toward the audience.

A. The tone is ironic since nothing that the author said can be understood literally.

B. A Gothic tone would be characteristic of a Gothic novel. Since this is a parody, the tone cannot be Gothic.

C. Derision (the noun form of the adjective derisive) expresses contempt and mockery. Jane Austen's humour is not contemptuous or mocking, even though she is having a lot of fun with the conventions of the Gothic heroine.

D. Insincere means false, not genuine. Although none of the words mean what they say, the intent is not falsehood. The irony is completely sincere.

8. A

Today, sensible means having common sense. However, in this context, sensibility means something very different. The sentence that contains sensibility has a parallel structure that could be simplified like this: without sensibility, without real passion, without real admiration.* The three phrases are not identical, but they are about feelings. In this context, sensibility means feelings. The context has nothing to do with social rank, which is not mentioned until several sentences later. Admiration is only one example of sensibility.

*On an exam, be careful not to misapply word meanings that you already know. A common word can have several unusual meanings. Always pay attention to context.

9. C

This question refers to the entire reading and it requires a judgement. What is the extract about?

A. The only mention of education is in its most limited form: reciting, arithmetic for the purpose of keeping household accounts, French, music, and drawing.

B. The qualities necessary for heroism are the subject of the extract, but only in the context of being a Gothic heroine, and the author is making fun of Gothic heroines.

C. It is the absurdity of Gothic novels that is the writer's subject.

D. In the early 1800s, boys and girls received very different kinds of education (when they received any at all) but that subject is not even mentioned.

10. C

All the choices are literary genres.

A. Burlesque is the humorous treatment of serious matter through grotesque exaggeration or some other incongruity, often mocking. Burlesque does not fit. Jane Austen is often witty and always restrained; she is never grotesque or exaggerated.

B. Romantic can refer to several kinds of stories: love stories, heroic adventure, or medieval adventure. Although Northanger Abbey is in fact a love story, this extract does not allow that judgement.

C. Parody is a humorous imitation of another work or of a genre. This extract parodies the Gothic novel that was common in Jane Austen's day.

D. Gothic depends on certain motifs: a brooding castle (or at least a huge mansion or an ancient abbey), a heroine in distress, a brooding, mysterious hero, curses and prophecies, overwrought emotions, thunder, lightning, torrential rain, gloom, and supernatural horror. The tone of Northanger Abbey does not qualify it as Gothic.

11. B

The question is about limited perception. All of the quotations come from Socrates' description of the cave. However, only one makes it clear that, being unable to turn around, the prisoners can only see what is in front of them. Their perception is limited by their chains: "here they have been from their childhood, and have their legs and necks chained so that they cannot move, and can only see before them, being prevented by the chains from turning round their heads."

12. C

The liberated prisoner will be confused and uncertain (lines 34 to 36), will have to be forced out of the prison (lines 42 to 43) and will experience pain. In the end, the prisoner will congratulate himself on his release (lines 59 to 60).

A. The liberated prisoner will not regret his liberation; in the end the prisoner will be happy about being freed.

B. He will not throw caution to the wind—no, at every step progress is slow.

C. The prisoner would be so used to the imprisonment that he would have to be forced into freedom (line 43).

D. The liberated prisoner will feel pain at first, but notice the words more intense levels. More intense than what? More intense than the earlier levels; but there are no earlier levels of pain.

13. A

All the responses are mentioned as being likely after the prisoner's return. Which is least likely?

A. He would be least likely to be put to death, because this is mentioned only as a threat to stop him talking about what he had seen.

B. He would be unable to see as well as the others because his eyes would now be adjusted to light.

C. He would appear ridiculous because the others would have no context through which to understand his descriptions of the real world.

D. Because he could not see as well in the darkness, he would be at a disadvantage compared to those who had never left.

14. A

Notice the words *in this context*. Myths have more than one purpose, and this "myth" was invented for a particular purpose.

A. The myth does express a truth about the human condition and the limited perception that we all experience.

B. Yes, the myth does provide a vivid image that the reader can "see," but the purpose of the image is to express a truth. The image is not invented for its own sake.

C. Yes, the myth presents a thought that is too difficult for ordinary words, but what kind of thought is it? The thought is a truth about the human condition (A).

D. The moral principle is derived from the truth that has been expressed. The myth is designed to lead up to the truth, but it does not summarize the truth.

15. C

The first paragraph explains "how far our nature is enlightened or unenlightened." Each of the responses has some truth. Which is the best?

A. We are unenlightened because of the immobilizing chains, but is this the complete answer?

B. The shadows give some information, but they also deceive because they are so limited. This response not the best because "enlightened" means more than just having partial, limited knowledge.

C. "Unenlightened because of external causes beyond our control," is a better answer because the chains are only a metaphor for external causes that we do not control.

D. There is some enlightenment because of the shadows of cast by the fire, but consider that a few shadows show very little of the reality outside the cave. We are both enlightened and unenlightened.

16. C

Plato's *Republic*, from which this dialogue is taken, is largely a collection of dialogues, because Plato was recording Socrates' teaching method. These dialogues had a definite purpose.

A. They do help to simplify the story, but the story itself is not really complicated.

B. The reader is not left to infer the meaning of the argument, for Socrates himself explains what the images in the story stand for.

C. This is a technique (the Socratic method) of teaching by proceeding one step at a time through question and answer. At each stage, Glaucon (and the reader) is given a chance to respond to what has just been said.

D. One method of persuasion is to arrange for constant agreement by asking a series questions that will almost certainly be answered affirmatively (Isn't this a beautiful car? Isn't it fun to drive? I bet you'd like to own it?). Thus a final agreement is set up without the need for honest argument and clear logic. An inattentive reader could just agree along with Glaucon. However, the questions are simple and the whole argument is laid out carefully, with every step clearly explained. It seems that the purpose is instruction, not persuasion.

17. B

This question about the narrator's view of human nature requires a value judgement based on understanding of the whole extract.

A. Cynical means distrusting or contemptuous of other peoples motives. But Socrates believes that other people are unenlightened because of factors beyond their control. Even the prisoner who escapes has to be helped (forcibly) to make the first steps. The anger of the prisoners who are told about the real world is also seen as inevitable under the circumstances. So Socrates is not cynical.

B. However, Socrates seems to be realistic about human nature: there are real problems and improvement is hard.

C and D. Optimism and pessimism can describe certain philosophical viewpoints, but in ordinary speech, they simply mean having positive or negative thoughts about life. Not being given any information about the two philosophies, it is best to use the everyday meanings. Socrates is neither optimistic nor pessimistic, he simply describes the situation and says what ought to be done. He does not say how likely or unlikely he thinks the desirable outcome to be.

18. C

This question requires a judgement about degrees of unreality. The most real location is the world outside the cave, but this is not one of the responses. The best answer must be selected from among the choices given. The most real location is the one closest in some way to the real world.

A. The den (cave) is the image of unreality, so it cannot be real at all.

B. The fire casts shadows, and is itself an image of the sun. However, approaching the fire will not bring anyone closer to reality.

C. On the other side of the wall, people from the real world come and go. The objects they carry are only images, but they are more real than shadows, and they come directly from the real world. This is the most real location.

D. Shadows of images are a limited representation of images, not even a representation of reality.

19. D

The meaning of the phrase "show in a figure" must be understood by inference.

A. The shadow play is what is seen when objects are carried past the fire. These shadows are part of the story and it is the story, not just one of its parts, that is "showing in a figure."

B. A figure is like a figure of speech that contains some truth, only figure is larger—this figure is the entire story (myth). So this response is related to the answer, but is not the answer.

C. A figure is the result of calculation in arithmetic, but this meaning has nothing to do with the story.

D. This story is all about explaining a difficult truth. An illustration that demonstrates the truth describes *figure* very well.

20. D

In lines 88 to 89, Socrates is saying that anyone who wants to behave rationally should do something. All of the responses are related to this something.

A. Yes, we should be guided by the light of the sun, but that light is a figure that represents the light of truth.

B. Yes, we should remember that the world is a prison and that the things we see are like the prison in the story.

However, knowing we are in a prison leads to thoughts of escape or at least of the outside.

C. Yes, we should understand that nothing that we see is really true—but this is another way of saying what has been said in response B

D. What Socrates is saying is that good is the source of truth in everything. Good is like the light of the sun by which we see the physical world. Good enlightens us in looking at the real world outside of the cave.

21. A

According to Socrates, there is a way to understand truth.

A. Socrates uses the word *inference* to describe how we come to realize that good is the author (the maker) of what is all that is beautiful and right and the source of the power to act rationally.

B. Socrates explained the truth through a figure, but not through figures of speech, which are much more limited.

C. It is very clear that studying shadows is only studying a limited part of what is real—the prisoners never see the shapes that throw the shadows.

D. The light of the sun is only a figure for the light that comes from the knowledge of good.

22. D

The tone of this poem helps to establish the theme.

A. The inevitable is not directly mentioned, although it might reasonably be inferred as part of the poet's thought as he wrote the poem.

B. The silence of eternity is a commonplace phrase, a cliche, but it is not mentioned directly or indirectly in the poem. The images of silence represent peace.

C. There is no way of inferring from the poem that death is approaching the poet (except in the general sense that death is at this moment approaching all of us). This poem could be a work of keen imagination written early in life.*

D. The images in lines 5 to 6, 7 to 8, and 15 to 16 clearly show the acceptance of death, expressed peacefully and hopefully.

*Tennyson was indeed fairly old when he wrote this, and we can infer that he saw death approaching, but that inference comes from other writings, not from this poem.

23. B

"Moaning of the bar" is a personification, a figure of speech. What does it mean? First of all, the bar is the ridge of gravel found at the shallow mouth of a harbour. Lines 5 to 6 refer to the tide, which would make a noisy rushing over the bar when rising and falling. Lines 2, 4, 8, 10, 12, 14, and 16 contain figures of speech for death. (The regularity of the numbers is probably no accident, of course. Great artists and writers do nothing by accident.)

A. Weeping is suggested by the personification in moaning, and the rush of water over the bar suggests weeping. This may be a secondary meaning implied in the metaphor (especially considering "sadness of farewell" in line 11).

B. Suffering is the best answer, since "crossing the bar" is death itself (lines 4, 8, 13, 14, 16). The surface meaning (see D) is the sound of the tide over the bar, but it is immediately followed by lines 5 to 6: "But such a tide as moving seems asleep, / Too full for sound and foam." The tide is moving the ship out of the harbour of this life, across the bar, which is death, into the wide sea, which is eternity.

The poet hopes to be swept out of life on a full tide and to sweep over the death silently, "too full for sound or foam."

C. There would be shipboard sounds accompanying the leaving of harbour, but the word moaning disqualifies anything to do with a ship.

D. The rush of the tide over gravel is the surface meaning; however, since the poem is about death, the surface meaning is not enough.

24. A

The poet left the exact meaning of Pilot to be inferred by the reader.

A. God is the most likely choice. Pilot is capitalized because it has special importance—this is no ordinary ship's pilot. Some other figure of great significance, an angel, or an already dead friend might also fit, but they are not in the responses.

B. Eternity is the destination. It cannot be the guide as well.

C. and D. These both refer to guides—but only at the level of the surface meaning.

25. C

An expression of attitude is closely related to tone, although tone is not asked for.

A. and B. are closely related in thought (see question 24). Both refer to a hope for a peaceful death.

C. The last expresses the hope that underlies everything in this poem. The poet refers to himself going home. The image of returning home best expresses his attitude.

D. These lines seem to be sombre, full of gloom: twilight, evening bell, and the dark. Life draws to a close, the first signs of death appear, then death itself.

26. C

Determining the reason for the three non-standard capitalizations requires a judgement of the author's intent.

A. Poetic licence refers to a non-standard usage in a poem, either for a special effect or to make the poem conform to a pattern of metre or rhyme. The three capital letters do produce an effect—but why is the poet taking poetic licence?

B. Yes, proper nouns are always capitalized, but these are not proper nouns—at least, not in the sense that is meant when quoting the rule.

C. "Time," "Place," and the "Pilot" are all very important in the poet's thought. In fact, because of that, they assume the status of proper nouns. That is why they are capitalized.

D. English did once have different rules for capitalization, but if you have read anything old enough to follow those rules, you will know that those rules are not followed in this poem. Otherwise, it is easy to see that all the other nouns are treated exactly as they are today: lower case letters for common nouns. Only three are different.

27. C

The word "that" does not have an antecedent. The poem itself makes the unexpressed antecedent clear.

A. The "I" who is embarking on a journey would be a good choice, but the word journey is too general. This is the last journey, the one that takes us beyond time and space. Alternative C is a more complete.

B. The tide is the image that fills the poem, but there are enough clues that the that is being carried by the tide. It is not the tide.

C. The soul leaving the boundary of time and space is "that which drew from out the boundless deep."

D. The pilot is met only after the ship leaves harbour.

28. A

Tone is an indication of what a speaker or author is thinking; tone indicates attitude toward the subject and toward the audience.

A. Calm means peaceful, quiet, without anxiety.

B. Anxious means uncertain, worried, afraid.

C. Grieving means feeling great sadness or sorrow.

D. Hopeless means without hope, despairing. Any of these might be a normal reaction when someone faces death. Of these, calm, peaceful, without anxiety best describes the poet's attitude and the tone of the poem.

29. B

This question must be answered by studying the printed words and lines and the scansion of the poetry.

A. When something is edited out of a text, the printers close up the space. Also, Shakespeare used so few directions that any he did use are valuable and unlikely to be discarded.

B. Look again at the lines of both the speaker and the speaker before. Counting the syllables shows that Shakespeare was indeed preserving the metre, the five feet of two syllables each, that make up iambic pentameter. The printing makes this clear to both readers and actors so the lines can be delivered properly.

C. A few lines have more or less than ten syllables to avoid monotony; otherwise, only a few lines vary in length.

D. There is sometimes a slight variation in length of line that relieves the monotony that would be produced by mechanically even lines. However, the short first line actually preserves the standard line. (See B).

30. C

Gonzalo's words have two purposes. On the one hand, he is speaking to his companions, on the other hand, he starts the scene and gives some important information.

A. The phrase contains two, possibly three, figures of speech. It is not itself an example of a figure of speech.

B. The whole play is an example of dramatic poetry.

C. Gonzalo is scene-setting. He is saying to the audience, in words that sound natural when directed to his companions, that they have been walking in circles. The audience is now filled in on what has been happening with this group of characters.

D. The words maze, forth-rights, and meanders might be considered to be metaphorical, but it is better to regard them as simple nouns. For example, a winding path may be called a meander after the winding River Meander (in Asia Minor, in what is now Turkey) or a twisted, confusing path might be called a maze, after the hedge-mazes planted as puzzles. When such a noun is used for the first time, it is a metaphor, but if such metaphors are useful, they become standard nouns and the origin is forgotten. Are these nouns examples of dead metaphors? It is hard to say. Alternative C remains the best answer.

31. D

Only one of the responses is connected both with hope and also with Alonso's lines spoken just before Antonio speaks.

A. No doubt Alonso is weakened by exhaustion; he says as much. However, although exhaustion may have caused his loss of hope, exhaustion has nothing to do with the fact that he had been hoping for something.

B. No doubt Alonso does feel trapped on the island, and losing hope could refer to losing hope of escape. However, there is evidence that Alonso's hope was for something else.

C. Remorse will come later, after Ariel speaks.

D. Alonso does think that his son is dead: he is drown'd / Whom thus we stray to find. That is the reason he has lost hope.

32. A

Notice that the question contains the word examples. A single example will not be sufficient.

A. An allusion is an indirect reference to something—often historical, classical, or biblical—that the writer assumes will be familiar to the audience. Unicorns and the phoenix (there is only one) are creatures of fable and legend. They are not explained, merely alluded to.

B. A metaphor is a comparison made as a direct statement rather than by using either of the words like or as.

C. Metonymy is a figure of speech that replaces the name of one thing with the name of something closely associated with it.

D. Synecdoche is a figure of speech similar to metonymy. Synecdoche replaces the names of something with the name of a part of that thing.

33. D

A careful reading reveals Alonso's statement of his reason for his exit. Although two of the responses give reasons that are related to Alonso's actual purpose, his own words give the correct answer.

A. Alonso does go to look for his missing son, but only in the sense that he thinks his son is drowned at the bottom of the sea and he is going to join him.

B. Because the depth and subtlety of Shakespeare's writing allows layers of interpretation, fleeing from his guilt would be a defensible answer. Alonso admits his guilt and then rushes away, intending to die. A close reading of lines 92 to 102 shows that Ariel threatens Alonso (and the others) with lingering perdition (slow damnation) which he can only avoid by repenting and living an honest life from now on. We might say that in admitting his guilt, but then planning suicide, Alonso shows remorse, which is often only regret at being caught out, but not repentance, which includes sorrow and the intent to do better. So in a sense Alonso is fleeing from his guilt. However, there is a simpler answer.

C. It is Antonio and Sebastian who want to fight. They respond to the exposure of their crimes with anger, not remorse. They call the spirits fiends (demons) and want to fight them.

D. Alonso does go to seek death: *my son i' the ooze is bedded, and / I'll seek him deeper than e'er plummet sounded / And with him there lie mudded.*

34. C

Ariel appearing like a harpy and making the food vanish actually suggests all the responses. Skilled writers often pack multiple meanings into images, actions, and scenes. However, one response fits the question best.

A. The shipwrecked men who have been wandering the island to the point of exhaustion are certainly hungry. That is part of the reason for the scene.

B. Naturally, a recognizable image from mythology is an allusion to mythology. The point of an illusion is to make some connection between things—in this case the action of Ariel in making the food vanish is in some ways like the actions of the harpies in a Greek myth. The point of the connection is found in alternative C.

C. Whether or not we know the story of Jason and the Argonauts, we know that the harpies stole food from King Phineas as a punishment for a crime. * So Ariel, like a harpy, takes away the food that King Alonso is about to eat.

D. The harpies in Greek mythology were images of horror. This fact, also known to the audience, echoes Alonso's horror when he is forced to face his crimes. Like alternatives A, B, and C, that echo is part of the reason for the scene.

35. C

Gonzalo's words to Alonso are another example of dialogue that has purposes on different levels.

A. Gonzalo certainly wants to know the reason for Alonso's strange look. Changing Alonso's mood would have to wait on learning what it is all about.

B. Alonzo is indeed on the point of confessing his crime, but Gonzalo cannot know that.

C. The simplest and clearest answer is that only the three guilty ones see and hear Ariel. Gonzalo and the others see the food disappear and they see the spirits take away the table. They are still staring when Gonzalo notices Alonso's strange look. In the story, Gonzalo's words to Alonso are his natural reaction—as part of the structure of the play, Gonzalo's words to Alonso are Shakespeare's way of making sure that we know that Ariel was seen only by the three guilty men.

D. Gonzalo's comment "I' the name of something holy" suggests that he is alarmed.
We might suspect that he has doubts about Alonso's sanity—after all, they have only just survived a shipwreck and Alonso has just given up hope for his son. However, Gonzalo has hardly had time to think about the situation.
At this point, he is simply reacting.

36. D

All the lines show some change in Alonso. Alternatives A and B show that he has given up hope of finding his son alive. Alternative C shows his loss of hope in general—since the best part of his life is past, he might as well eat the magical food; the danger doesn't matter. Alternative **D** shows that he recognizes his crimes: he has driven Prospero from Milan and he believes that he has murdered both Prospero and his infant daughter. Mourning and loss of hope are not as great a change as admitting guilt. This is made especially clear in the lines that follow the quote in alternative **D** when Alonso, convinced of his guilt and convinced that his crimes have caused the death of his son, decides to drown himself.

37. B

The word "ecstasy" has all the meanings that are given in the responses. Gonzalo's meaning is made clear by his other words and by the words and actions of the others.

A. Alonzo, moved by guilt and grief, has rushed off to throw himself into the sea (lines 124 to 125). He is moved by intense feeling. Antonio and Sebastian have rushed off, sword in hand, to fight. They are moved to intense activity, but not to intense feeling—for they will not admit their guilt. Thus this response applies only partially.

B. Rushing headlong to suicide or to fight spirits is a clear example of loss of self-control. Gonzalo sends off the younger lords to stop Alonso, Antonio, and Sebastian from harming themselves or others.

C. Feelings of remorse, guilt, and despair (Alonso) or violence (Antonio and Sebastian) are not examples of spiritual uplifting.

D. Remorse, guilt, despair, and violence are not examples of intense delight.

38. C

When a tableau is staged, the actors are motionless and silent. For as long as the tableau lasts, the audience simply watches.

A. There is no doubt that tableaux would add variety to a play. However, an author usually has some other purpose besides variety. In a carefully constructed play, everything has dramatic purpose.

B. The set designer would probably take the opportunity to have costumes and sets worth showing off. In some productions, such an opportunity might be reason for inserting tableaux; however, this would not be a dramatic reason—it would not likely be part of an author's intention while writing a play.

C. The titles of the tableaux presented in the whole play and the content of the first tableau show that they are a dramatic way of presenting the situation. The first tableau is the presentation of a family scene in the house of a well-to-do tradesman—and we are aware that it is one half of a double life.

D. Tableaux could be used as an ironical commentary on the audience's expectations, but there is no evidence of that in this extract. In fact, the audience knows what is going on: Brodie was infamous in his day, and the title of the play itself gives away his secret.

39. B

Satire uses some form of laughter to attack or to expose wrongdoing.

A. Leslie is not inviting laughter at Mary's wrongdoing—if her admiration is excessive, it is still not a proper object of satire.

B. The question, "Are you sure sacred is strong enough?" means the opposite of their literal meaning. Ironic would be the accurate description. This is an example of gentle irony.

C. Sarcasm is like irony but it is obvious, it is usually delivered in an unpleasant tone, and it is intended to hurt.

D. Satire sometimes makes use of ridicule, but the rest of Leslie's lines make it clear that he genuinely loves Mary. Ridicule is cruel and hurtful. Ridicule is not likely.

40. B

Leslie's tone as he speaks to Mary in the dialogue beginning in line 2 is best described as teasing.

A. *Jeering* is laughing at or shouting insults at someone in order to show lack of respect.

B. *Teasing* has several meanings. One is to playfully joke with or make fun of. Leslie's words to Mary show love and affection, so when he is laughing at her excessive respect and admiration for her brother, he is teasing.

C. Satirical has been fully answered in the solution to question 39.

D. *Mocking* means scornful laughing or jeering.

41. B

The context of Brodie's remark about his attacks is his declining to join Leslie and Lawson in a drink, saying, "Oh no, thank you, not any for me. You strong people have the advantage of me there: With my attacks, you know, I must always live a bit of a hermit's life."

A. *Attacks* might suggest *injuries*, but there is no suggestion of violence here.

B. An episode of poor health or of a health crisis is sometimes called an attack. Brodie also says "You strong people have the advantage of me," alluding to some weakness in himself. Thus, the best answer is poor health.

C. Since stealing was at that time punishable by death, the Deacon would have been very foolish to allude to his criminal behaviour. His earlier comment, "Why, I could do it better myself!" was different; it was a way saying that the robberies were clumsy, not the work of a master craftsman like himself.

D. Brodie may or may not disapprove of liquor. There is no evidence that he does. The fact that he has bottles and glasses ready to offer drinks to visitors suggests that he does not.

42. C

Each detail shows that Brodie has a hold over his family.

A. Sacred means holy, a strong word to use about one's brother's room. Still, Mary might be using hyperbole. She might even be laughing at herself, or joking with Leslie.

B. Here Mary is remembering her younger self, who was proud to carry out her older brother's orders. That was years ago, and her tone suggests that she is not quite the same now.

C. Mary will not marry without her brother's approval. This is the clearest example of Brodie's hold over his family. To be ready to refuse to marry the man that she loves in order to please her brother shows Brodie's strong influence over his family.*

D. "We are all Deacon-mad" suggests a degree of understanding. Mary is aware that her feelings are unusual.

*At one time, anyone under the age of 21 was a minor and could not marry without the consent of a parent or guardians. If Mary is underage, then since her mother is dead (lines 87 to 88) and her father mentally incapacitated, her brother would be her guardian. But we do not know Mary's age, so C remains the best answer.

43. C

Which detail most strongly shows Brodie's dislike?

A and D. Brodie calls Leslie superficial and idle (line 109) as Leslie owns enough profitable land that he does not have to work with his hands, and he tells Lawson, the Procurator, that he does not want to discuss the subject of Mary and Leslie marrying. These points show his dislike, but do not show just how strong his feelings are.

B. This detail has nothing to do with Leslie and Mary.* It is about Leslie's interest in the burglaries, and it is a foreshadowing of something that will be important later in the play.

C. Brodie is so upset that he unconsciously tightens his grip on his father's hand and doesn't notice, even though he is hurting the old man. This is the strongest indication of his feelings.

*But at a glance, this detail might appear to mean that Brodie is telling Leslie that he is more fortunate than he deserves in winning Mary's love.

44. D

We cannot be entirely sure why the procurator uses Latin phrases, but we can determine the most likely reason.

A. The procurator is old, but he seems too shrewd and humorous for pomposity (an exaggerated manner that shows self-importance).

B. Deacon Brodie has established himself as a leader in the community. He exhibits self-confidence and the habit of giving orders. It is unlikely that the procurator would think that a display of knowledge would impress such a man.

C. The procurator hints strongly at one point that he would like a drink, and he raises his glass with obvious pleasure. He also has a lot to say about Leslie's wine cellar. All this is evidence that he likes "to take a glass," but it is not evidence that he actually drinks too much.

D. Since he is a magistrate and at least some of his Latin is law-related, we can infer that professional habit is the reason for his using Latin.

45. D

Dramatic irony is found when the audience knows something that the characters do not, or when everyone knows something that one character does not.

A. This is Leslie's gently ironical teasing of Mary. It is not dramatic irony unless Leslie suspects Brodie, and we cannot know that from this excerpt.

B. Ironically, the Deacon has no principles. But alternative A is a far stronger example, because it comes from Deacon Brodie himself.

C. Brodie's practical tool-mongering interest is more directly practical than anyone yet realizes. Again, alternative A is a stronger example of dramatic irony, because it is a direct statement about his ability to carry out clever burglaries.

D. Do it better himself? Brodie is the thief. All the burglaries are his work. Since the words are from his own mouth, this is the strongest irony, and therefore the best example.

46. D

The Procurator is very talkative. What is the best example?

A. The Procurator's interest in the burglaries is sensible and natural, and he expresses no more than his interest.

B. Here the Procurator is telling a joke but he is not saying too much.

C. His words about Leslie and Mary wanting to marry are a sensible observation and possibly helpful.

**D. The Procurator starts by telling Brodie that Leslie is a desirable match because he has some good land. Then he goes on at length about the Bordeaux wine in Leslie's wine cellar before remembering that he is arguing the case for Leslie and Mary marrying.
This is the Procurator being talkative.**

47. D

The tone of this extract is best seen in the early conversation between Leslie and Mary, and in the character of the Procurator.

A. There is nothing grim (depressing, forbidding, sternly serious) about this extract. We may infer that the rest of the play will be grimmer, but this extract is from the opening.

B. Some of the dialogue is funny, but not enough to be comic (funny enough to cause laughter).

C. The dramatic irony of the conversation about the burglary is an important element in the extract, but see D.

D. The Procurator gets some of the longest speeches, and he is intended to be a humorous character. Also the exchanges between Leslie and Mary are both loving and light-hearted—people in love do feel light-hearted.

48. C

To answer a question like this, it is necessary to understand the form of an Elizabethan (also called Shakespearean) sonnet.

A. All closing lines provide closure in some way.

B. The sonnet (and thus the couplet) is about making the memory of the poet's love deathless until the Day of Judgement at the end of the world—not forever. When she is raised from the dead, then the poet will not care about memory.

C. In all sonnets, the function of the couplet is to summarize the earlier ideas.

D. None of the imagery in this sonnet suggests despair. The word "doom" is used merely to signify the end of time, and in the final judgement, the poet's love will rise to new life.

49. A

What is the best interpretation of the phrase, "and dwell in lovers' eyes"?

A. The whole of line 14 states that the poet's love will live in the poem and in lovers' eyes. The two statements are intended to be similar in meaning.

B. Lovers' is the plural possessive. It cannot refer to the author's love herself.

C. The subject will not be immortalized by simply stating that she will be. She will be immortalized by the power of the sonnet (lines 1–4).

D. This line is plausible only because of the invented synonym for judgement. Judgement does not mean standard.

50. A

A. The immortality of art is most clearly described in the words that say that this "powerful rhyme" will outlive marble and gilded monuments.

B, C, and D all refer to the beloved, not to art.

51. D

A. Although the sonnet describes its own lasting qualities, it is really about the poet's love, not about itself.

B. The poet's love is addressed as though she is the reader of the poem, but the actual reader is not addressed.

C. Posterity is only mentioned as an example of how long the poet's love will be praised.

D. The woman that the poet loves is addressed throughout the poem: "you pace forth . . . your praise . . . you live in this"

52. C

Again, the words most complete show that all the responses could be defended as statements of the controlling idea.

A. That love is stronger than death is an old theme, but it is not love as an abstract (but real) thing that is celebrated in this sonnet, it is the poet's love—a real woman.

B. The woman herself will not be made immortal by the poetry. Instead, her living memory will last until the Day of Judgement. After that, when the poet's love rises from the dead, we may assume that he has no further need of poetry.

C. That this poem will keep the lover alive in memory until she lives again is clearly stated in the last couplet.

D. The sonnet does claim that it is stronger than war and death and lasts longer than brick or marble—but the poem is important only as far as it preserves the living memory of the beloved.

53. D

This is one of Shakespeare's sonnets, so we can be sure it follows a sonnet form; however, there are variations within that form.

A. Shakespeare wrote sonnets of this kind, but this particular example does not contain a logical argument.

B. There are no contradictory statements in this sonnet.

C. This is a description of the form of a Petrarchian (also called Italian) sonnet.

D. All three quatrains of this sonnet express the same idea of the beloved's memory being kept alive by the power of the verse. This is one of the sonnet forms: the main idea is repeated with variations in all three quatrains, and a rhyming couplet sums up the idea.

54. D

Thoreau states over and over that tradition, the community, and the old are all unreliable guides. The only guidance he values is his own, and he recommends similar free choices to his readers.

55. B

The speaker recommends that people, instead of listening to advice from elders should look for guidance somewhere else.

A. Listening to the wisdom of youth is a modern idea. It is not part of Thoreau's thought.

B. Personal experience is the only guide that Thoreau recognizes.

C. Thoreau did live close to nature, and although he recommends a simpler life, he does not talk about leaving civilization.

D. Although Thoreau is clearly giving advice, he does not speak of setting an example.

56. C

There is one very notable thing about Thoreau's comments about the elderly.

A. Since Thoreau suggests that the old have nothing valuable to pass on, one might infer limited contact with the elderly, but there is nothing in this extract to suggest that the inference is likely.

B. Thoreau's words do suggest the possibility of bias, but if such bias exists, there is no way to judge its origin from this extract.

C. Thoreau does completely reject any advice that might come from the old. The old have no very important advice to give the young, their own experience has been so partial, and their lives have been such miserable failures.

D. There is no evidence in this extract that Thoreau feared anything the elderly might say.

57. C

The advice of the old is completely rejected. Then why would Thoreau mention the famous names of long-dead people?

A. There are no quotations from the people alluded to.

B. The names alluded to were distinguished for wisdom of one kind or another, but Thoreau is not interested in that. If anything he is suggesting that the wisest did not have much to say about important matters. Hippocrates' advice on trimming fingernails seems to be sensible, but that is not what interests Thoreau. It is perhaps the most trivial of Hippocrates' teachings that has been mentioned. That is why Thoreau chose to mention it.

C. He is citing examples of the emptiness of common experience: undoubtedly, the very tedium and ennui* that presume to have exhausted the variety and the joys of life are as old as Adam.

D. The brief mention of ancient ideas is not given in contrast to current opinion. See alternative C.

58. D

Thoreau has a very distinct tone in his writing.

A. Genial means kind, good-natured, pleasant. Thoreau's tone (see line 1) is not genial.

B. Spite is petty malice. Despite some of Thoreau's comments (see line 15), the tone is not spiteful.

C. There is nothing even mildly funny about this excerpt.

D. Thoreau is writing to persuade people to agree with his point of view. He makes statements and gives examples and evidence. His tone is argumentative.

59. B

All four responses show the poet's mood of melancholy and feelings of loss. Three of them refer to his absent friends, and one refers to the imagined experience of nature. The extract itself contains 20 lines, of which 6 lines contain references to the friends. The remaining 14 lines are about nature and contain clear images of trees, plants, stone, and water. There is no doubt about the poet's main interest in this extract. Thus alternative B is the best answer.

60. A

The best response to this question depends on information that in not stated in the poem—the reader needs some background information of the kind that is included in the introduction and footnotes.

A. A garden shelter (bower) under a tree noted for its beauty and the scent of its flowers (in July, when the poem was written) would usually be thought a very pleasant place to be.* The exclamation mark emphasizes the irony of the lime-tree bower now being a prison.

B. The poet does express feelings of self-pity (the pain of the burn may have had something to do with it), but this is not as strong a reason for the exclamation mark as is the irony.

C. "Well, they have gone, and here must I remain, / This lime-tree bower my prison!" Although the absent friends are mentioned, notice how the placement of the exclamation mark emphasizes the lime-tree bower rather than the friends.

D. Both alternatives A and D refer to prison, but alternative D is in general terms. As a rule, a specific response is better.

*lime-tree—recall the footnote attached to the poem. This is a good example of the importance of paying attention to extra information that may be given by examiners.

61. C

The answer to this question depends on knowledge of different styles of poetry.

A. The first two lines with their exclamation mark are enough to show that the poem is not meant to be sober and rational.

B. Memory and blindness lie in the future. The "beauties and feelings" that the poet has missed would be a comfort in old age—this is another example of the Romantic belief in the importance and power of nature. See alternative C.

C. During the Romantic period, natural beauty and the emotions it inspired were very important, especially to poets. The words "Beauties and feelings, such as would have been / Most sweet to my remembrance" are good examples of the Romantic attitude.

D. The poet's friends have gone for a walk; there is no mention of a disagreement.

62. C

Sometimes it is necessary to read carefully to decide who (if anyone) is being addressed in the poem.

A. The poet could be said to be addressing no one, in the sense of no one in particular. However, see alternative B. The poet is speaking to someone, even if the someone is invented for the purpose of the poem.

B. The phrase "of which I told" (line 9) shows that the poet is not speaking to himself; he is reminding someone of what he has already said.

C. The phrases "Well, they are gone" (line 1) and "of which I told" (line 9) clearly indicate that the poet is addressing someone. That someone is the reader, since he is not speaking to himself or to his friends.

D. "Well, they are gone" (line 1). If the friends were being addressed, the pronoun would have to be different: Well, you have gone.

63. D

Coleridge follows his friends in his imagination and describes what his mind's eye sees. Careful reading will show what he knows and what he supposes.

A. and C. If the friends went into the dell, then they would see the things mentioned in these responses, but we do not know for sure where they have gone.

B. A careful reading shows that there is no bridge and no word about crossing—bridge is a figure of speech. Also see alternatives A and C.

D. In the quotation "and wind down, perchance, / To that still roaring dell," the word "perchance" makes the answer clear.
They might have gone to the dell, we cannot know for certain.

64. C

A. and B. The lines do describe nature and reinforce the romantic mood of the poem, but both of these responses are too general.

C. The narrow, dark, damp, dell (narrow valley) with its branchless, almost leafless ash tree all match the author's melancholy feelings.

D. Lines 10 to 17 contain melancholy images, but these images would have been / Most sweet to my remembrance (lines 3–4). The melancholy images would have been pleasant to remember even when old and blind—melancholy feelings can be pleasant and not necessarily the result of age.

65. B

A. The tone of the poem is romantic, but this description is too general. In what way is the tone romantic?

B. A pleasant melancholy when contemplating nature was a feeling valued—even indulged in—by the Romantic poets.
All the thoughts and images in this poem suggest a melancholy tone.

C. Reminiscent (suggesting or recalling the past) does not fit: the poet is imagining the present, not remembering.

D. There may be self-pity in the poem, but nearly all the words and images are about nature, not about the poet and his feelings.

PRACTICE TEST—WRITING

WRITING TASK:

Throughout your life, certain people have influenced your development in positive ways. Think about someone who has been a particularly significant role model for you. What caused you to look up to this individual?

Write an essay in which you discuss a person who has been a positive role model for you. Explain what has made this person such a meaningful influence. Use details and examples to support your ideas.

ANSWERS AND SOLUTIONS—PRACTICE TEST—WRITING

PROFICIENT

STUDENT RESPONSE

The most significant role model in my life has been my mother's older sister, Aunt Ena. Aunt Ena was consistently fashionable, a stylish person who taught me that you don't have to be a celebrity to look your best for your audience. With her globe-trotting confidence, she inspired me to be a world traveller. Aunt Ena was a family leader in cultural sophistication. To her dying day, though, my Aunt's greatest gift was the importance she placed on family.

As a grade one teacher for more than 40 years, Aunt Ena once told me that she dressed up for her students. "The children are just learning their primary colors. When I dress in bold red and black, with shiny red earrings and matching beads, they just stare! Then we talk about all the red things in the classroom, at home, and the red apples in their lunch kits. They love it!" Even when she was finally in a wheelchair, Aunt Ena and I were still shopping for a yellow blouse to wear with her wide-brimmed yellow hat and navy suit.

Aunt Ena also inspired me to become a seasoned world traveller, to explore those magic kingdoms and exotic places she first saw in her National Geographic magazine. Every summer brought a new trip—by air, by land, by sea. Walking along the Great Wall of China, relaxing in a gondola on the canals of Venice, marvelling at the treasures of the Louvre, or lingering in the factory that produced her favourite English bone china, Aunt Ena was a lifelong learner who brought home pictures, experiences, and mementos we could share through the winter at one of her lively dinner parties. When I finger the sparkling stones of an Austrian Crystal necklace she left me, or walk past a small Japanese print on my guest bedroom wall, I remember those times.

Probably because she had travelled so extensively, Aunt Ena loved culture. Whether it was attending Agatha Christie's The Mousetrap in London or a performance by our hometown symphony orchestra, my aunt basked in the riches of art, music, literature, and theatre. If a show came to town, Aunt Ena bought tickets. Well into her eighties, she could join in a knowledgeable discussion of cultural experiences and trends.

Lastly, and most importantly, Aunt Ena taught me to celebrate family. She kept in touch, by letter and phone, across the country, with loved ones near and far. Aunt Ena was the driving force behind her father's 100th birthday party. In a well-guarded journal, she kept track of birthdays, marriages, births, deaths, and milestones. We were a large and extended family, and postage kept going up, but, as well as I can remember, there were always cards in the mail for those special occasions. Single by choice all her life, she hosted grand games nights at Christmas, where we shouted at boisterous games of Rook and devoured abundant plates of Christmas goodies.

A wonderful fashion sense, love of the world's unexplored corners, passion for culture, and devotion to family live on in my memories of Aunt Ena. To be seen as "a bit like your Aunt Ena" is the ultimate compliment for me. The giant atlas she once used lies open on a table in my home, to a map of Italy… where my travels will take me this fall. Where I would take her, if only I could.

In this response, the writer responds to the writing task meaningfully with a thesis that directly addresses the prompt to write about a significant role model.

The thesis is supported by four main ideas: the aunt is a role model in fashion, in travelling, in appreciating culture, and in making family a priority. These ideas are elaborated on throughout the essay with specific examples and details from the writer's memory.

The organization is purposefully controlled by following the order established in the opening paragraph. The focus on the "role model" is maintained throughout by using a personal tone ("Aunt Ena once told me") that reminds the reader that this role model was an important part of the writer's life. The writer seems to have a clear sense of a comfortable, accepting audience that is receptive to the writer's ideas and memories.

There are a variety of sentence types: "The most significant…," "As a grade one teacher…," "They love it!" The writer tries to use precise, descriptive language. Examples of this are "Shiny red earrings," "wide-brimmed yellow hat," and "gondola on the canals of Venice."

The essay shows some signs of being a first draft piece of writing. Some of the wording, for instance, could be rearranged or tightened, but it is essentially error-free. The essay is an example of a **proficient** response.

ACCEPTABLE

STUDENT RESPONSE

Throughout your life, several people will have influenced you as a positive role model. My Aunt Ena was one of those people. She influenced me in her role as an educator and also as a person.

As an educator, my aunt was quite remarkable. She taught children their primary colors by modelling bright clothing with colour-matching jewellery. She designed picture flashcards at home and made learning numbers into a game. She brought a friend who was an author to class to inspire her students to read good books.

I absorbed my aunt's love of reading, but she was more than an educator. Aunt Ena was also an amazing human being. She loved departing on trips, but after all the sightseeing was done, arriving home beat out the Eiffel Tower. Her love of family was legendary. Here was a woman who never forgot a birthday or special occasion.

I miss her, & I miss her extraordinary influence in my life, I hope & pray that I may be more like her as I grow older. Role models are great!

In this response, the writer adequately responds to the prompt—to write about a role model with a thesis paragraph that introduces the aunt's two main roles that influenced the writer's life: her role as an educator and as a fine human being.

The writer is able to support the main ideas introduced with somewhat general details and examples such as "modelled bright clothing" and "loved departing on trips."

The focus on the aunt as a role model is consistent throughout the essay, as is the tone of summarizing for the reader the key influences in the writer's life. There is a general sense of writing for an unknown audience, although it lapses somewhat in the impulsive-sounding outburst at the end: "Role models are great!"

The writer does endeavour to provide some variety in sentence types: "Throughout your life," and "I absorbed." The essay also includes some descriptive language such as "my aunt was quite remarkable" and "her extraordinary influence."

The essay contains a few errors in conventions (such as using the symbol "&" in the last paragraph), but the errors do not interfere with the reader's understanding of the essay. The response is characteristic of a **acceptable** essay.

LIMITED

STUDENT RESPONSE

In my life I have had a lot of role models and I learnt a lot from them, but my best role model was probally my aunt, I learnt a lot from her.

My aunt was a great person. When I saw the question I knew she would be the one, cause her role is more clear than anyone els. I did love her, I realy did, cuz she always sent us kids gifts & cards, rain or shine. She was a great teacher too, the little kids loved her bright cloths.

Well anyway, that's about all there is to say on this topic. I think we shuld all have a role model. All's well that ends well, as they say. Thanks for the Canct to write about my aunt. She was a great lady.

This response does provide a thesis that is related to the writing task: "my best role model was probally my aunt, I learnt a lot from her." The somewhat brief response includes some limited details/examples such as "always sent us kids gifts & cards" and "kids loved her bright clothes."

The focus on the aunt is inconsistent with unrelated statements such as "All's well that ends well." This also makes the tone inconsistent—at times, the writer is enthusiastic about the subject ("I did love her"), and at other times vague and dismissive ("Well anyway, that's about all there is to say on this topic"). The inconsistent focus and tone contribute to a rambling style that demonstrates little or no sense of audience. There are few types of sentences—most are simple subject/verb patterns or run-ons. The language is basic and predictable: "learnt a lot," "us kids," "great teacher," "great lady." The writer makes fairly frequent errors in conventions. The spelling errors in particular may interfere with the reader's understanding of the response. Generally, this response contains characteristics typical of a **limited** essay, which does not measure up to Grade 11 expectations.

Appendices

Some Common Literary Terms

Abstract	Abstract terms and concepts name things that are not knowable through the senses; examples are love, justice, guilt, and honour. See CONCRETE.
Allegory	A story or visual image with a second distinct meaning partially hidden. It involves a continuous parallel between two or more levels of meaning so that its persons and events correspond to their equivalents in a system of ideas or chain of events external to the story.
Alliteration	Repetition of initial consonant sounds
Allusion	Indirect or passing reference to some person, place, or event; or to a piece of literature or art. The nature of the reference is not explained because the writer relies on the reader's familiarity with it.
Analogy	A comparison that is made to explain something that is unfamiliar by presenting an example that is similar or parallel to it in some significant way
Anecdote	A brief story of an interesting incident
Antecedent Action	Action that takes place before the story opens
Antithesis	A contrast or opposition of ideas; the second part of a statement that contrasts opposite ideas
Apathy	Lack of interest
Apostrophe	A speech addressed to a dead or absent person or to an inanimate object (Do not confuse this use of apostrophe with the punctuation mark.)
Archaic	Belonging to an earlier time; words or expressions that have passed out of use are said to be archaic
Aside	Comment made by an actor and supposedly not heard by other actors
Assonance	Repetition of similar or identical vowel sounds
Ballad	A narrative poem that tells a story, often in a straightforward and dramatic manner, and often about such universals as love, honour, and courage. Ballads were once songs. Literary ballads often have the strong rhythm and the plain rhyme schemes of songs. Songs are still written in ballad form, some old ballads are still sung, and some literary ballads have been set to music. Samuel Taylor Coleridge's "The Rime of the Ancient Mariner" is an example of a literary ballad.
Blank Verse	Poetry written in unrhymed iambic pentameters
Caricature	A distorted representation to produce a comic or ridiculous effect
Chronological	In order of time
Cliché	An overused expression; one that has become stale through overuse
Colloquial	Informal, suitable for everyday speech but not for formal writing
Concrete	A concrete thing exists in a solid, physical; and is knowable through the senses; trees, copper, and kangaroos are all examples of concrete things. See ABSTRACT.
Connotation	Implied or additional meaning that a word or phrase imparts. Such meaning is often subjective. See also DENOTATION.
Deduction	A conclusion reached by logic or reasoning, or by examining all the available information
Denotation	The explicit or direct meaning of a word or expression, aside from the impressions it creates. These are the meanings listed in dictionaries. See also CONNOTATION.
Discrepancy	Distinct difference between two things that should not be different, or that should correspond
Dissonance	Harsh sound or discordance; in poetry, a harsh jarring combination of sounds

Epic	A long poem that is often about a heroic character. The style is elevated and the poetry often represents religious or cultural ideals; the *Iliad* and the *Odyssey* are examples of epics
Epilogue	A final address to the audience, often delivered by a character in a drama
Fantasy	A literary genre; generally contains events, characters, or settings that would not be possible in real life
Foreshadowing	A storytelling technique; something early in the story hints at later events
Free Verse	Is usually written in variable rhythmic cadences; it may be rhymed or unrhymed, but the rhymes are likely to be irregular and may not occur at the end of lines
Hyperbole	A figure of speech that uses exaggeration for effect
Imagery	Language that evokes sensory impressions
Imitative Harmony	Words that seem to imitate the sounds to which they refer; *buzz* and *whisper* are examples of imitative harmony; also called ONOMATOPOEIA.
Interior Monologue	Conversation-like thoughts of a character
Irony	The difference—in actions or words—between reality and appearance. Authors use irony for both serious and humorous effects. Irony can also be a technique for indicating, through character or plot development, the writer's own attitude toward some element of the story.
Jargon	Special vocabulary of a particular group or activity; sometimes used to refer to confusing or unintelligible language
Justification	The giving of reasons or support; for example, giving an argument or reason that shows that an action or belief is reasonable or true
Juxtaposition (or contrast)	The deliberate contrast of characters, settings, or situations for effect; the effect may be a demonstration of character or heightening of mood
Lyric	A poem that expresses the private emotions or thoughts of the writer; sonnets, odes, and elegies are examples of lyrics
Metamorphosis	An alteration in appearance or character
Metaphor	Comparison without using the words *like* or *as*
Metrical poetry	Is written in regular, repeating rhythms and may be rhymed or unrhymed; when rhymes are used, they are generally regular, like the rhythm, and are often found at the end of the line
Monologue	A literary form; an oral or written composition in which only one person speaks
Mood	In a story, the atmosphere; when a writer orders the setting, action, and characters of a story so as to suggest a dominant emotion or patterns of emotions, this emotional pattern is the mood of the story. Also a person's state of mind or complex of emotions at any given time.
Motif	A recurring theme, situation, incident, idea, image, or character type that is found in literature
Ode	A poem expressing lofty emotion; odes often celebrate an event or are addressed to nature or to some admired person, place, or thing; an example is "Ode to a Grecian Urn" by John Keats
Onomatopoeia	Words that seem to imitate the sounds to which they refer.
Oxymoron	A combination of two usually contradictory terms in a compressed paradox; for example, "the living dead." An oxymoron is like a metaphor in that it expresses in words some truth that cannot be understood literally; *truthful lies* is an oxymoron that describes metaphors

Parable	A short, often simple story that teaches or explains a lesson—often a moral or religious lesson
Paradox	An apparently self-contradictory statement that is, in fact, true
Parallelism	The arrangement of similarly constructed clauses, verses, or sentences
Parenthetical	A word, phrase, or passage (sometimes within parentheses) that explains or modifies a thought
Personification	The giving of human attributes to objects or to abstract ideas
Prologue	An introduction to a play, often delivered by the chorus (in ancient Greece, a group, but in modern plays, one actor) who plays no part in the following action
Pun	A humorous expression that depends on a double meaning, either between different senses of the same word or between two similar sounding words
Rhetoric	The art of speaking or writing
Rhetorical Question	A question for which a reply is not required or even wanted; the question is asked for effect. Often, a rhetorical question is a way of making a statement: *Is there anyone who does not believe in freedom?* really means *Everyone believes in freedom.*
Ridicule	Contemptuous laughter or derision (contempt and mockery); ridicule may be an element of satire
Satire	A form of writing that exposes the failings of individuals, institutions, or societies to ridicule or scorn in order to correct or expose some evil or wrongdoing
Simile	Comparison using the words *like* or *as*
Soliloquy	A speech by a character who is alone on stage, or whose presence is unrecognized by the other characters; the purpose is to make the audience aware of the character's thoughts or to give information concerning other characters or about the action
Sonnet	A lyric poem fourteen lines long and usually written in iambic pentameter. The Shakespearean sonnet consists of three quatrains (four-line stanzas) and a couplet (two lines), all written to a strict end-rhyme scheme (abab cdcd efef gg). The development of the poet's thoughts is also structured. There are several methods: one method is to use each quatrain for different points in an argument and the couplet for the resolution of the argument. Because of the complexity of the sonnet, poets sometimes find it a suitable form for expressing the complexity of thought and emotion.
Symbol	Anything that stands for or represents something other than itself. In literature, a symbol is a word or phrase referring to an object, scene, or action that also has some further significance associated with it. For example, a rose is a common symbol of love. Many symbols, such as flags, are universally recognized. Other symbols are not so universally defined. They do not acquire a meaning until they are defined by how they are used in a story. They may even suggest more than one meaning. For example, snow might be used to symbolize goodness because of its cleanness, or cruelty because of its coldness. Symbols are often contained in story titles; in character and place names; in classical, literary, and historical allusions and references; in images or figures that appear at important points in a story; and in images that either receive special emphasis or are repeated.
Thesis	A statement that is made as the first step in an argument or a demonstration
Tone	A particular way of speaking or writing. Tone may also describe the general feeling of a piece of work. It can demonstrate the writer's attitude toward characters, settings, conflicts, and so forth. The many kinds of tone include thoughtful, chatty, formal, tragic, or silly; tone can also be a complex mixture of attitudes. Different tones can cause readers to experience such varying emotions as pity, fear, horror, or humour.

Directing Words

The following list of directory words and definitions may help you plan your writing. For example, a particular discussion might include assessment, description, illustrations, or an outline of how an extended argument could be developed.

Agree Or Disagree	Support or contradict a statement; give the positive or negative features; express an informed opinion one way or the other; list the advantages for or against
Assess	Estimate the value of something based on some criteria; present an informed judgement. The word "assess" strongly suggests that two schools of thought exist about a given subject. Assessing usually involves weighing the relative merit of conflicting points of view; e.g., negative vs. positive, strong vs. weak components, long-range vs. short-term
Compare	Point out similarities or differences; describe the relationship between two things; often used in conjunction with CONTRAST
Contrast	Show or emphasize differences when compared; see COMPARE
Describe	Give a detailed or graphic account of an object, event, or sequence of events
Discuss	Present the various points of view in a debate or argument; write at length about a given subject; engage in written discourse on a particular topic
Explain	Give an account of what the essence of something is, how something works, or why something is the way it is; may be accomplished by paraphrasing, providing reasons or examples, or by giving a step-by-step account
Identify	Establish the identity of something; establish the unique qualities of something; provide the name of something
Illustrate	Give concrete examples to clarify; provide explanatory or decorative features
List	Itemize names, ideas, or things that belong to a particular class or group
Outline	Give a written description of only the main features; summarize the principal parts of a thing, an idea, or an event
Show (that)	Give facts, reasons, illustrations or examples, to support an idea or proposition
State	Give the key points; declare
Suggest	Propose alternatives, options, or solutions
Support	Defend or agree with a particular point of view; give evidence, reasons, or examples
Trace	Outline the development of something; describe a specified sequence

Credits

Every effort has been made to provide proper acknowledgement of the original source and to comply with copyright law. However, some attempts to establish original copyright ownership may have been unsuccessful. If copyright ownership can be identified, please notify Castle Rock Research Corp so that appropriate corrective action can be taken.

Some images in this document are from www.clipart.com, © 2013 Clipart.com, a division of Getty Images.

"Charles Dickens—Chronicler Of His Times, from *Made in the USA 1st edition* by GAE MACKWOOD. 1990. Reprinted with permission of Nelson, a division of Thomson Learning: www.thomsonrights.com. Fax 800-730-2215.

Poster "Rules to be Observed" from "The United States An Economic Perspective" by Victor A. Zelinski, © 1990, John Wiley & Sons Limited. Reproduced with permission.

"Hard, Hard Times" by William Emberley

"The Blind Men and the Elephant" by John Godfrey Saxe

Cartoon "The Summit at Last" from *The New Zealand Graphic*, Saturday, 21 July, 1894, Reference No: PUBL-0126-1894-01 Alexander Turnbull Library, Wellington, New Zealand.

"The Highwayman" by Alfred Noyes

"Skating" from "The Prelude" by William Wordsworth

"A Thunderstorm" by Archibald Lampman

"On His Blindness" by John Milton

"To Autumn" by John Keats

Excerpt from "The Tell-Tale Heart" by Edgar Allan Poe

Excerpt from "A Tale of Two Cities" by Charles Dickens

"Nothing Gold Can Stay" by Robert Frost, first published in the *Yale Review* October 1923

Excerpts from "MacBeth" by William Shakespeare

"We Real Cool" by Gwendolyn Brooks, from *The Bean Eaters* by Gwendolyn Brooks, published by Harpers. © 1960 by Gwendolyn Brooks. All rights reserved.

"The Conqueror Worm" by Edgar Allan Poe, first published in Graham's Magazine 1843

"The Bells" by Edgar Allan Poe, first published in *Sartrain's Union Magazine* November 1849

"Where There's a Wall" by Joy Kogawa, published at http://library.utoronto.ca/canpoetry/kogawa/poem4.htm

"The Step Mother" by Suzanna Moodie, published at http://rpo.library.utoronto.ca/poem/1484.html

"Inukshuk" by Daniel David Moses, published at http://www.danieldavidmoses.com/the-white-line-inukshut.shtml

Excerpt from "Miss Brill" by Katherine Mansfield, first published in *Athenaeum*, November 26, 1920

Excerpt from "Northanger Abbey" by Jane Austin, first published December 1817

Excerpt from "The Republic" by Plato

"Crossing the Bar" by Alfred, Lord Tennyson

Excerpt from "The Tempest" by William Shakespeare

Excerpt from "Decon Brodie, or The Double Life: A Melodrama in Five Acts and Eight Tableaux" by William Ernest Henley and Robert Louis Stevenson

"Not Marble, Nor the Gilded Monuments" by William Shakespeare

Excerpt from "Walden, or Life in the Woods" by Henry David Thoreau

Excerpt from "This Lime-Tree Bower My Prison" by Samuel Taylor Coleridge

NOTES